THE MI   OF JESUS

Books available from Marshall Pickering
in the
Evangelical Heritage Series

E. H. Broadbent
The Pilgrim Church

A. M. Hodgkin
Christ In All The Scriptures

F. B. Meyer
Great Men of the Bible (one volume)

Andrew Murray
Abide in Christ
Absolute Surrender
An Apostle's Inner Life
The Blood of the Cross
Christ is All
The Coming Revival
Consecrated God
The Cross of Christ
The Full Blessings of Pentecost
Humility
The Ministry of Intercession
The Prayer Life
Prayer's Inner Chamber
The Promise of the Spirit
The Reign of Love
Waiting on God
Working for God
You Will Be Done

Henry Pickering
1000 Subjects for Speakers and Students

W. E. Sangster
The Craft of Sermon Construction
The Craft of Sermon Illustration

C. H. Spurgeon
Cheque Book of the Bank of Faith
Lectures to My Students on the Art of Preaching
Morning and Evening

R. A. Torrey
What the Bible Teaches

THE
MIRACLES
OF JESUS

C. H. SPURGEON

Selected and Edited by
Charles T. Cook

MarshallPickering
An Imprint of HarperCollins*Publishers*

William Collins Sons & Co. Ltd
London · Glasgow · Sydney · Auckland
Toronto · Johannesburg

First published in the Kelvedon Edition
by Marshall, Morgan & Scott in 1958
This edition first published in Great Britain in 1991
by Marshall Pickering

Marshall Pickering is an imprint of
Collins Religious Division,
part of HarperCollins Publishers Ltd,
77–85 Fulham Palace Road,
Hammersmith, London W6 8JB

Printed and bound in Great Britain by
HarperCollins Manufacturing, Glasgow

CONDITIONS OF SALE

CONTENTS

I

THE BEGINNING OF MIRACLES

"This beginning of miracles did Jesus in Cana of Galilee, and manifested forth his glory; and his disciples believed on him."—John 2: 11.

AT this time I shall not consider the relation of this miracle to total abstinence. The wine which Jesus made was good wine. What is now called wine is a very different liquid from that which our Lord divinely produced. We use our Christian liberty to abstain from wine, and we judge that our Saviour would approve of our avoiding that which, in these days, makes our brother to offend. We who quit the intoxicating cup of to-day have our ways of viewing our Master's action in this instance, and we do not find it difficult to see wisdom and holiness in it; but even if we could not so interpret what he did, we should not dare to question HIM. I pursue a spiritual theme, and pray for help from on high to treat it aright.

We find this miracle only in John; neither Matthew, nor Mark, nor Luke, has a word of it. How did John come to know of it? In part it was because of his being present; but the preface in reference to the mother of Jesus came to him in another way, we think. Remember our Lord's words to John from the cross, and how it is written, "From that hour that disciple took her unto his own home." I believe that no one heard the word of Jesus to his mother but Mary herself. It was after the manner of his delicacy to utter a reproof to her alone. But when John and the honoured mother conversed together, she, in all probability, reminded him of the miracle, and told him of her mistake. If my conjecture be correct, I see the holy modesty of "the mother of Jesus"—that she narrated her own fault, and did not forbid John to mention it. The Holy Spirit moved the evangelist to chronicle not only the miracle, but the error of Mary. It was wise; for it is a conclusive argument against the notion that the mother of Jesus can intercede for us with her Son, and use authority with him. It is evident from this narrative that our Lord would tolerate no such idea, either in her mind or in ours. "Woman, what have I to do with thee?" is a sentence which rings the deathknell of any idea of our Lord's being moved by relationships according to the flesh. With all loving respect, he yet very decidedly shuts out all interference from Mary; for his Kingdom was to be according to the spirit, and not after the flesh.

Let it never be forgotten that "the mother of Jesus" had a very firm and practical faith in her Son, concerning whom angels and prophets had borne witness to her. She had seen him in his infancy, and watched him as a child; and it could not have been easy to believe in the divinity of one whom you have held as an infant to be nourished at your breast. From his marvellous birth she believed in him; and, now that she receives a kind of rebuff from him, her faith does not fail her; but she calmly turns to the servants and bids them stand ready to obey his commands, whatever they might be. She felt that he was quite certain to do the kind and needful thing. Even from his word, "Mine hour is *not yet* come," she probably gathered that his hour to work would arrive. Her faith was accompanied with imperfection, but yet it was of the right kind. It persevered under difficulty; and in the end it was triumphant, for the wine which had failed became plentiful again, and that which he provided was of surpassing quality.

May we have a faith which will outlive a rebuke. May we, like Mary, sing, "My spirit hath rejoiced in God my Saviour"; and may Jesus be to us, as he was to her—a trusted and beloved one upon whom our soul has learned to wait with confidence.

To begin with, let us think upon THE SIGNIFICANCE OF THIS BEGINNING OF SIGNS. May the Holy Ghost graciously assist our thoughts, and warm our hearts!

The first sign-wonder that Christ wrought was the turning of water into wine at the wedding at Cana of Galilee; and as we may often judge of a man's course by its beginning, and the beginning is often the key of all that follows, so we may learn the whole tenor of our Lord's miracles from this one.

Note, first, that this miracle *displayed his self-denial*. Our Lord had been a few days before in the wilderness, and after forty days' fasting he was an hungered. It was in his power to have commanded the stones to become bread; and had he done so the beginning of signs would have been a miracle wrought for his own necessities. But such a beginning would not have been like his life-course, and especially would it have been wide apart from the conclusion of his life when it was said of him, "He saved others; himself he cannot save." He would not make bread for himself, but he will make wine for others; and the fact that it was wine, and not bread, that he made, makes the miracle all the more remarkable. He did not merely make bread for men, which is a necessity; but he even went further, and made wine for them, which is a luxury, though he would not make even bread for himself.

You see the sharp contrast between his refusal to help himself even to a crust of bread, and his readiness to give to men, not only what might be needful for life, but that which was only needful to their joy. When the wine failed, the only danger was that the bride and bridegroom would be pained, and the wedding dishonoured; and this our Lord prevents. He would not allow the humble festival of two villagers to come to an untimely end, when they had so kindly invited himself and his disciples. He repaid their courtesy by his spontaneous bounty. How greatly is our divine Lord to be admired and beloved by us! Behold his kindness! We can each one cry, "He loved me, and gave himself for me." He laid down his life for men—he gave his all to others. No selfish aim ever tinctured that consecrated life of his. For himself he reserved no measure or degree of power: for others he used that power without stint. Thoughtfulness for others shone in that miracle like the sun in the heavens.

Next, observe that this miracle *was marked with beneficence*. Happy are we that the first miracle is full of blessing! Moses commenced his work in Egypt with a miracle of judgment. He cast down a rod and it became a serpent, and he turned water into blood: but Jesus overcomes the serpent with the rod of Scripture, and turns water into wine. He works no plagues, but heals our sicknesses. Blessed Master,

> *Thine hand no thunder bears,*
> *No terror clothes thy brow.*

The mission of Jesus is a happy one, and it opens at a marriage feast; it is intended to bring joy and gladness to heavy hearts, and so it begins with a deed of royal bounty. At the coronation of kings the conduit in Cheapside has run with wine, and here the waterpots are filled with it to the brim. The after-miracles were all beneficent. True, he withered a fruitless fig-tree, but it was a beneficent act to wither a tree which drew men out of their way by false promises of fruit, and so caused bitter pangs of disappointment to hungry and fainting way-farers. It was a good thing to teach us all a practical lesson of sincerity at so small an expense as the withering of a good-for-nothing tree. All our Lord's actions towards men are full of royal benevolence and grace. There will be a day when the Lamb will be angry, and, as a Judge, he will condemn the ungodly; but while this dispensation lasts, he is to us all mercy, love, kindness, and bounty. If you will come to him, you will find that his heart will go out to you; and he will freely bless you with life, and rest, and peace, and joy.

This beginning of miracles was wrought at a wedding to show great beneficence. Marriage was the last relic of paradise left among men, and Jesus hasted to honour it with his first miracle. Marriage is his Father's ordinance; for he it was that brought Eve to Adam; and our Lord wrought in harmony with the Father. He symbolically touched the very springs of manhood, and gave his sanction to that ordinance whereby the race is perpetuated. Jesus comes to a marriage, and gives his blessing there, that we may know that our family life is under his care. How much we owe to the joys of our domestic relationships! Thereby life is raised from water into wine. We have sometimes thought it was almost a proof of the divinity of Christianity, that there could be homes so happy as some of our homes have been made by the presence of our dear Lord, whom we invited to our wedding-feast, and who has never gone away since, but has stayed with us all these happy years. It was a miracle which, by honouring marriage, confirmed an institution fraught with happiness to our race.

But, next, it was *a miracle most compassionate.* Our Lord's miracles were wrought in each case to meet a need. The wine had failed at the wedding-feast, and our Lord had come in at the time of the pinch, when the bridegroom was fearful of being made ashamed. That need was a great blessing. If there had been sufficient wine for the feast, Jesus had not wrought this miracle, and they had never tasted this purest and best of wine. It is a blessed need which makes room for Jesus to come in with miracles of love. It is good to run short, that we may be driven to the Lord by our necessity, for he will more than supply it. If you have no need, Christ will not come to you; but if you are in dire necessity, his hand shall be stretched out to you. If your needs stand before you like huge empty waterpots, or if your soul is as full of grief as those same pots were filled with water up to the brim, Jesus can, by his sweet will, turn all the water into wine—the sighing into singing.

Be glad to be very weak, that the power of God may rest upon you. We are likely to do our work best when we feel most our insufficiency, and are driven in upon God for help. If we have a great need, if something essential has given out, if we are likely to be despised for failure, let us in faith expect the Lord Jesus to come for our deliverance.

Further, I cannot help noticing *how condescending was this miracle*! We are told, twice, that it was performed at Cana in Galilee. Twice is this mentioned, that we may observe it well. Our Lord did not choose the high places of Jerusalem, nor any of the notable cities of Palestine, as the scene of his first miracle: but he went to a quiet village in Galilee, Galilee of the Gentiles, a district much despised, and there he wrought his first miracle at the city of rushes and canes—even Cana in Galilee. He wrought the sign, not on a spiritual and sacred occasion, nor before ecclesiastics and scientists. Some seem to fancy that all our Lord does must be done in churches or cathedrals. No, no: this miracle was in a private house, and that not at a Prayer-Meeting, or a Bible-reading, but at the marriage of a couple of poor peasants, names unknown. See how Jesus condescends to the commonplaces of life, and sheds a blessing upon the secular side of our existence!

Those who gave that feast were people of slender means. The wine would not have been so soon exhausted if they had been very rich. It is true that seven more came to the wedding than they had expected; but still, if they had been wealthy people, they would have had more than enough to satisfy seven extra guests; for Easterns kept open house for almost everybody during the marriage week. They were by no means an aristocratic party, or a set of Israel's notables. Why did not our Lord begin his miracles before the king, or the governor, or at least in the presence of the high priest, and the scribes and doctors of the law? Our Lord chose not to make his first appeal to the great and dignified. Jesus can come to you, though you are only a labourer, or a servant, or a poor tradesman, or the wife of an artisan. Our Lord loves the poor. He is a great frequenter of cottages. He stops not for grand occasions; but he makes his abode with the lowly.

This first of miracles was most munificent. He did not at the wedding multiply the bread; but he dealt with a luxury, and rejoiced their hearts with that which was as the pure blood of the grape. When our Lord fed the multitudes in the wilderness, he might have given them each a bit of bread to keep them from famishing; but he never does things in a beggarly, workhouse style, and therefore he added fish, to be a relish with their bread. Our Lord not only gives existence, but happy existence, which is truly life. He does not give to men just enough for their necessity, but he gives up to the higher degree which we call enjoyment. Our dear Master will give to all those who are his followers a joy unspeakable and full of glory. They shall not only have enough grace to live by so as barely to hope and serve; but they shall drink of "wines on the lees well refined," and shall have grace to sing with, grace to rejoice with, grace to fill them with assurance, and cause them to overflow with delight. Our Beloved has not only brought us to the house of bread, but to the banquet of wine. We have heaven here below. Jesus does not measure out grace by the drop, as chemists do their medicines; but he gives liberally, his vessels are filled to the brim. And the quality is as notable as the quantity: he gives the best of the best—joys, raptures, and ecstasies.

What a gracious miracle it was! How free! How unconstrained! He did not need pressing to do it. Mary must not interfere. You think perhaps that you must pray up to a certain quantity; but the Lord is much more ready to give than you are to pray. It is not your prayer that will make him willing to bless you; for he is willing even now to do for you exceeding abundantly above what you ask or even think.

To obtain the supply of wine, it is noteworthy that nothing was required from men but what was very simple and easy. Hasten, ye obedient servants, to fetch water: just draw it from the well; pour it into those large waterpots: that is all you have to do! The Lord Jesus does not come to us with hard conditions and exacting terms. Dream not that, to be saved, you have to do or feel some great thing. As you are you may believe in Jesus to eternal life. Have faith enough to draw out at the Lord's bidding, and, to your own amazement, there will be wine where aforetime there was only water. The Lord, by his Spirit, can come and change your heart, and renew your spirit, so that where only a little natural thought has been, there will be spiritual life and feeling. He will do this without pressing and persuading. Grace is free.

The first miracle was *prophetic*. At a wedding our Lord begins his signs; to a marriage-feast he invites us now; at a glorious marriage-supper all will end. The story of our Bible ends like all well-told tales, with—they were married, and lived happy ever afterwards: for proof read the Book of the Revelation. Our Lord will come to celebrate a wedding between himself and his Church, and all the wine they will drink at that high festival will be of his own providing, and all the joy and bliss will be of his own giving.

Secondly, I want you to notice in this miracle ITS SPECIALITY AS A MANIFESTATION. "This beginning of miracles did Jesus in Cana of Galilee, and manifested forth his glory." I believe that there is a very clear connection between the first chapter of this Gospel and the passage before us. John in the first chapter said, "And the Word was made flesh, and dwelt among us, (and we beheld his glory, the glory as of the only begotten of the Father,) full of grace and truth." Here you have an unveiling of that grace and glory.

Observe that *he manifested forth his glory*. Truly, he glorified the Father, for that was his great end and aim; but yet he manifested forth his own glory in that very act. Notice that it was his own glory which was manifested. This was never said of any prophet or saint. Moses, Samuel, David, Elias—none of these ever manifested their own glory; indeed, they had no glory to manifest. Here is one greater than a prophet; here is one greater than the holiest of men. He manifested his own glory: it could not be otherwise. I feel that I must adore my Lord Jesus while I read these words. Jesus revealed his own glory as God and man. During all those former years it had been veiled. He had been a boy obedient at home, a young man industrious as a carpenter at Nazareth; then his glory was a spring shut up, a fountain sealed; but now it began to flow forth in the ruddy stream of this great miracle. If you will think of it, you will see more clearly what glory it was. He was a man like other men, and yet at will he turned water into wine. He was a man with a mother: his mother was there as if to remind us that he was born of woman. He was a man with a mother, and yet he was so truly "God over all," that he created, by his will, an abundance of wine. He was but one among many wedding guests, with his six humble followers; but yet he acted the Creator's part. He was simply a man among men, and yet he was God among men. His wish was law in the world of matter, so that water received the qualities of wine. Adore him, brethren! Adore him, reverently! Worship him who counts it not robbery to be equal with God, and yet is found among the guests at a lowly marriage, manifesting his glory even there.

Observe, *he manifested his glory by operating beyond the power of nature*. Nature does not in an instant turn water into wine: if this be done, it must be by the direct hand of the Lord. It is true there are processes by which the dewdrop enters the berry of the grape and is gradually, by secret arrangements, turned into refreshing juice; but by what power could water be taken from an earthen vessel and be transmuted into wine while being carried to the table? None but God himself could do this, and as Jesus did it, he therein displayed his Godhead. By doing this he showed that he had all power on earth.

And *he operated so easily and so majestically*, that he therein reminds us of the method and way of the great God. He simply says, "Fill the water-pots," and the servants do his bidding with enthusiasm, for he is Master of all minds. "Draw out now," he says, and in the process of bearing it to the ruler of the feast, the water is turned into wine. Here is no effort, no breathing as of one gathering up his strength to perform a feat. The earth revolves, but the wheel of nature never grinds upon its axle. God acts by his laws in a perfectly natural and unconstrained manner. All goes easily where God is. With his own will he can do all things *for us*, and in a moment turn the waters of our grief into joy.

Our Lord manifested his glory by *operating naturally and without display*. I really believe that if you could have worked this wonder, you would have said to the ruler of the feast, "Call upon all the guests to remark that the wine has failed, and I am about to create a new supply. See this huge waterpot. Mark how I have it filled with water, that you may know that there is no wine in it. Observe me while I work the transformation." Then you would have spoken aloud, or you would have gone through a series of performances. Jesus did nothing of the kind. He hates display. He will not have his kingdom come with observation. He shuns pomp, noise, and ceremony; but acts like a God whose wonders are too many to be made matters of note to himself. It was Godlike on our Lord's part to perform so great a work without appearing to be doing anything uncommon.

That he did literally perform the miracle, was certified by impartial witnesses. John, or Philip, or the whole six, might have said, "Master, we will fill the water-pots with water." But this must not be so, lest there should be a suspicion of collusion between the Master and the disciples. The ordinary servants must fill the water-pots with water. Again, the disciples would have been very pleased to bear the wine to the ruler of the feast, saying, "Here is the wine which our great and good Master has made for you." No; the servants shall bring in the wine, and say nothing at all about whence it came; and the chief witness that what they bring is really wine, and wine of the best quality, shall be the master of the ceremonies— a gentleman not at all spiritually-minded, but one who has been at many such feasts, that knows the custom of them, and has a proverb ready to set it forth. He was evidently a man who was a judge of the quality of wine, and we may safely accept his verdict—"Thou hast kept the best wine until now." The less spiritual the man in this case, the better the witness to the reality of the miracle. If he had been a follower of Jesus he might have been suspected of being in the swim with him and his disciples; but you can see he is a man of another mould altogether. God's work is fact, not fiction: it appeals to faith, not to imagination. God doth his transforming work in such a way that he will have witnesses ready to attest it. As when Christ rose from the dead there were appointed witnesses to certify it, so his first miracle is certified beyond all question as real and true by the best of witnesses.

Oh, if you come to Christ he will not deceive you; his blessings are not dreams. If you will come and trust in Jesus, the work he will do for you will be as real as what he did at Cana. Even the ungodly shall be obliged to see that God has made a change in you. When they see your new life, they will say, "Here is something good, the like of which we never saw in him before." Come, I pray you, and take Christ to be your all; and he will be, in very truth, all that you need. Trust him with your sin, and he will bring real pardon. Trust him with your trouble, he will give you perfect rest. Trust him with your evil nature, he will renew you. He is no pretender to deeds which he does not perform. He did by the witness of everybody at the marriage actually turn water into wine of special quality; and so he can now transform your character and make it such as nature, when best educated, can never produce. He raises the poor from hunger to feasting. He uplifts fallen humanity into something so glorious that it stands, in his person, near to the throne of God. In all this Christ is revealed, and his name is glorified.

And now, lastly, I think we have here A SUFFICIENCY FOR THE CONFIRMING OF FAITH. It is said, "And his disciples believed on him."

How did John know that the disciples believed on him? Why, because he was one of them, and he himself believed on him. The best witness is that of one who has a share in the fact. When you feel a thing yourself, you have a full assurance of it. John knew that the other five disciples believed on Jesus by what they said to him; for their feelings coincided with his own. Let us see to it that we also share in the faith which the marvels of our Lord are designed to produce.

Note, that the guests at that feast all partook of the wine, but the disciples at that feast had something far better; they had an increase of faith. An increase of faith is better far than all the dainties of a feast. Others ate and drank; but these men saw God in Christ Jesus manifesting his glory.

Our enquiry is, What was there in this miracle which would tend to confirm their faith? Notice that I say *to confirm* their faith. It did not originate their faith, but it established it.

Their faith had been originated by the word of the Lord, preached by John the Baptist: they had believed in Jesus as the Lamb of God which taketh away the sin of the world. Secondly, they had enjoyed personal intercourse with Jesus, by going to him, and dwelling with him. This had strengthened their faith greatly. And now they begin to taste of the benefit of being associated with Jesus, and to see for themselves what Jesus was able to do. This miracle confirmed their confidence.

The miracle abundantly justified the disciples in implicitly believing in Jesus; for it is manifest that *one miracle proves the power to work every miracle.* If Christ can turn water into wine by his will, he can do anything and everything. If Jesus has once exercised a power beyond nature, we may readily believe that he can do it again: there is no limit to his power. He is God, and with God all things are possible. Thus, the first miracle rightly confirmed their faith.

But, next, *it showed their Master's readiness to meet unexpected difficulties.* Nobody had foreseen that the wine would fail. Jesus had not gone to the marriage prepared and primed, as we say among men. The demand came all of a sudden, and the supply came too: the wine ran out, and he was ready for the difficulty. Does not this confirm your faith? Christ is always ready for every emergency. Something may happen to-morrow that you have not thought of; Christ will be ready for the unexpected. Between here and heaven you will meet with a great many unlikely events; but they will not be surprises to him. He has clear foresight: when the trial comes he will provide: "In the mount of the Lord it shall be seen" (Gen. 22 : 14).

Again, their faith was confirmed because *he had showed that he would allow nothing to fail with which he was connected.* I like to feel sure that Jesus is with me in any business, for then I know that the pleasure of the Lord will prosper in his hand. True, it was not the wedding of one of his relatives or disciples, but still it was a marriage at which he was a guest; and he would not suffer it to be said that they ran short of provisions when he was there. His connection with the feast may seem to have been remote, but it was a connection; and slight connections are observed by our Lord Jesus. O my soul, if I can but touch the hem of his garment, virtue will come from him to me. I get into the same boat with Jesus, and if I drown Jesus must drown too: and therefore I know that I am safe! O my heart, if I do but get the hand of Christ in my hand, or my hand in his hand, I am linked with him, and none can separate us. In that union is my life, my safety, my success; for nothing that he touches, or that touches him, will ever fail. He is only one of a party at a wedding, but because he is there things must go well. I think this must have encouraged the disciples much when, in after days, they began to preach: their confidence would be that Jesus was with them, and they must prevail. They were poor, unlearned men, and all the scholarship of the age was arrayed against them; but they said to themselves, "We fear not, for Jesus is in this controversy, and he will see it through." Let us get Christ into our quarrel for God's covenant and truth, and the battle is no longer doubtful. If in the matter of your salvation faith brings the Saviour into the business, you may rest assured of eternal life.

It showed to them, next—and this must have greatly confirmed their faith—that *he could use the poorest means*. To make wine the Lord had only water and six large water-pots. Yes, but he can make better wine out of water than men can make out of grapes. Behold his vats and his winepresses, six water-pots of stone. You and I—what are we? Well, we are poor earthen vessels, and a little cracked, I fear. There is little enough in us, and what there is is weak as water; but the Lord can bring forth from us a wine which will cheer the heart of God and man—words of faith which will please God and save man. The disciples would in after days know themselves to be nothing but earthen vessels, but they would remember that their Lord could work miracles with them.

When they saw *the majestic ease of his working*, do you not think it confirmed their faith? He did not call for angels, he did not deliver a long prayer, much less repeat a sacred incantation. He did but will it, and the deed was done. Next time they came into a difficulty, the disciples would believe that the Lord could easily enough appear for them. They would stand still and see the salvation of God. In some way or other the Lord would provide, and he would do wonders without trouble to himself.

It showed to them, also, that henceforth *they need never be anxious*. Will you that read your Greek Testament notice the expression here? Is it said, "His disciples believed him"? No. Is it "Believed *in* him"? No. "Believed *on* him"? Yes. It is so in our version; but *into* would be more correct: his disciples believed "*into* him." They so believed that they seemed to submerge themselves in Jesus. "Into him"—think what that means! John, and Andrew, and Nathanael, and the others, cast their life-long concerns upon Jesus, and felt that they need never have another care. Jesus would see them through to the end. They would leave everything to him. Mary took the matter a little into her own hands, but she erred therein; the disciples entered into Jesus by the open door of this confirming miracle, and there they rested. Be this your condition— "Casting all your care on him, for he careth for you" (1 Pet. 5 : 7). They believed right into Jesus. It is one thing to believe in him, and another thing to believe him; it is a restful thing to believe on him, but best of all to believe right into him so that your very personality is swallowed up in Christ, and you feel the bliss of living, loving, lasting union with him. Those six men could not have produced a drop of wine for the wedding; but count their Master in with them, and the seven could flood the streets with it, if there had been need. Entering into partnership with Jesus, their faith rose as a morning without clouds. Now were they sure, steadfast, strong; for their weak and watery faith had gained the fullness and richness of generous wine.

Jesus Christ will come and visit such as you are. He is willing to go to plain men's houses, even when they have a feast going on. Ask him to come to you just as you are.

See how he is able to bless human joy! You think, perhaps, that you will go to Jesus next time you are in sorrow; but I say to you, come to him at once, while you are in joy. You that are getting on in business, you that rejoice over a new-born child, you that are lately married, you that have passed an examination with honours, come to Jesus in your joy, and ask him to raise your happiness to a higher degree and quality, and elevate it till it touches the joy of the Lord. Jesus is able to raise you, beloved friend, from what you now are into something better, fuller, grander, nobler, holier, and more God-like. May he do it now!

II

THE NOBLEMAN'S FAITH

"There was a certain nobleman, whose son was sick at
Capernaum. When he heard that Jesus was come out of Judæa
into Galilee, he went unto him, and besought him that he
would come down, and heal his son: for he was at the point of
death. Then said Jesus unto him, Except ye see signs and
wonders, ye will not believe. The nobleman saith unto him,
Sir, come down ere my child die. Jesus saith unto him, Go thy
way; thy son liveth. And the man believed the word that
Jesus had spoken unto him, and he went his way. And as he
was now going down, his servants met him, and told him,
saying, Thy son liveth. Then enquired he of them the hour
when he began to amend. And they said unto him, Yesterday
at the seventh hour the fever left him. So the father knew that
it was at the same hour, in the which Jesus said unto him, Thy
son liveth: and himself believed, and his whole house."—
John 4: 46–53.

THIS narrative illustrates the rise and progress of faith in
the soul. We want to come to real business, and to make
the things of God matters of downright fact to ourselves: not
only to hear about this nobleman from Capernaum, or anybody
else, but to see in our own souls the same work of grace as was
wrought in them. The same living Christ is here, and his help
we as greatly need as ever did this nobleman. May we seek it
as he sought it, and find it as he found it!

Observe, at the commencement, that *trouble first of all led this
courtly personage to Jesus.* Had he been without trial, he might
have lived forgetful of his God and Saviour; but sorrow came
to his house, and it was God's angel in disguise. It may be that
you are in trouble this day; and, if so, I pray that affliction may
be the black horse upon which mercy shall ride to your door. It
is a sad, sad thing with some men that, the better the Lord
deals with them in providence, the worse return they make.
On the other hand, there are hearts that turn to the Lord when
he smites them. When they drift into deep waters, when they
can scarcely find bread to eat, when sickness attacks their

bodies, and especially when their children are smitten, then they begin to think of God, and better things. Blessed is the discipline of the great Father in such a case. It is well for the troubled if their tribulation bruises their heart to repentance, and repentance leads them to seek and find pardon.

The particular form of trial which visited this nobleman was the sickness of his child. A little son he had, whom he dearly loved, and he was down with a deadly fever. The father appears to have been a naturally kind and affectionate person. His servants evidently took a great interest in him, and in the domestic affliction which grieved him; for you observe with what eagerness they came to meet him, to tell him of the recovery of his child. The father's heart was sadly wounded because his dear boy was at the point of death. No doubt he had tried all the remedies known to the times, had sent for every physician that could be found within miles of Capernaum; and now, having heard of one Jesus of Nazareth, who at Cana had turned water into wine, and at Jerusalem had done many mighty works, he resorts to him with eager petition and desperate hope. He might never have thought of seeking Jesus if it had not been for that dear dying boy. How often does it happen that children, though they are not angels, yet are used to do better work than angels could accomplish; for they sweetly lead their parents to God and heaven! The prayers that come from many hearts are, under God, fetched forth by grief for little ones most dearly loved. Is it not written, "And a little child shall lead them"? It was so with this man; he was brought to Jesus by anxiety about a child. I have it strongly upon me at this moment that I am speaking to certain persons who are not converted, but they have come hither because they are in great sorrow: possibly a dear little one is pining away, and their hearts are crying to God that, if possible, the precious life may be spared. In the house of prayer they feel somewhat comforted; but their hearts are ready to break because of the loss they so much dread. How much I pray our Lord to make this trouble a means of grace!

Trial was the occasion, the preface to the work, of divine grace. I want you carefully now to mark THE SPARK OF FAITH, all the while saying—I am going to look and see if I have such a spark of faith; and if I find it, I will prize it much, and pray the Holy Spirit to breathe softly upon it, that it may rise to something more permanent and powerful.

The faith of this nobleman *rested, at the first, entirely upon the report of others*. He lived at Capernaum, down there by the sea; and amongst the newsmongers it was common talk that there had arisen a great prophet who was working great wonders. He himself had never seen Jesus, nor heard him speak; but he believed the report of others; and he was right in doing so, for they were credible persons. No doubt many are in the early stages of faith: they have heard friends say that the Lord Jesus receiveth sinners; that he calms the conscience; that he changes the nature; that he hears prayer; that he sustains his people under trouble: these things they have heard from persons of good repute, whom they esteem, and therefore they believe them. Friend, are you saying to yourself, "I have no doubt it is all true; I wonder whether it ever would be true to me. I am in trouble this day: will the Lord Jesus help me? I have a present pressure upon my spirit: will prayer to him relieve me?"

Well, faith often begins in that way. Men believe the report which is brought to them by well-known persons who have experienced the power of divine love, and thus at first, like the Samaritans, they believe because of the woman's report. In future time, they will come to believe because of having heard, and seen, and tasted, and handled, for themselves: but the beginning is good. This faith which comes of a report by others is a spark of true fire. Take care of it. May God grant you grace so to pray about it, that that spark may increase into a flame!

Observe that this faith was such a little faith that *it only concerned the healing of the sick child*. The nobleman did not know that he needed healing in his own heart; he did not perceive his own ignorance of Jesus, and his own blindness to the Messiah; he did not perhaps know that he needed to be born again; neither did he understand that the Saviour could give him spiritual life and light. What he did believe was that the Lord Jesus, if he would come to his house, could prevent his child from dying of the fever. He had reached as far as that; and such faith as he had, he turned to practical use at once. You do not as yet know how great my Lord is, and what wonderful things he doeth for those who put their trust in him;

but you are saying, "Surely he could help me this day in my present trial, and deliver me out of my present difficulty." So far, so good. Use what faith you have. Let me encourage you to do so. If you cannot come to him for heavenly things, you may, for the present, begin with the sorrows and trials of earth: if you cannot come to him for an eternal blessing, you may come to him for a passing favour, and he is ready to hear you. Though that faith will be only a spark, and nothing more, I would not blow it out; nor will the Lord Jesus do so, for he hath said that a smoking flax he will not quench.

The nobleman's faith was so feeble that *he limited the power of Jesus to his local presence*. Hence his prayer was, "Sir, come down ere my child die." If he could but induce the Lord Jesus to enter the room where the sick child lay, he believed that he would speak to the fever, and the fever would be allayed; but he had no idea that the Lord Jesus Christ could work at the distance of twenty-five miles: he had no notion that the word of the Lord could operate apart from his presence. Still, it was better to have that limited faith than to have none at all. Therefore I say to you, in whom the Lord is beginning to work, if you have no more faith than just to say, "The Lord Jesus could heal me if he were here: the Lord would help me, and answer my cry, if he were here"—it is better to have such a faith than to be unbelieving. Your narrow faith limits him exceedingly, and shuts him up in a very close place; and therefore you may not expect him to do many mighty works for you: and yet up to the measure of your faith he will go with you and bless you. As a matter of unpromised sovereign grace, he may even do exceeding abundantly above what you ask or even think. Therefore I would treat your faith like a little babe: I would nurse it until it can stand alone, and hold out my finger to help it till its tottering steps become firm. We will not blame the babe because it cannot run or leap, but we will cherish it, and urge it to greater strength; to which strength it will come in due time. Our Lord Jesus Christ deserves the largest faith from each one of us. Give him what faith you have, and ask for more.

His faith in the Lord Jesus Christ, though it was only a spark, yet *influenced this nobleman*. It led him to take a considerable journey to find our Lord. From Capernaum he went up the hills to Cana, that he might plead with Jesus. And he went personally. This is the more remarkable because he was a man of rank and position. I do not know whether he was Chuza, Herod's steward. I should not wonder if he was, because we do not hear of any other noble family being on the side of Christ; but we do hear of the wife of Chuza, Herod's steward, as amongst those that ministered to our Lord of their substance. We hear also of Manaen, foster-brother to Herod. It may have been one of these. Now noblemen do not, as a rule, think of taking journeys themselves while they have so many servants at their disposal; but this nobleman came himself to Christ, and personally besought him that he would come and heal his son. If your faith is weak in some respects, and yet strong enough in others to drive you personally to Christ, personally to pray to him, it is faith of an acceptable order. If it leads you to beseech Christ to have mercy upon you, it is the faith which saves the soul. It may be little as a grain of mustard-seed, but its importunity shows that there is pungency in it—it is true mustard. Are you beginning to pray at this time because of sorrow? In the silence of your soul are you crying, "O God, save me to-day! I have come up to London to see other things, but oh, that this may be the day in which I shall be helped out of my trouble, and myself be saved"? If your faith brings you to prayer, it is the acknowledged child of grace; for true-born faith always cries. If your faith helps you to lay hold of Jesus with a resolute grip, saying, "I will not let thee go, except thou bless me," it may be little faith, but it is true faith. It is wrought in your soul by the Spirit of God, and it will bring a blessing with it. You shall be saved by this faith, to our Lord's glory, and to your own comfort.

I notice that *this man's faith taught him how to pray in the right style*. Notice the argument he used: he besought him that he would come down and heal his son, for he was at the point of death. He urged no merit, but pleaded the misery of the case. He did not plead that the boy was of noble birth—that would have been very bad pleading with Jesus; nor did he urge that he was a lovely child—that would have been a sorry argument; but he pleaded that he was at the point of death. His extremity was his reason for urgency.

When you are taught by grace to pray aright, you will urge

those facts which reveal your own danger and distress, and not those which would make you appear rich and righteous. Remember how David prayed. "Lord," he said, "pardon mine iniquity; for it is great." Plead with God, poor sinner, the greatness of your necessity, the direness of your need; say that you are at the point of death, say that the matter about which you plead is a matter of life and death: this will be an argument calculated to move the heart to infinite compassion. Any tint of goodness that your pride would tempt you to throw into the picture would spoil it: lay on the black colours thick and three-fold. Plead with God for his mercy's sake, for mercy is the only attribute which you can hopefully address while you are a sinner unforgiven.

Do you follow me, you that are not yet converted? Is there, at any rate, in you some desire to come to the Lord Jesus Christ, though it be only because a temporal trouble is pressing you sorely? A horse does not want a dozen spurs to make it run. The one which now wounds your flank is sharp enough, and it is plunged in so deep that you must feel it. Yield to it, lest there should be need of whip as well as spur to make you stir. If you are the Lord's chosen, you will have to come, and the more readily you do so the better will it be for you. Come just as you are, and look up to Jesus, and pray; for in that prayer shall lie the hope, nay, the certainty of relief. The great heart of Jesus will feel your prayer, and say, "Go in peace."

Secondly we will now look at THE FIRE OF FAITH, struggling to maintain itself, and gradually increasing. Let us see how the fire smoulders, and the heap begins to smoke, and thus betrays the inner fire.

This man's faith was true as far as it went. That is a great thing to say. He stood before the Saviour resolved not to go away from him; his only hope for his child's life was in this great Prophet of Nazareth, and therefore he did not intend to leave him till his request was granted. He does not at first get the answer that he wants, but he perseveres, and pleads on. This showed that his faith had heart and vitality in it. What a mercy to be delivered from all sham faith! Better to have little faith, and that faith real, than to possess a great creed, and give the Lord Jesus no hearty credit. Tell me, have you any real practical faith in the Lord Jesus?

His faith was true as far as it went: but *it was hindered by a desire for signs and wonders*. Our Lord therefore gently chided him, saying, "Except ye see signs and wonders, ye will not believe." Now I know that many of you believe that the Lord Jesus can save, but you have fixed in your mind the way in which he must do it. You have been reading certain religious biographies, and you find that such a man was driven to despair, had horrible thoughts, and so on: therefore you settle it in your minds that you must have similar horrors, or you will be lost. You lay it down as a programme that you must be saved in that way, or not at all. Is this right? Is this wise? Do you mean to dictate to the Lord?

Perhaps you have read or heard that certain eminent persons were converted through singular dreams, or by remarkable movements of providence, and you say to yourself, "Something equally singular must happen to me, or I will not believe in the Lord Jesus." In this you err like the nobleman. He expected the Saviour to come down to the house, and perform some act peculiar to his prophetic office. In fact, this nobleman is the New Testament reproduction of Naaman in the Old Testament. You remember how Naaman said, "Behold, I thought, he would surely come out to me, and stand, and call on the Lord his God, and strike his hand over the place, and recover the leper." Naaman had planned it all in his own mind, and had no doubt arranged a very proper and artistic performance; and, therefore, when the prophet simply said, "Go and wash in Jordan seven times," he could not receive so simple and bald a gospel: it was too common-place, too free from ritual. Many persons, by their mental prejudices, would bind down the Lord of mercy to such and such a way of saving them; but our Lord will not be thus laid under constraint; why should he? He will save whom he wills, and he will save as he wills. His Gospel is not, "Suffer so much horror and despair, and live"; but, "Believe on the Lord Jesus Christ, and thou shalt be saved." He comes to many, and calls them effectually by the soft whispers of his love: they do but trust him, and they enter into immediate rest. Why should it not be so with you? Let him save you as he wills. Away with foolish prejudices!

Yet this is to be said of the nobleman's faith: *it could endure a rebuff*. Think of the Master only saying to this poor anguished

father, "Except ye see signs and wonders, ye will not believe."
It was sadly true, but it sounded honestly sharp. He was like
that woman for whom the Lord said, "It is not meet to take
the children's bread, and to cast it to dogs," and yet she said,
"Truth, Lord: yet the dogs eat of the crumbs which fall from
their masters' table." This man answered our Lord by still
greater importunity. He would not go away; not he. Oh, dear
heart, may you have such faith in Christ that, though he should
rebuke you, you will not leave him! Jesus is your only hope;
therefore do not turn away from him. Imitate Bunyan when
he spake words to this effect:—"I was driven to such straits
that I must of necessity go to Jesus; and if he had met me with
a drawn sword in his hand, I would sooner have thrown myself
upon the edge of his sword than have gone away from him;
for I knew him to be my last hope." O soul, cling to thy Lord,
come what may!

Then see *how passionately this man pleaded*. He cried, "Sir,
come down ere my child die"; as much as if he had said,
"Lord, do not question me just now about my faith. O my
Lord, I pray thee do not think of me at all, but heal my dear
child, or he will be dead! He was at the point of death when I
left him: do hasten down and save him." Note how intense,
how eager, how persevering was his pleading. If his faith failed
in breadth, it excelled in force. Dear anxious friend, keep close
to the example now before us. Pray, and pray again; hold on,
and hold out; cry on, and cry out; never cease till the Lord
of love grants you an answer of peace.

We come to a higher stage, and watch thirdly, THE FLAME OF
FAITH. The spark increased as a smouldering fire, and now the
fire reveals itself in flame. Observe that Jesus said to the peti-
tioner, "Go thy way; thy son liveth." And the man truly
believed, and went his way.

Here note that *he believed the word of Jesus over the head of all
his former prejudices*. He had thought that Christ could heal
only if he came down to Capernaum; but now he believes,
though Jesus remains where he is, and only speaks the word.
Friend, wilt thou, at this moment, believe the Lord Jesus Christ
on his bare word? Without laying down any rules as to how he
will save thee, wilt thou trust him? Thou hast prescribed dark
convictions, or vivid dreams, or strange sensations; wilt

thou cease from such folly? Wilt thou believe in Jesus Christ as he is revealed in the Scriptures? Hast thou not heard of his passion and death upon the Cross for the guilty? Hast thou not heard it said that all manner of sin and of iniquity shall be forgiven unto men if they believe in him? Dost thou not know that he that believeth in him hath everlasting life? Thou shalt be saved as surely as thou dost trust.

The next thing this man did to prove the sincerity of his faith was that *he at once obeyed Christ*. Jesus said to him, "Go thy way"; that is, "Go home"—"thy son liveth." If the man had not believed the word he would have lingered there, and kept on pleading, and looking for favourable signs; but as he has believed, he is satisfied with the word of the Lord, and goes his way without another word. "Thy son liveth" is enough for him. Many of you have said, when you have heard the Gospel preached, "You tell us to believe in Christ; but we will continue in prayer." That is not what the Gospel commands you. Do I hear you say, "I shall continue to read my Bible, and attend the means of grace"? That is not the precept of the Saviour. Are you not satisfied with his word? Will you not take that word, and go your way? If you believe in him, you will go your way in peace: you will believe that he has saved you, and act as if you knew it to be true. You will joy and rejoice in the fact that you are saved. You will exclaim, "He tells me to believe him, and I believe him. He says, 'He that believeth on me hath everlasting life'; and I do believe in him, and therefore I have everlasting life. I may not feel any peculiar emotion, but I have eternal life. Whether I see my salvation or not, I am saved. It is written, 'Look unto me, and be ye saved, all ye ends of the earth.' Lord, I have looked, and I am saved. My reason for believing it is that thou hast said it."

Now, the nobleman's faith has flamed up indeed. He believes not upon mere report, but upon the word of Jesus. He does not wait for a sign, but he hears the word, and on that word he hangs his confidence. Jesus said, "Thy son liveth; go thy way"; and he goes his way, that he may find his son alive. Still, I am bound to say concerning his faith at this stage, that *it still fell somewhat short of what it might have been*. It was a great thing for him to have come so far; but he had farther yet to go. He expected less than he might have expected, and therefore, when he saw his servants, he asked them when the dear child began to amend. He was overjoyed when they virtually said, "He never did begin to amend; the fever left him all at once; at the seventh hour he recovered."

You see he expected a gradual restoration. He looked for the ordinary course of nature; but here was a miraculous work. He received far more than he reckoned on. How little we know of Christ, and how little we believe in him even when we do trust him! We measure his boundless treasure by our scanty purses. Yet the faith that saves is not always full-grown: there is room for us to believe more, and to expect more, of our blessed Lord. Oh, that we would do so!

But one thing I want to mention here, though I do not quite understand it; perhaps you can make it out. *The father travelled with the leisure of confidence.* It was about twenty-five or thirty miles to Capernaum, and I have no doubt the good man started off directly the Master said, "Go thy way." No doubt he would go at once in obedience to such a command, and make progress on the road home. But we read that the servants met him. Did they start as soon as the child was cured? If so, they might meet him half-way, or thereabouts. It was uphill: say, therefore, that they came ten miles; and that fifteen, or even twenty, remained for the nobleman to travel. The servants said, "Yesterday at the seventh hour the fever left him." The seventh hour was about one o'clock in the day, and that day was "yesterday." I know that the day closed at set of sun, yet one would hardly talk of "yesterday" without a night between. Did he take fifteen or sixteen hours for that part journey? If so, he did not travel with any excessive speed. It is true that twenty-five miles was a good day's journey for a camel, for in the East the roads are execrable; but still it does seem to me that the happy father moved with the ease of a believer rather than with the hurry of an anxious parent. A nobleman's usual progress through the villages was slow, and he did not alter the usual pace, because he would not even seem to hurry now that his mind was believingly at rest. He felt quite sure that his son was all right, and therefore the fever of anxiety left the father, even as the fever had left his child.

I like this consecrated restfulness; it befits a solid faith. I want you all, when you believe in Jesus Christ, to believe right

up to the hilt. Give him not a half faith, but a whole faith;
whether about a child, or about yourself, believe in earnest.
Say, " 'Let God be true, but every man a liar.' On his bare
word my soul reposes. I will 'rest in the Lord, and wait
patiently for him.' What though no amazing joys flash through
my spirit? What if I do not rise up, and dance for joy? Yet
will I sit still, and sing within my soul, because God has visited
his believing servant. I will wait until high joys shall come to
me, but meanwhile I will trust, and not be afraid."

So far the nobleman's faith has grown, but now fourthly,
we shall see it become THE CONFLAGRATION OF FAITH. As he
went home, his servants met him with good news. In the
quietude of his faith he was exceedingly delighted when they
said, "Thy son liveth." The message came upon him like the
echo of the word of Jesus. "I heard that," said he, "yesterday,
at the seventh hour; for then Jesus said, 'Thy son liveth.'
Another day has come, and, behold, my servants salute me
with the same word, 'Thy son liveth.'" The repetition must
have astonished him. I often notice about the preaching of
the word, how the sentences strike you as to their very words
when God blesses them. People say to me, "You said, sir, the
selfsame thing that we were talking of when we were on the
road: you described our cases even to our thoughts, and you
mentioned certain expressions which had been used in our con-
versation; surely God was speaking through you." Yes, it is
often so; Christ's own word finds many echoes from the mouths
of his commissioned servants.

Now the nobleman's faith is *confirmed by the answer to his
prayers*. His experience has come in to the aid of his faith. He
believes in a more assured sense than he did before. He has
proved the truth of the Lord's word, and therefore he knows
and is persuaded that he is Lord and God. The faith of a sinner
coming to Christ is one thing; the faith of a man who has come
to Christ, and has obtained the blessing, is another and stronger
matter. The first faith, the simpler faith, is that which saves;
but the further faith is that which brings comfort, and joy,
and strength into the spirit.

"My prayer is heard," said he; and then he spoke to the
servants, and *after enquiry his faith was sustained by each detail*.
He cried, "Tell me all about it: when was it?" When they

replied, "At the seventh hour the fever left him," he remembered that at that very moment, when over there above the hills at Cana, the Lord Jesus Christ had said, "Go thy way; thy son liveth." The more he studied the case the more wonderful it became. The details were singularly confirmatory of his confidence, and by their means he rose to a clearer and firmer faith. How many such confirmations some of us have had! Doubters attempt to argue with us about the simplicities of the Gospel; and they want to fight with us upon their own ground of mere speculative reasoning. This is hardly fair to us. Our own ground is of quite another kind. We are not strangers to the business of faith, but adepts in it; and you ought to allow something for our personal experience of the faithfulness of the Lord our God. We have a thousand treasured memories of happy details which we cannot tell you. We do not call you swine, but at the same time we dare not throw our pearls before you. We have a host of things laid by; but we cannot repeat them, for to us they are too sacred: thus we are not able to use those reasons which to our own hearts are the most convincing. We have other arguments than we choose to bandy in open court. Be not surprised if we seem obstinate; you do not know how intensely sure we are. We know, and are sure; for we have seen, and heard, and tasted, and handled of the good Word of the Lord. Certain things are so intertwisted with our lives that we are anchored by them. "Coincidences," you say. Ah well! say what you please; to us they are other than to you! Our soul has cried out, time after time, "This is the finger of God." A man who has been helped out of a very severe trouble cannot forget his deliverer. Do you reply, "You were fortunate to get out of it"? O sir; this seems a very cold-blooded remark!

If you had been where I have been, and experienced what I have experienced, you would own that the Lord stretched out his hand, and saved his servant: you would have the same solemn conviction as I have that God was there, working out salvation. I know that I cannot create those convictions in you by telling you my story. If you are determined not to believe, you will not accept my testimony, but will think me a deluded person, though I am no more apt to be deluded than you are. However, whether you are inclined to believe or to disbelieve, I am in no such hesitation. I am forced to believe, for the more carefully I examine my life, the more I am convinced that God must have been at work with me and for me.

At the same moment that Christ said, "Thy son liveth," the nobleman's son did live. Strengthened in his faith by his experience, after having believed the bare word of Jesus, the good man now sees that word fulfilled, and *he believes in Jesus in the fullest sense*; believes for everything; for his body, and for his soul; for all that he is, and for all that he has. From that day forth he becomes a disciple of the Lord Jesus. He follows him, not as a Healer only, nor as a Prophet only, nor as a Saviour only, but as his Lord and his God. His hope, his trust, and his confidence are fixed upon Jesus as the true Messiah.

What follows is so natural, and yet so joyous, that I pray it may be true to all of you: his family also believe. When he gets home, his wife meets him. Oh, the delight that sparkles in that woman's eyes! "The dear boy is well," she said, "he is as well as ever he was in his life. Oh, my dear husband, what a wonderful Being this must be who has heard your prayers, and at all that distance has spoken our child into health! I believe in him, husband; I believe in him." I am sure she would speak in that fashion. The same processes which had been working in her husband had been working in her.

Now, think of the little boy. Here he comes, so happy and cheerful; and his father tells him all about his fever, and his going to see that wonderful Prophet at Cana, and how he said, "Thy son liveth." The little boy cries, "Father, I believe in Jesus. He is the Son of God." Nobody doubts the dear child's faith: he was not too young to be healed, and he is not too young to believe. He had enjoyed a special experience, more personal than even that of his father and mother. He had felt the power of Jesus; and it was no marvel that he believed.

But we are not at the end of the matter, for the servants standing around exclaim, "Master, we cannot help believing in Jesus, also; for we watched the dear child, and saw him recover, and the power which healed him must have been divine." One and all, they emulate their master's faith in Jesus. "I sat up with the dear boy," says the old nurse; "I would not go to sleep, for I felt that if I did sleep I might find him dead when I awoke. I watched him, and just at the seventh hour I saw a delightful change come over him, and the fever left him." "Glory be to Jesus!" shouted the old woman, "I never saw or heard of such a thing; it is the finger of God." All the other servants were of the same mind. Happy household! There was a grand baptism soon after, when they all went to confess their faith in Jesus. Not only was the child cured, but the whole household was cured.

May the Lord work such a wonder as that in all our houses! If any of you are groaning under a burden of grief, I trust you will be so relieved that, when you tell your wife of it, she will believe in Jesus too. May the dear child of your care believe in Jesus while yet a child; and may all who belong to your domestic circle also belong to the divine Lord!

III

"NEVERTHELESS AT THY WORD"

"Nevertheless at thy word."—Luke 5 : 5.

OUR Lord Jesus Christ had preached a sermon to the multitude while he was sitting down in Peter's boat; and after the people had gone, he had a private message for Simon. He said to him, "Launch out into the deep, and let down your nets for a draught." Christ's discourses to the general public were all full of most blessed teaching, but his little private talks to his intimate acquaintances were even more helpful and precious. They were important truths which he proclaimed to the many, but the choicest things he reserved for the few. Many a parable, which he addressed to the crowd, he explained only to his own disciples, and many a thing which he never said to the crowd at all, because they could not understand it, and it would have been like casting pearls before swine, he whispered in the ears of his disciples. So it was with Simon Peter at this time. There was the sermon to the many first, and after the sermon this word to Peter about launching out into the deep. Mind that you, who love the Lord, always look for the private piece after the public sermon. Watch for the sweet word which your Master is always willing to utter, and do not be satisfied unless you hear it.

Then, if the message that he gives you shall be a precept, or a command, like that addressed to Simon, bidding him let down his nets, be careful that you at once obey it. Be not negligent of the special voice of God in your own heart and conscience, for God intends thereby to bestow a great blessing upon you, even as he did upon Simon whose boat was filled with fish almost to sinking. If you give heed to that special private word of your Lord to your own heart and soul, many a boatful of fish shall you have, or, rather, many a heartful of untold blessing which otherwise you might never have received.

Peter, being exhorted to launch out into the deep, and to let down his nets for a draught, reasoned that, according to the ordinary course of events, it would be of very little use to do so, for he and his comrades had been toiling hard with their great seine net all through the night, yet they had caught nothing, and it did not, therefore, seem probable that they would catch anything now. However, feeling that Christ was his Master and Lord, and that it did not become him to raise any question about the matter, he just stated the facts of the case, and then added, cheerfully, "Nevertheless at thy word I will let down the net."

Those four words, "Nevertheless at thy word," seem to furnish me with a topic upon which I shall try to speak thus:— First, *the word of Christ is our supreme rule:* "At thy word." Secondly, *the word of Christ is our sufficient warrant.* If we have that at our back, we may well say, "Nevertheless at thy word I will let down the net"; and, thirdly, *to keep that word will always ensure a reward.*

First, then, THE WORD OF CHRIST IS THE SUPREME RULE OF THE CHRISTIAN.

Time out of mind have we spoken to you about the precious blood of Christ that cleanses from all sin, and about the blessings that Jesus brings to you when he becomes your Saviour; but we are bound also to remind all of you, who profess to have believed on him, and to have become his disciples, that you must not only own him as your Master and Lord, but that you must do whatsoever he bids you.

> *Faith must obey the Saviour's will,*
> *As well as trust his grace.*

The moment we become Christians, who are saved by Christ, we become his servants to obey all his commandments. Hence, it is incumbent upon us to search the Scriptures that we may know what our Master's will is. There he has written it out for us in plain letters, and it is an act of disobedience to neglect this search. By refusing to learn what the will of our Lord is, the sin of ignorance becomes wilful, because we do not use the means by which we might receive instruction. Every servant of Christ is bound to know what he is to do; and then, when he knows it, he should at once do it. The Christian man's business is, first, to learn Christ's will, and, secondly, to do it. Once learnt, that will is the supreme law of the Christian whatever may seem to oppose it.

Let me just mention a few of the times when it seems difficult to conform to that will, but when we must say, "Nevertheless at thy word."

First, we must do this with regard to great Gospel truths *when our own reason is staggered*. No thoughtful person can seriously consider the doctrines of grace without often crying out, "They are high; I cannot attain to them." There are many things revealed to us in the Scriptures which we cannot understand; nay, not even though we give all our mind to endeavour to comprehend them. There are difficulties in theology. This doctrine does not appear to square with that, or that one with the next. One truth, perhaps, appears inconsistent with the love of God; or we may sometimes wonder how certain events in God's providential dealings can be consistent with his goodness or justice. Well, whenever you put your hand to your brow, and say, concerning anything revealed in the Scriptures, "I cannot comprehend it," lay your other hand upon your heart, and say, "Nevertheless I believe it. It is clearly taught in the Bible; and although my reason may find it difficult to explain it, and I may not be able to discover any arguments to prove the truth of it, yet I lay my reason down at my infallible Master's feet, and trust where I cannot see." For a man to take his creed blindly from a pope or a priest, is to degrade himself, because he receives that teaching from his fellow-man; but for him to lay his whole mind down at the feet of Jesus Christ, is no degradation, since Christ is the wisdom of God, and all wisdom is infallibly gathered up in him. I do not expect fully to understand my Lord's will, I only ask to be informed what that will is. I do not suppose that I can comprehend it, but I say, "What is thy will, my Master? If thou wilt reveal it to me, I will believe it."

We must adopt a similar course *when we are exposed to the quibbles of our fellow-men*. Many young persons, especially, find themselves unable to answer all the objections that are raised by those who oppose the Gospel. It would be a marvel if they could for the old proverb says, "One fool can ask more questions than fifty wise men can answer." It is not likely that those who are just beginning to learn divine truth should be able to overcome all its opponents. When a question has sometimes staggered me, I have felt, "Well, I cannot answer that, but I believe that it can be answered. I thank God that I have heard it asked, for it has taught me my ignorance upon that point, and I will sit down, and study God's Word till I can answer it; but even if I cannot answer it, it does not signify. Somebody can do so; and, above all, God himself can. Be it mine sometimes to leave the arrows of the adversary sticking in my shield; they will do no harm there. If he likes to see them there, let him be amused by it; but as long as I cling to Christ's infallible teaching, they will not hurt me. So let him shoot, and shoot again." You will find, beloved, that this will be good exercise for your humility, and good exercise for your loyalty to Christ. It will be shown that you are, after all, a follower of Christ, and not a believer in your own infallibility, or relying upon that reason of yours which, at best, is but a dim candle, but that you have really yielded up your mind to the lordship of your Saviour.

Sometimes we shall have to say, "Nevertheless at thy word," *when the command of Christ seems contrary to our own experience.* It would become a dangerous thing if we were always to follow the experience even of Christians, for the experience of one man might teach us one thing, but the experience of another might teach us the very reverse; and to make experience the basis of theology, though it is often a helpful illustration of it, would lead to great mistakes. I must never say, "I did such-and-such a thing; I know it was not right, yet good came of it, and, therefore, I feel that I may do the same thing again." Neither ought I to say, "I did so-and-so, which I knew was right, but I suffered great trouble as the result of it, and, therefore, I ought not to do it again." No, no; whatever happens to us, our only course is to pursue the right path, and to avoid all that is wrong. Let each of us say, "My Master, if any act of obedience to thee were to cost me many a pang—to cost me my liberty—,to cause me to be put into prison"—and it has done so to many of the saints of old—,"yet I will do as thou commandest me, whatever the consequences may be."

What said Master John Bunyan, after he had lain in prison many years simply for preaching the Gospel? The magistrates said to him, "John, we will let you out, but you must promise not to preach again. There are the regular divines of the country; what have you, as a tinker, to do with preaching?" John Bunyan did not say, "Well, now, I can see that this preaching is a bad thing. It has got me into prison, and I have had hard work to tag enough laces to keep my wife and that poor blind child of mine. I had better get out of this place, and stick to my tinkering." No, he did not talk like that, but he said to the magistrates, "If you let me out of prison to-day, I will preach again to-morrow, by the grace of God." And when they told him that they would not let him out unless he promised not to preach, he bravely answered, "If I lie in gaol till the moss grows on my eyelids, I will never conceal the truth which God has taught to me."

We are, therefore, not to put our own past experience in the way of obedience to our Lord's will, but to say to him, "Nevertheless, however costly this duty may prove to be, at thy command I will let down the net, or do whatsoever thou biddest me do." But, sometimes, people get remarkably wise through experience, or they think that they do. Old sailors, for instance, fancy that they "know a thing or two"; and Simon Peter, who had been fishing in that lake for a long while, thought he knew all that could be known about fishing. And Christ interfered with Peter just in Peter's own line, and gave him a command about fishing. The fisherman might have said, "What is the good of casting the net? We have been fishing all night long, and have taken nothing; what is the good of our fishing any more?" Peter did not talk so, though he may have thought like that; but he said, "Nevertheless at thy word, since thou knowest far more about fish than I do,—since thou didst make them, and canst make them come wheresoever thou wilt,— since, Lord, thou commandest it,—I would not do it at anybody else's bidding, but I will do it at thine, I will let down the net." So, sometimes, there may be something in God's Word, or some path of duty clearly indicated to you, which does not seem to carnal judgment to be very wise; but you are to say, "Nevertheless at thy word,—no other authority could make me do it;—but thy law is the supreme rule for my conduct, and I will do whatsoever thou dost bid me."

This great principle ought also to prevail *when self-love is in the way.* Sometimes, the command of Christ runs completely contrary to what we should ourselves like, and obedience to it involves self-denial. It threatens to take away from us much that was very pleasurable to us; and then, very likely, something within us says, "Do not obey it; it will go very hard with you if you do." Nevertheless, may the Holy Spirit so mightily work upon you that you will do anything and everything that Christ commands, however galling to the flesh it may be. We are not our own; so let us never act as if we were. The mark of the precious blood of Jesus is upon us; we have been bought with it, so it is not right for us to make provision for the flesh, or to be looking out for our own ease or aggrandisement. It is our duty to do whatever our Lord bids us do, and to take the consequences, whatever they may be. So let us each one say, "I know that it will cost me much, my Master; but, nevertheless, I will do whatever thou commandest me."

Sometimes, there is a more powerful opposition still to the will of the Lord; that is, *when love of others would hinder us from obeying it.* "If I do so-and-so, which I know I ought to do, I shall grieve my parents. If I carry out that command of Christ, the dearest friend I have will be very angry with me; he has threatened to cast me off if I am baptized. My old companions, who have been very kind to me, will all consider that I have gone out of my mind, and will no longer wish to have me in their company." If a person has a genial heart, and a loving spirit, this kind of treatment is very trying, and there is a strong temptation to say, "Well, now, how far can I go in religion, and yet just manage to save these fond connections? I do not wish to set myself up in opposition to everybody else; can't I, somehow or other, please God, and yet please these people too?" But if we are indeed Christians, the supreme rule of our Lord's will drives us to say to him, "Nevertheless, I will do whatever thou dost command." Farewell, our best-beloved, if they stand in the way of Christ our Lord, for he said, "He that loveth father or mother more than me is not worthy of me: and he that loveth son or daughter more than me is not worthy of me." Everyone else and everything else must go, that we may keep company with Christ.

It sometimes happens that we have God's Word pointing us to a certain course of action, but we do not follow it because of *the faintness of our own heart.* Do you ever feel faint-hearted? There are some people who seem as if they were born without nerves, or feeling, for they never appear to be downcast. But some of us, at times, shrink away, and seem to be dried up, as if the marrow were gone from our bones, and the strength from our hearts. At such a time as that, we know what Christ would have us do, but we hesitate to do it; we feel as if we could not; not that we would not, but that we really could not. There is a want of courage, a lack of confidence; we are timid, and cannot dash into the fray. Then is the time, when heart and flesh fail, for us to take God to be the strength of our soul by resolving, let our weakness be what it may, that we will obey the command of Christ. When thy heart is faint, still follow Christ; when thou feelest as if thou must die at thy next step, still keep close at his heel; and if thy soul be almost in despair, yet hold on to him, and keep thy feet in his ways. If anyone, who feareth the Lord, still walketh in darkness, and hath no light, let him trust in the name of the Lord, and stay upon his God, for so shall his light break forth as the morning, and his heart shall be once more glad in the Lord.

So, you see, whatever obstacle there may be in the way of our obedience to the command of Christ, let each one of us still say to him, "Nevertheless at thy word, I will do whatever thou commandest. That shall be the supreme rule and guide for all my actions."

Now, secondly, I want to show you that THE WORD OF CHRIST IS OUR SUFFICIENT WARRANT, as well as our supreme rule.

This is, first, our warrant for *believing on him.* If the Lord Jesus Christ has bidden thee do this, thou certainly mayest do it; and if any shall ask thee why thou dost believe on him, this shall be thy triumphant answer, "The King gave me the command to do so." Listen to this, all ye who desire to have eternal life, and who have not yet obtained it. The Gospel commission is, "Go ye therefore, and teach all nations, baptizing them in the name of the Father, and of the Son, and of the Holy Ghost"; and this is the Gospel command, "Believe on the Lord Jesus Christ, and thou shalt be saved." The poor timid soul says, "How can I venture to trust my guilty soul with Christ? It would be presumption upon my part. What right have I to come and rely upon him?" It must be right for thee to do it, for he biddeth thee do it; and if he biddeth thee do it, this is warrant enough for thee. Every sinner under heaven, who hears the glad tidings of salvation, is commanded to believe on Jesus; and he is warned that, if he does not believe on him, he shall be damned. "God now commandeth all men everywhere to repent." This is the very widest form of command, so I bid each one of you to say, this very moment, "Lord, I am not worthy to be thy disciple; but, nevertheless, at thy command, I will believe in thee. I feel that it will be a wonder of grace if I am saved, and it is almost incredible that it should ever take place; nevertheless, at thy command, I let down my net; I even dare to trust thy precious blood and thy spotless righteousness, and to expect that thou wilt save me." Is not that a blessed form of argument? I pray that some of you may feel its force, and act upon it even now.

Next, *this is an excellent reason for being baptized if you are a believer in the Lord Jesus Christ.* Somebody may say to you, "What is the good of baptism? It will not save you; to be immersed in water will not wash away your sins." I hope you will be ready to reply, "No, I know all that; nevertheless, at Christ's command, I mean to do it. I ask not what will be the gain to me of obeying his orders. That would be sheer selfishness; he bids me be baptized, and that is enough for me." "But such-and-such a church does not ordain the baptism of believers, or baptism by immersion." No, but Christ has ordained it. By his own example, by his plain precept, by the preaching and practice of his apostles, he has revealed his will to us, and therefore it is for us to obey that will. If any shall accuse us of making too much of the baptism of believers, we reply, "Our Lord has said, 'He that believeth and is baptized shall be saved,' and we have no more right to leave out one portion of his words than the other; so, at his command we do this, and let men say what they will."

This, beloved, is also *the great argument for our taking up the position which we hold as Dissenters.* Is it not a bad thing to dissent from other people? Yes, of course it is, if they are right, and we are wrong; but it is just as bad for them to dissent from us if we are right, and they are wrong. I am not to say, "I will be singular, and keep myself separate from other people." It would be wrong for me to act like that; but it is right to say,

"Whatsoever Christ commands is law in his Church." What synods command, or bishops command, or popes command, is not worth the paper it is written on; there is no authority in it to a Christian. He is free from all such control as that; but the law of Christ, as he finds it revealed in the Bible, is binding upon him. I should honour any man who stood absolutely alone, without another individual to support him in his opinion, for having the courage to do so, if he justified his action by the Word of God. To run with the multitude is only too often to go in the wrong road. To believe a thing because the many believe it, is a coward's reason. To slink away from truth because she stands in the pillory, because she is unpopular, because the crowd cries her down, oh, this is a craven spirit! I would rather be on the side of truth with half a dozen paupers than be on the side of a lie with all the kings and prelates who ever rode in their pomp through the streets of this world, for, at the last, they who were on truth's side, and on Christ's side, shall be honoured, and they who had not the conscience and the courage to follow the Lamb shall be dishonoured and covered with everlasting shame and contempt.

This principle can also be applied to many other matters. "Nevertheless at thy word" ought to be *an argument for keeping on praying*. If you have been asking, for seven years, for the salvation of a soul, and yet that soul is not saved, you may be tempted to say, with Peter, "We have toiled all the night, and taken nothing"; but if you do, mind that you also add, "Nevertheless at thy word I will let down the net." Pray on still; if thou hast begun to pray for any man, keep on praying for him as long as thou livest and he lives. Or if it is some choice blessing for the Church or for the world, which God has evidently promised, and it is laid on thy heart to ask it, intercede still even though for years thou shouldst receive no answer to thy petition. Still knock at mercy's door; wrestle till the break of day, for, if in the night the blessing comes not, ere the morning sun has risen the Lord will give thee the desire of thy heart.

So, too, is it *with regard to Christian service*. I will suppose that you have begun to labour for Christ, and that you feel very stupid at it. You have not much talent; and what little you have, you hardly know how to put to the best use. Well, it looks as if you had better not try again; yet I would advise you to say to your Lord, "Nevertheless at thy word I will go to work again, I will try once more; nay, I will try many times more." Suppose you have been working in a certain district, or class, and you have not succeeded; do not yield. Many a hard piece of soil has, after many efforts, at last brought forth a harvest. If Jesus bade thee sow there—and he did, for he told thee to sow beside all waters—, go thou, and say, "Nevertheless at thy word I will do what thou commandest." When I come to address this congregation, I like to feel that I come because I am told to do so. One of you may say, "If I go to that dark village, and stand up on the green to preach, I expect I shall be mobbed, nevertheless at thy word I will do it." It is a blessed thing to render obedience to Christ under the most difficult circumstances. To obey him when it is pleasant to do so, when all that you do prospers, is good as far as it goes; but to obey him when everything seems against you, and nothing appears to prosper, to trust the Lord, and still to work on for him, this is indeed making Jesus Christ to be your Lord.

I must not dwell longer on this part of my theme, lest I weary you; so I will conclude with the last point, which is this, TO KEEP YOUR MASTER'S WORD WILL ENSURE A REWARD TO YOU.

You, who believe in Jesus, are already saved, so you will understand that I speak not of any legal reward, as of debt, for this is all of grace; but the man, who carefully and faithfully does everything according to Christ's word, shall have, first of all, *the reward of an easy conscience.* Suppose you go home, one night, and say to yourself, "I have done to-day something that I thought to be right, but I did not stop to enquire if it was according to my Master's will, I did not wait upon him in prayer for guidance";—you will feel very uneasy and uncomfortable in your conscience; and if any trouble shall arise through it, you will have to say, "I brought this on myself, for I took my own course." But if you can say, at nightfall, "What I have done to-day will probably be much discussed, and possibly it will be censured by some, and it may be that it will cost me much pain, and even pecuniary loss; but I know that, as far as I could judge, it was my Master's will"—you will sleep very sweetly after that. "Whatever comes of it," you will say, "I will take it from my Saviour's piercèd hand,

and reckon it to be part of the sacrifice that is necessary in being a Christian.'' It is better to be a loser in that way than to be a gainer in any other, for, as the old divine used to say, ''He that can wear the flower called heart's ease in his bosom is better off then he that weareth diamonds in his crown, but who has not true ease of heart.'' If a man goes up and down in his daily business in the world, and in his family, and is always able, by God's grace, to feel, ''I have laboured as in the sight of God to do that which is right according to the teaching and example of my Lord and Saviour,'' he has a reward in his own heart from that very fact even if he had no other.

But, next, there is a great reward in being enabled to obey the Master's word, because, rightly looked at, *it is in itself a blessing of divine grace.* When thou thankest God for the good things he has done for thee, thank him not only for keeping thee out of sin, but also thank him for enabling thee to do his will. No man has any right to take credit to himself for his own integrity, for, if he be a Christian, that integrity is the gift of God's grace, and the work of God's Spirit within him. If thou didst, in thy youth, form a candid, honest judgment of the Word of God, and then, burning all bridges and boats, and severing all connection with that which was behind thee, if thou didst dare to cast in thy lot with the despised people of God, bless him for it, and count it as a great favour which he did thee in that he enabled thee to act thus; and if, when tempted with heavy bribes, thou hast hitherto been able to say, ''Get thee behind me, Satan,'' and to follow close to the heels of Christ, give God all the glory of it, and bless his holy name. In such a case as this, virtue is its own reward. To have been obedient to Christ, is one of the highest blessings that God can have bestowed upon any man. There are some of us, who have to thank God that, when there were pinching times, we did not dare to yield; but when friends and enemies alike pointed out another way, we saw what was our Master's way, and followed it by his grace. We shall have to thank him to all eternity for this. Once begin to parley with the foe, to stifle your conscience or hide your principles, young man, once begin to follow trickery in trade, once begin to dally with the wrong, and you will soon find that you are sowing thorns that will pierce through your pillow when you grow old. Be just, and fear not.

Follow Christ though the skies should fall; and in doing this, you will be rewarded, for it is a blessing in itself.

But, more than this, *no man does his Master's will fully without getting a distinct reward.* Simon Peter's boatful of fish was his reward for launching out at Christ's word; and in keeping his commandments there is always a great reward. There is usefulness to others, there is happiness to yourself, and there is glory to God. I sometimes fear that we, ministers, do not preach enough about practical godliness. We tell you about justification by faith, and the doctrines of grace, and we cannot too frequently discourse upon such topics as these; but we must also insist upon it that, where there is faith in Christ, there will be obedience to Christ; and we cannot too often insist upon it that, while the everlasting salvation of the Christian does not depend upon what he does, yet his own comfort, his own usefulness, the glory which he will bring to God, must depend upon that. Therefore, look ye well to it, beloved, young and old, rich and poor, and henceforth, as long as you live, take the Word of God to be the pole-star to you in all your sailings across the ocean of life, and you shall have a blessed voyage, and reach the port of peace, not with rent sails and broken cordage, a dismasted wreck, but "an entrance shall be ministered unto you abundantly into the everlasting kingdom of our Lord and Saviour Jesus Christ."

IV

COMFORT FOR THE FEARFUL

"He saith unto them, Why are ye fearful, O ye of little faith?"—Matt. 8: 26.

THE winds were howling, the waters were roaring, and the disciples thought that the little ship must surely be engulfed in the raging sea, so they aroused their Master from his sorely-needed sleep, and cried to him, "Lord, save us: we perish." Note well the first words that he speaks to his frightened followers. Generally, when a man is in trouble, it is best first to help him out of it if we can, and then to give him any rebuke that he may deserve. Yet we may be quite sure that our Lord Jesus Christ followed the wisest order in every case. Being aroused because there was danger, he dealt first with the chief cause of danger; what was that? Not the winds or the waves, but the disciples' unbelief. There is always more peril, to a Christian, in his own unbelief than in the most adverse circumstances by which he may be surrounded.

I think I may venture to say—though, to omnipotence, all things are possible—that it was an easier task for Christ to calm the winds and the waves than to still the tumult raised by doubt in his disciples' minds; he could more swiftly cause a calm to fall upon the stormy surface of the Galilean lake than upon the perturbed spirits of his terrified apostles. The mental always excels the physical; the ruling of hearts is a greater thing than the governing of winds and waves. So, when we have to battle with trouble, let us always begin with ourselves—our own fears, mistrusts, suspicions, selfishness, and self-will,—for the chief danger lies there. All the trouble in the world cannot harm you so much as half a grain of unbelief. May God grant you grace to take this estimate of unbelief; and because Christ first rebuked that, and then the winds and the waves, so do you first seek to have yourself under proper control, so that, afterwards, you may be able to overcome your difficulties, whatever they may be. He who is, by the grace of God, enabled to master his own soul, need not doubt that he shall also be master of everything that opposes him.

First, I shall apply the question in my text to THOSE WHO REALLY ARE THE LORD'S PEOPLE; those who are in the boat with Christ, his disciples, who follow him, and keep near to him: "Why are ye fearful, O ye of little faith?"

First, *why is it that you doubt his love?* He brought you on to this stormy sea, he bade you take ship, and he knew all about this storm coming on. Do you think, because of your present experience, that he does not love you? You dare not utter such a calumny. Look back at your past life, and see how patiently he has borne with you. Your slowness in learning has not made your Divine Teacher angry, but he has still gone on teaching you. Do you remember when he first called you by his grace, and what you were when he called you? Do you recollect what you have been since he called you? Yet he has still continued to love you and has not cast you away. Look back, I pray you, upon the many times in which he has appeared for you, bringing you through very severe trials, and sustaining you under very heavy burdens. After all this, do you mistrust him? Do you suspect that he has brought you thus far, encouraging you with many hopes, allaying your fears, and supplying your necessities, on purpose that he might overwhelm you with disappointment? Has he been trifling with you in all this, exciting desires and expectations in you which, after all, are not to be fulfilled, but you are to be left to perish? Oh, no! It is impossible that he can have done this; it is altogether unlike him, and inconsistent with all his past treatment of us, and with his well-known character. Come, child of God, you know that he loves you, after all. The proofs and pledges of that love rise up before your memory, so you cannot think that he will suffer you to be cast away. Will he allow your present troubles to destroy you, when so many others have not been able even to hurt a hair of your head? Trust in his love, and dismiss your fears.

Let me turn to another side of this truth. *Do you doubt your Lord's power?* These disciples ought not to have done so, for they had lately been eye-witnesses of many remarkable displays of his power. Had they not seen him cast out devils? Had they not been with him when a touch of his hand healed the leper; when, another time, the laying of his hand upon the fevered brow had raised the sick one from her bed? Had they not come fresh from a mass of miracles where, in the crowded street, he had dealt out healing to all manner of sufferers? How could they doubt his power when, before their own eyes, they had seen it so wonderfully displayed? Is he Master of devils, and not of winds? Can he cast out diseases, and not lull to sleep the roaring billows? It was both absurd and wicked for them to think of setting a limit to his unbounded power.

And now, you dear child of God, after the experience you have had of his goodness, and after what you know the Lord did for you by his redeeming love in ages past dare you say that he has not power to deliver you now? Is anything too hard for the Lord? You say that you are poor; but can he not supply your need? Are not the cattle upon a thousand hills his own? Does he not claim the silver and gold as his treasure? He can feed the universe; he has done it these many centuries, and he is still doing it. And will not he, who supplies the wants of all living creatures by simply opening his hand, find food enough for his own child? Will you doubt his power? Is your case a very peculiar and difficult one? Do you draw a line, and say, "This God can do, but that he cannot do"? Is that right? Is it reasonable? Granted that he is omnipotent,—and he is omnipotent, whether you admit it or not,—and you have done away with difficulties. O thou with little faith in God's power, wherefore dost thou doubt? He can—he will—help thee, if thou wilt but trust him to do so.

Peradventure, however, your doubt may touch another point. *Have you any suspicion of God's wisdom?* Possibly, these disciples may have thought, "It was very unwise of our Master, just at eventide, to bid us cross this lake, which, lying low in a hollow surrounded by hills, is subject to very sudden and fierce gusts of wind, that catch a ship, and twist her round, so that no steersman can tell how to cope with the various currents and winds which are so extraordinary in their course. It was unwise of him to bring us here." Yet, if they did talk like that, they ought to have known better, for they had sat at his feet, and listened to the wondrous wisdom which poured from his lips. They knew that he was supremely wise; how, then, could they doubt? And dost thou, O child of God, think that the Lord is dealing unwisely with thee? Darest thou charge the all-wise Jehovah with folly? What is thy life but a constant repetition of floundering and blundering? But he, who has shown his marvellous skill in creation, and his wondrous wisdom in redemption, and also in providence,—dost thou think that he miscalculates, or misses the mark he aims at, or that he can in any way err? Oh, cast away this dishonouring reflection upon the Lord, as thou hearest him say to thee, "Why art thou fearful, O thou of little faith?"

There are some other things which might very well have smitten the consciences of these fearful followers of Christ; and among them were these considerations which I suggest to you as worthy themes for your meditation. It is true that it was a terrible storm; but, then, *they were in the same boat with their Lord*. Whenever a foaming billow smote the ship, and agitated the breasts of the disciples, it moved their Master also. He had to bear all the tossing of the waves, the wild leaping of the vessel from the billow's base to the billow's crown; he must have felt it just as much as they did. If the little vessel went down with them, it must go down with him also, for they were in the same boat. How this thought ought to have lulled their fears to rest! And, beloved Christian, dost thou not know that he that believes in Jesus is sailing in the same ship with him? Remember how Paul writes, "For ye are dead, and your life is hid with Christ in God." "Because I live," said Jesus himself to his disciples, "ye shall live also."

It was a bold saying of one that he had trusted Christ to save him, so he knew that he could not be lost. "But," asked someone, "suppose, after all, that you are lost?" "Well, then," he replied, "Christ would lose more than I should; for while I should lose my soul, he would lose his honour. If he did not save one who trusted him, he would lose his character as Saviour, he would lose the most precious jewel in his crown; and that can never be."

Another reflection is that, although they were in a great storm, *the power that made the storm was the very power to which they had to trust*. There was not a single blast of the tempest but

Jehovah's might had sent it, nor did a single wave leap up, in apparent wrath, but with God's permission, or at his command. It was his power, outside the peril.

It is the same in your case; you are in great trouble, but does trouble spring out of the ground? Does it come by chance? Nay, God's hand is in it all. I know men talk of the laws of nature, but the laws of nature have no force in themselves; the whole force that carries out a law of nature is a divine force. So, your difficulties are of God's sending, trials of God's making, and they are all still in the hand of the all-powerful One to restrain, or mitigate, or increase, or direct according to his own will.

You have often heard, I daresay, that pretty little story which I cannot help telling again, of the woman, on board ship, who was much disturbed in a storm, while her husband, the captain, was calm and restful. She asked him why he was so placid when she was so distressed. He did not answer in words, but he took down his sword, and held it to her breast. She smiled. He said, "Why are you not afraid? This is a sharp sword, with which I could slay you in a minute." "Ah!" she replied, "but I am not afraid of a sword when it is my husband who wields it." "So," said he, "neither am I afraid of a storm when it is my Father who sends it, and who manages it." Now, since all the trials and troubles of this mortal life are as much in the hand of the great God as that sword was in the hand of the good woman's husband, we need not be afraid of them, for they are all in his power.

> *The God that rules on high,*
> *And thunders when he please,*
> *That rides upon the stormy sky,*
> *And manages the seas.*
>
> *This awful God is ours,*
> *Our Father and our love.*

There was another thing that ought to have kept those disciples from being afraid, and it was this. Suppose they had sunk—, still, having put to sea at his command, and with him on board—, *all would have been well with them.* I have heard of a sailor, who was very calm in a storm; and someone asked him,

"Why are you not afraid? Can you swim?" "No," he said, "I cannot swim; but if I were to sink to the bottom of the sea, I should only sink into my Heavenly Father's hand, for he holds the waters in the hollow of his hand." That is a sweet thought; and if the worst comes to the worst with you, well, you would only die. You would go as low as the grave; but, blessed be God, you would never go any lower; and, in due time, even your body will come up again from that grave, and, re-united with your soul, be "for ever with the Lord." "Wherefore, comfort one another with these words." But suppose you should die, your soul will then leap away from death into eternal life in a moment. Death would end all your troubles, rid you for ever of all your burdens, and you would be at home, to go no more out for ever.

There was one other reason why these disciples ought not to have been at all alarmed; and that was, *because their Master was asleep.* "Oh!" say you, "I do not see what comfort that was to them." Well, let me tell you what happened to me, one night, when I was on board ship. In my sleep, I started because I thought I heard something slip. Something had slipped; it was the anchor that had been cast overboard. I called out to one who slept near me, "What is the matter?" He said, "There is something the matter, I feel sure." "Why?" I asked, and he replied, "Because the captain is up." It was in the middle of the night, but the captain was up, so I was also up very soon, and saw that the captain was up, and that the sailors were quietly getting out a boat. If my friend had told me that the captain was asleep, I might have slept on, for I should have said, "It is all right if he is asleep. I need not trouble myself to know what is the matter"; but when I heard that he was up, I thought it was time for me to be up, too. But if, at any time, you were at sea, and you said to another passenger, "Where is the captain?" and the reply was, "Oh, he is in his berth, sound asleep!" you would say, "Oh, then, it is all right!" Why did the Lord Jesus Christ go to sleep in a storm? Why, just because he knew that all was right; why should he not go to sleep? The great loving heart of Christ would not have rested if his children had been in any danger. It was because there was no danger, either to him or to them, that he went to sleep.

Perhaps you are saying to yourself, "I have not had any wonderful deliverance from this trouble. I have had, in times gone by; but, now, the Lord does not seem to work any great marvel for me." No, because there is not any need for it. And you may rest assured that, if he does not come to help you, it is because there really is not any urgent need for his inter-position, as you are not in any great danger. Possibly, the Lord sees that it will be best for you to bear your troubles a little longer, for you are getting good out of them. He means to leave you in the furnace for a little while because he can see that your dross is being taken away; but if the good metal in you were being injured in the slightest degree, he would lift you out of the furnace directly. I hope that you can see now that the sleep of Jesus ought to have given rest to the minds of his disciples; but it did not, and he had to say to them, "Why are ye fearful, O ye of little faith?"

Thus I have spoken to the Lord's own people. May the Holy Spirit graciously bless the word to them!

Now I want to speak to THOSE WHO CANNOT SAY THAT THEY ARE CHRIST'S DISCIPLES.

There is a story told of Dr. John Owen, who was then Mr. John Owen, that he had been for two or three years in great distress of mind. He went to London, hoping to hear a very famous divine; but, on arriving at the meeting-house, he found that the doctor was not preaching. A man, whose name Mr. Owen never knew, preached from the text from which I am now preaching: "Why are ye fearful, O ye of little faith?" He was a man of no great ability; but it pleased God, that night, to break John Owen's fetters by means of the remarks that were made by the stranger-preacher, which were exactly suited to the condition of John Owen's mind at that time; and so, that mighty master of theology, perhaps the grandest of all English divines with whom God has ever favoured us, was brought into light and liberty through the instrumentality of that stranger-preacher.

You are seeking Christ, dear friend, and longing to be saved; but, for want of faith, you are still in trouble of soul. What is your real condition? Perhaps you say, "*I labour under a deep sense of sin, I have been exceedingly guilty.*" Possibly, some one sin specially troubles you; or, more probably, a number; it may be that you know that you have sinned against light and knowledge, and you are aware of the peculiar provocation of having sinned, as you have done, after enjoying Christian teaching from your youth up. You feel that there is some special aggravation about your transgression, and you say to yourself, "I can scarcely believe that there is pardon for me." My dear friend, I put it to you, "Why art thou fearful, O thou of little faith?" Did not Jesus Christ come into the world to save sinners? I am afraid that you do not think enough of the greatness of the Saviour, that he is God as well as man. Consider the dignity of his person as God over all blessed for ever; yet, nevertheless, stooping to bear human sin! Think of your sin as much as you will, but do also think much more of the Sin-bearer, and his vicarious sufferings. Weep at the remembrance of your guilt; but weep on Calvary, weep with the wounds of Christ before you. But, Oh! I pray you, do not do my Lord the great dishonour to say that he cannot forgive you. It is you who will not believe in him; it is, certainly, not with him that the difficulty lies. "He is able to save them to the uttermost that come unto God by him, seeing he ever liveth to make intercession for them" (Heb. 7 : 25). It is not possible that you are beyond his ability to save. There have been other persons saved, and many of them, who have sinned just as much as you have done; and even if there had not been any such, yet recollect that, if you are a sinner beyond all others, your case presents an opportunity for Christ to exceed everything that he has ever done; and he would delight in that. He delighteth in mercy; so, if you are really what you suppose yourself to be, namely, something altogether extraordinary in the way of guilt, then there remains room for Christ to show in you the extraordinary power of his grace. I pray you to believe that he can do this; trust him to do it, and you shall find that he both can and will.

Possibly, someone says, "*My difficulty is not so much concerning the power of God to pardon, as concerning the strong propensities to sin which I find dwelling in me.* How can they be conquered? I have resolved, a great many times, to overcome them; but I find my sin to be like Samson; it is not to be bound with new cords and green withes, for it breaks loose from all its bonds. I cannot think that I can be saved with such an impetuous temper, or such a proud spirit,"—or whatever form your sin happens to take. Now it is well that you should see this difficulty; but is not he, who is mighty to save, quite able to grapple with it? Have you forgotten that text, "Behold, I make all things new"? Do you not know that the Spirit of God has been given that he may take away the heart of stone out of your flesh, and give you a heart of flesh? Have you never read the covenant of grace which says, "Then will I sprinkle clean water upon you, and ye shall be clean: from all your filthiness, and from all your idols, will I cleanse you. A new heart also will I give you, and a new spirit will I put within you." Is anything too hard for the Lord in this matter?

"*But*," says another, "*my trouble is, that I cannot find anything in me that Christ can work upon.* I perceive some redeeming feature in all converted people, but I do not perceive anything of the kind in myself. I seem to be weak where I ought to be strong, and strong where I ought to be weak. I am all that I ought not to be, and nothing that I should be." Ah, my friend, I want you to believe—to do my Lord Jesus the honour to believe—what he has a right to claim from you, namely, that he can deal readily enough with your case, for yours is just the typical case that he came to save. This may seem strange to you, but it is the very essence of the Gospel, even as Joseph Hart sings,

> 'Tis perfect poverty alone
>   That sets the soul at large;
> While we can call one mite our own,
>   We have no full discharge.
>
> But let our debts be what they may,
>   However great or small,
> As soon as we have nought to pay,
>   Our Lord forgives us all.

Well, now, you who thus condemn yourself, should see that your very condemnation of yourself gives you hope of salvation. Why, the devil himself, I should think, would hardly dispute with some of you the fact that you are sinners. On the contrary, he has often been to you, and said, "See what a great sinner you are!" For once, he spoke the truth, though he did even that with an evil intention. If he says that to you, say to him, "Yes, Satan, you have proved that I am a sinner, but that is my hope of salvation, for 'it is a faithful saying, and worthy of all acceptation, that Christ Jesus came into the world to save sinners.'" He who condemns himself God absolves. He who is shut up in the prison of the law, so that he cannot escape; he who writes his own death-warrant, and signs it, and feels that he deserves to die,—he is the man for whom the Lord Jesus Christ sets open the door of mercy, and says, "Come unto me, for I have absolved thee. Thou art a free man. Be of good comfort. I died to redeem just such souls as thou art." So again I say, "O thou of little faith, wherefore dost thou doubt?"

Another case I would like to meet is that of one who says, *"Oh, but I have such a lack of sensibility!* I am afraid I do not feel humble enough. Some sinners weep, but I cannot. Some have upon them an awful horror of great darkness, but I have not; I wish I had." Dear friend, dost thou think that would help Christ to save thee? Oh, then, thou dost malign my Lord, who wants no help from thee! He can save thee, stony-hearted as thou art. What canst thou do, poor fool? I cannot help calling thee "fool" if thou dost think that thou canst do any-thing to help him to save thee. A righteousness like his, wouldst thou patch thy rags upon it? Blood like his, wouldst thou bring some bottles full of thy tears to add to the merit of his great sacrifice? There is nothing good in thee; it is all in Christ. From first to last, it is grace, *grace*, GRACE; and grace, you know, takes no payments, for it would mar its glory and its freeness if it took from thee anything from a thread to a shoe-latchet. Be thou only emptiness, and Christ will be thy fullness.

"But I do not feel," thou sayest. Well, then, be so empty that thou art even empty of feeling; thy feelings cannot save thee, but Christ will give thee all the feeling that thou needest. Come unto him just as thou art, and trust him for everything. Out with thy confession! Let not sin be smouldering in thy bosom any longer. Tell the Lord how guilty thou art; tell him that thou deservest his utmost wrath; tell him that thou couldst not complain even if he should destroy thee, but tell him that thou dost cling to Christ, and to the promise of pardon made in his Word; say to him,

Thou hast promised to forgive
All who in thy Son believe;
Lord, I know thou canst not lie;
Give me Christ, or else I die.

That is the thing to do. God help you to do it! Away with everything but what Christ has done, and what Christ is, and the boundless love of the great forgiving God, whose bowels yearn over thee, and who cries, "How shall I give thee up, Ephraim? how shall I deliver thee, Israel? how shall I make thee as Admah? how shall I set thee as Zeboim? Mine heart is turned within me, my repentings are kindled together, . . . for I am God, and not man" (Hos. 11: 8, 9). "O thou of little faith, why art thou so fearful?" Trust thy God, and live.

But, lastly, I hear someone else say, "*My trouble is concerning the difficulties of a Christian life.* How can I, if I begin to be a Christian, hold on to the end?" Dear friend, I will not deny that there are difficulties, and that they are very great, much greater than you imagine; but your holding on is not the great matter; it is Christ who will hold you on. Your perseverance in grace is no more to be your own act, apart from Christ, than is your first hope in him. You are to look to Christ to be Omega as well to be Alpha,—to be the Z as well as to be the A of the Christian Alphabet; and if you come, and cast yourself upon him, it is not his custom to cast away any who come to him, neither at first nor yet afterwards. "Having loved his own which were in the world, he loved them unto the end." And he will do the same with you. He will subdue your corruptions, drive out your iniquities, and present you, at the last, "faultless" before his Father's throne. Oh, I can talk about this; but, after all, it is only the Lord and Giver of grace who can drive away your unbelief! May he do so now, and to his dear name shall be the praise for ever and ever!

V

RESISTANCE TO SALVATION

"What have I to do with thee, Jesus, thou Son of the most high God?"—Mark 5: 7.

WHEREVER Jesus comes, there is a commotion. No sooner does he set his foot on the shore at Gadara, than he is at once assailed by the powers of darkness, and it is no long before the whole population of the district is affected by his presence. However uninfluential other people may be, Jesus is never so. He is ever either "the savour of death unto death" or "the savour of life unto life." He is never a savourless Christ. Virtue is always going out of him, and that virtue stirs up the opposition of evil-doers, so that, straightway, they come forth to fight against him.

You remember that, when Paul and Silas preached at Thessalonica, the unbelieving Jews cried out, "These that have turned the world upside down are come hither also." Was that a wonderful thing? Nay, rather, was it not exactly what the Lord Jesus Christ had prophesied when he said, "I came not to send peace, but a sword"? He said that, because of him, there would be division even in families, so that a man would be at variance against his father, and a daughter against her mother, and a man's foes would be those of his own household. Christ must make a stir wherever he comes, and his Gospel must cause a commotion wherever it is preached. Stagnation is inconsistent with life. Deathlike slumber is the condition of those who are dead in sin; but to be aroused to action is the sure consequence of the Gospel coming with power to anyone.

Yet Jesus Christ's actions were, as a rule, very quiet; and, on this occasion, he merely landed at Gadara. He had no trumpeters to herald his arrival, and no squadron of cavalry to escort him. In fulfilment of the ancient prophecy, he did not strive, nor cry, nor cause his voice to be heard in the streets.

He was so gentle that a bruised reed he did not break, and the smoking flax he did not quench; yet, wherever he went, there was always a stir. Well, we might have expected that it would be so; the analogies of nature would teach us to look for that. When the morning sun arises, without sound of drum, or tramp of armed men, straightway it causes confusion among the doers of darkness. With a roar, the lion gets back to his den; and the wolf and the hyena fly before the eye of light. I daresay, too, that the owl and the bat have a very strong aversion to the rising of the sun. But the sunlight is only objectionable to creatures that delight in darkness; and so it happened that Christ's landing at Gadara was like the sun rising upon the thick darkness in which that poor tortured demoniac was dwelling, and like the sun rising upon the dense darkness of ignorance and sin in which the swine-keeping Gadarenes were dwelling, so there was quite certain to be a stir, and a commotion, and an opposition.

I trust that the Lord Jesus Christ will be with us here in the preaching of his Gospel; and if so, there will be a stir here; and if some opposition should be aroused, we shall not wonder at it; and if others should find their opposition to the truth disarmed by the power and grace of the Holy Spirit, we shall not marvel at that, for it is God's wont thus to overcome his adversaries.

The first point that I shall speak upon, in connection with the demoniac's question, is this, THE DEVIL DREADS ALL CONTACT WITH CHRIST, for he moved the poor man to cry out, with a loud voice, "What have I to do with thee, Jesus, thou Son of the most high God?"

The devil dreads all contact with Christ, and he does so because, first, *Christ's nature is so contrary to his own.* "Can two walk together, except they be agreed?" And these two, so far from being agreed, are absolutely opposed to each other in every respect. There is a very ancient warfare between them; a warfare which, so far as this world is concerned, was proclaimed in the garden of Eden when God said to the serpent, "I will put enmity between thee and the woman, and between thy seed and her seed; it shall bruise thy head, and thou shalt bruise his heel." Christ loves light, Satan loves darkness. Christ worketh life, Satan worketh death. Christ is love, Satan is hate. Christ is goodness, Satan is evil. Christ is truth, Satan is falsehood. Christ is God, and Satan labours to supplant God, to set himself up for an anti-Christ, exalting himself above all that is called God.

Moreover, in the next place, *Satan is well aware that the mission of our Lord Jesus Christ in this world is not for his good*. He has no share in Christ's incarnation, nor in his atoning sacrifice. This is one of the wonderful results of the election of grace. Those persons, who stumble at the election of some men rather than others, ought equally to stumble at the fact that Christ did not redeem the fallen angels, but only fallen men; for why God chose to save men, and not to save angels, who among us can tell? The only answer I know to that question is this, "Even so, Father, for so it seemed good in thy sight." The mighty angels were passed by, and we, who are but worms of the dust, were looked upon with eyes of favour and love; and Satan, knowing this, and being jealous of the love which lights upon men, cannot endure the presence of Christ.

Moreover, Satan knows that, not only is there nothing for his good in the mission of Christ, but *he understands that the whole drift of Christ's mission is against him*. "For this purpose the Son of God was manifested, that he might destroy the works of the devil." What horrible work the devil has already done in the world! Behold how the garden of Eden is withered, and blighted, and turned into a desert. See the fertile earth bringing forth thorns and thistles; and see man, who was made in the image of God, reduced to the position of a toiling sinner, earning his bread by the sweat of his face. See war, and famine, and pestilence, and all kinds of evil and woe thickly spread over the whole earth; and remember that all this has come as the result of that one disobedience into which man was led by the temptation of the evil one. But the evil one has little room to glory in the mischief that he has wrought, for Christ has come to undo it. In the person of the second Adam, the Lord from heaven, man is lifted up from all the sin into which he fell through the first Adam; and, as to this poor world itself, sin-blighted as it now is, it travails in anticipation of the new birth which yet awaits it, and the day shall yet dawn when new heavens and a new earth shall prove how completely Christ has cancelled the curse, and made the earth fragrant with blessing. It is for this reason that Satan hates the presence of Christ, because Christ is to destroy his evil work; and, therefore, he dreads that Christ should come near to him.

The whole wish of this particular legion of devils was concentrated into the one request that they might be let alone; and *Satan wishes to be let alone*, to be suffered to work his evil will, and to do whatever he pleases. He did not, at that time, want to come into conflict with Christ; he did not wish that Christ should be assailed; nor did he have any hope that Christ might be caused to suffer any sort of defeat: he was too craven to aspire to any such thing as that. That had been his dream, in earlier days, when he had met him in the wilderness; but, now, he only asked to be let alone, just to be allowed to skulk off, and hide away, and keep himself out of Christ's notice. That is very much what the devil wants nowadays, when Christ's power is manifestly working in his Church; but when the Lord has, in his gracious providence, given peace to the persecuted, and by his Spirit has given power to the preaching of the Gospel, then the devil whines out that he only wants to be let alone. All things will go on comfortably and pleasantly. He would have a kind of truce proclaimed between himself and Christ; he wants a little respite, and desires to be let alone.

One reason for this is that *he knows his own powerlessness in the presence of Christ*. In the presence of man, Satan is great, and strong, and crafty; but, in the presence of the Christ of God, he shrinks into utter insignificance. He knows that he cannot resist even a word from Christ's lips, or a glance from his eyes, so he says, "What have I to do with thee, Jesus, thou Son of the most high God?" The question appears as if Satan pleaded with Christ not to put forth his power, not to touch him, but just to let him alone as too insignificant to be noticed. Such is the craft of Satan, that he will whine like a whipped cur, and crouch at the great Master's feet, and look up to his face, and entreat to be let alone, for he knows well enough the power of the Son of God. Yes, the name of Jesus has wondrous power over all the hosts of hell; so, let us not be discomfited nor dismayed by all the armies of Satan, but let us, with holy courage, contend against all the powers of evil, for we shall be more than conquerors over them through Jesus Christ our Lord and Saviour.

Satan also fears the presence of Christ *because he dreads the doom which awaits him*. Those fallen spirits at Gadara were afraid that they were about to begin to endure the dismal fate which, certainly, will be theirs by-and-by. There will come a day when the arch-traitor, and all the multitudes of fallen spirits whom he dragged down with him from heaven, shall have to appear before the judgment-seat of Christ. The saints of God will take part in that judgment, for Paul wrote to the Corinthians, "Know ye not that we shall judge angels?" And then the devil shall receive his final sentence, and be for ever banished to hell. There will he be bound, no more to wander through dry places, seeking rest, and finding none,—no more to be able to molest the children of God, and disturb their devotions, no more to be able to lay traps for the ensnaring of the feet of God's elect, no more to beguile the multitude, and lead them astray, no longer able to go through Christ's fields by night, and to sow his tares in the midst of the good wheat, but kept in prison, for ever bound in chains, to continue as an eternal and awful evidence of the wrath of God against transgression. It is no wonder that, in anticipation of his ultimate fate in hell, the very shadow of the Lord Jesus, as it falls upon him, makes him tremble; and, although he cannot repent, and cannot turn from the evil in which his heart indulges, yet is he cowed as he feels how awful goodness is, and how majestic is the supremacy of Christ over all who oppose his almighty will.

There will, perhaps, be more practical teaching in the second part of my subject, which is this, WHEN SATAN GETS MEN INTO HIS POWER, HE LEADS THEM ALSO TO OPPOSE THE COMING OF CHRIST TO THEM.

First, *conscience is feared by them*. They have not quite lost all knowledge of right and wrong; and, sometimes, Mr. Conscience, though drugged with Satanic opiates, and very hoarse with the cold that he has taken in this sinful world, does cry out at such a rate that they cannot sleep at night, and they cannot feel comfortable by day; so they say to themselves, "If we begin to think of Jesus and his Gospel, this conscience of ours will grow more troublesome still, and we shall not have any peace or enjoyment at all. Even now, we cannot indulge in our cups and our merry dances as we used to do; and we cannot go with our former jolly companions. If our conscience should once become thoroughly alive and active, it would follow us at our heels like a bandog, and we should not know how to get away from it. We do not want to have that state of things, we just want to be let alone." So they carefully avoid attending a place of worship where there is likely to be anything to trouble and alarm their conscience. They try to keep clear of preaching that is plain and outspoken against sin. There are some men, who seem as if they would not mind six months' imprisonment if, thereby, they could escape six months' thinking about their character and their state before God. May the Holy Spirit graciously save all of us from getting into that terrible condition! That is one reason why men cry out, as this demoniac did, "What have I to do with thee, Jesus, thou Son of the most high God?"—because conscience is feared by them.

Then, next, *change is dreaded by them;* they are content to remain as they are. In certain stages of a sinner's life, he feels as if he does not want to be anything but just what he is. He has succeeded in business, he is merry of heart, he is enjoying himself. I pity the man who never has any troubles. I believe that there are some people who never will have the heartache till they have known what it is to be hungry almost to starvation. It was so with that poor prodigal; he never thought of going back to his father till "he would fain have filled his belly with the husks that the swine did eat: and no man gave unto him." Poverty, sickness, bereavement, and sorrow of heart are often God's angels that come to smite men on the side and wake them up, as the angel awoke sleeping Peter, and delivered him from prison, whence he was to have been led forth to die on the morrow.

Some of you ought to thank God that he does not let you have a very easy or merry time. The reason for this is that he has designs of love for you, and he means that you never should rest till you rest in him. But it is often because of the pride which comes of fullness of bread, and the fatness of heart, which grows out of worldly prosperity, that many a man says to the Lord Jesus Christ, "What have I to do with thee, Jesus, thou Son of the most high God?"

And then, if you try to probe such people a little deeper, and begin to talk to them about death and judgment, they probably turn upon you with great indignation, for *they claim the right to be let alone*. "Surely," they say, "this is a free country, so we ought to be let alone, and not be interfered with." You will hear them say, concerning a certain preacher, "Why does not that man preach his own religion, and let other people alone?" Yes, that is the old cry, "Let us alone! Let us alone!" If you will only let the devil alone, the devil will let you alone; but if you once attack him, he will be certain to attack you. But just think for a moment what this foolish sinner claims; he claims the right to live in blindness! You who can see must not tell him that he is blind; if you do so, he says you are infringing his rights. He says that he has a right to lie in prison, if he chooses to do so; and if you come and hammer at the door, or shout to him through the iron bars that there has come One who can let loose the captives, he complains that you are disturbing him. Here is a man on the verge of destruction, asleep on the edge of a precipice. If you wake him, he tells you that he has a right to sleep there if he likes, and that he does not want you to rouse him up in that rough way, and talk to him about his imminent danger. If he does get up, he abuses you, and says, "Mind your own business. You go your way, and let me alone."

That is the style in which sinners talk when they claim the right to be let alone, but everybody who has any sense knows that such talk is the language of a fool, for a man has not the right to be damned, he has not the right to destroy himself eternally. Our law very properly withholds from a man the right to commit suicide; if he be caught in the act of attempting to take his own life, he is punishable as a criminal. The act of suicide is a grave offence against the laws of God and man, and no man has the right to damn his own soul, and so to commit spiritual suicide.

What a blessing it is that although some of us were once of that way of thinking, our Lord Jesus Christ would not let us alone! We were sheep away on the mountains, and we did not want the good Shepherd, but he came after us; and even when we saw him coming, we wandered further and further away from him, yet he would not let us wander away from him altogether. He followed us in all our devious tracks, and at last he found us, and laid us on his shoulders, rejoicing, and carried us back to the fold where he still watches over us.

Once again, some of these people, who entreat Christ to let them alone, do so *because they fear that he will torment them*. The demoniac at Gadara said to Christ, "I adjure thee by God, that thou torment me not." Many people seem to think that it is a very sorrowful thing to be a Christian, that believers in Christ are a miserable, unhappy lot of folk who never enjoy themselves. Well, I must admit that I do know some little communities of people, who reckon themselves the very pick of Christians, and who meet together on a Sunday to have a comfortable groan together; but I do not think that the bulk of us, who worship in this place, could be truthfully charged with anything like that. We serve a happy God, and we believe in a joyous Gospel, and the love of Christ in our hearts has made us anticipate many of the joys of heaven even while we are here on earth. "The peace of God, which passeth all understanding," keeps our hearts and minds through Christ Jesus; and "the joy of the Lord is our strength." Perhaps, if we were to let the ungodly know more about this joy and peace, they would throw down the weapons of their rebellion, and say, "We did not know that the religion of Jesus Christ was so blessed as this. We did not know that there was such music as this in the great Father's house. We did not know that there was a fatted calf waiting to be killed for us, and that the whole household would begin to be merry over us. Now that we know what joy there is, we will enter, and go no more out for ever."

Now I turn to the third part of the subject. I want to show you that SANE MEN MAY PUT THE DEMONIAC'S QUESTION, AND ANSWER IT: "What have I to do with thee, Jesus, thou Son of the most high God?"

First, *what have I, whoever I may be, inevitably to do with thee?* This is a question which concerns every person. Suppose that you are a stranger to these things of which I have been speaking, I beg you to give me your earnest attention; for, whether you believe in Jesus Christ or not, you cannot escape from having some connection with him, because, first of all, he has come into the world to save sinners, and that good news has been made known to you; and everyone who hears that Gospel message, and refuses to believe it, is responsible to God for that rejection. Remember how the Lord Jesus Christ said, concerning those cities in which his mighty works had been wrought, that it would be more tolerable for Sodom and Gomorrah in the day of judgment than it would be for Capernaum and Bethsaida where he had so often been. Christ has been near to you, and you have heard his Gospel, which many poor heathens have not heard. Now that you have heard the Gospel —the Gospel of the atoning sacrifice of Christ—his blood will cry out against you, as the blood of Abel cried out against Cain, if it is not applied to you to cleanse you from sin. You cannot escape from the Lord Jesus Christ. You are caught in the meshes of the great net which he has cast over all those who have heard the Gospel. "He that believeth not is condemned already, because he hath not believed in the name of the only begotten Son of God. And this is the condemnation, that light is come into the world, and men loved darkness rather than light, because their deeds were evil" (John 3:19). If you do not believe on the Lord Jesus Christ, you resolve not to be saved by him, but to remain in the condition in which you now are, that is, "condemned already."

There is another connection between you and Christ which you cannot get away from, for there is a sense in which you belong to Christ, whether you believe in him or not. In one of the last prayers he offered before his death, he said, "Father, the hour is come; glorify thy Son, that thy Son also may glorify thee: as thou hast given him power over all flesh, that he should give eternal life to as many as thou hast given him" (John 17:1, 2). For the special purposes of his grace to his own elect, Christ has received from his Father power over the whole human race; and it is in this sense that it is said "that he by the grace of God should taste death for every man"; for, although the full saving results of his death will come only to his chosen and redeemed people, "even to them that believe on his name," yet that wondrous work of his upon the Cross has a relation to all the sons of men. You cannot, therefore, get away from some connection with Christ even though you refuse to believe in him; so I put the definite question to you: Will you receive him, or will you reject him? Will you be his subject, or will you be his foe? The marriage supper is spread, and you are bidden to come to it; you are not in the position of those who never were bidden, so beware lest this sentence should be applied to you, "I say unto you, that none of those men which were bidden shall taste of my supper."

Remember, too, that all here, whether they receive Christ or reject him, will have to stand before his judgment-seat. The day cometh when not only the sheep, but the goats also, shall be gathered before him, so you must all be there; there is no way of escape for any one of you. It used to be said of the whole world, under the Roman Empire, that it was one great prison for any man who had offended Cæsar; for, wherever he might go, the officers of Cæsar could follow him, and arrest him. And, in a similar sense, the whole universe is, to an ungodly spirit, but one great house of detention, where that spirit is awaiting the last dread assize. In that day, the ungodly shall know that they cannot escape from Christ. Oh, that they would be wise enough to run to his open arms, and find salvation there!

It is much more sweet to turn to the other form of the question, *What connection is there between me and Christ by way of grace?* I believe my text might be read in two ways, and that in either sense it would be equally true to the original, for the Greek runs something like this, "What to me, to thee?" And that may mean, "What hast thou to do with me?" or, "What have I to do with thee?"

Put it the first way, "What hast thou to do with me?" Why, since I have believed on thee, thou hast had everything to do with me; and I know now that, even before I believed in thee, thou hadst everything to do with me. Didst thou not choose me, or ever the earth was created? Did not thy Father give me to thee? Didst thou not enter into covenant with him on my behalf? Didst thou not, in the fullness of time, redeem me with thy precious blood? Hast thou not called me by thy grace, and renewed me by thy Holy Spirit, and interceded for me in my times of temptation and upheld me in my hours of trials? If there be anything good in me, thou hast put it there.

And, then, what have I to do with thee? I have to receive my life from thee, my food from thee, my drink from thee; I have to receive my cleansing from thee, and my keeping from thee, and everything else that I need in time or in eternity. Thou art now my example, and thou art for ever to be my exceeding great reward. What have I to do with thee? I find in thee my All-in-all. I am to sit at thy feet, and learn of thee.

What have I to do with thee? I am to serve thee all my days, glad to be thy servant; and then I am to be for ever with thee where thou art, that I may behold thy glory.

I now refer very briefly to my last point, which is this: WHEN MEN ARE BLESSED BY JESUS, THEY CHANGE THEIR MINDS WONDERFULLY WITH REGARD TO HIM.

Can you picture to yourself the change between that poor demoniac, as he was when he first spoke to Christ, and the same man when he was clothed, and in his right mind, sitting at the feet of Jesus? If I were able to give you a graphic sketch of that man in all the agony of his delirium, you would be sick at heart as you looked upon the picture. See him there, with unkempt locks, beard all matted and grimy, face covered with filth, eyes starting out of their sockets, limbs twisted with hideous contortions, and the whole man a picture of horror. If you have ever had the misery of looking into the face of a man when he was in a delirium, you know what an awful sight it is. How glad you were to get away from that fearful spectacle! But this man had a whole legion of devils within him, and must have looked a frightful object as he fell down before Jesus, crying, "What have I to do with thee, Jesus, thou Son of the most high God?"—vociferating with all his might in horrible tones which must have seemed terribly sad to all who were near.

But Jesus has said, "Come out of the man, thou unclean spirit." And now see him. He has been washed, he has put on some garments though he has not worn any for years, and he sits down at the feet of Jesus, calmly, collectedly; and when he gets up, he falls on his knees to pray; and what is his petition? "Lord, let me be with thee; do not send me away from thee. Thou hast done so much for me, let me always abide with thee. Let me loose the latchets of thy shoes; let me wash thy feet; let me be the servant of the servants of my Lord; let me do what thou wilt, only do let me stay with thee."

Is not that a wonderful change? It is just the same with us who have come to Christ. Once, we wanted to get away from him; but now that we know him, we cannot get near enough to him. And, sometimes, we even carry that prayer of ours too far, as this man did, because he wanted to be near to the person of Christ as to the flesh; and, at times, I am afraid that our

desires concerning going to heaven savour a little of that spirit.
When we are saying,

> *Let me be with thee, where thou art,*
> *Thy unveiled glory to behold;*

we must recollect that, possibly, it is not the right thing for us,
or for the kingdom of God at large, that we should go to heaven
just yet. There is something more to be done by us down here,
and we ought to be just as happy to have Christ with us in
spirit as we should be if we were actually with him in heaven.

Notice, also, that this man promptly obeys the Lord Jesus
Christ in something which must have been very unpleasant to
him. In answer to his petition, Christ said, "No, you must not
stay with me. Go home to your friends." That looked, on the
face of it, rather a harsh answer. It seemed such a beautiful
desire on the man's part, "Let me abide with thee"; and it
seemed in opposition to the finest instincts of his newly-created
nature to send him away. But it was not for this man to judge
what was best for him, nor is it for us to judge what is best
for us. We are to do *what* Jesus tells us, *as* Jesus tells us,
because Jesus tells us. That is what this man did.

And that led, in the last place, to this man's glorifying of
Christ, for he went home to his friends, and told them what
great things the Lord had done for him; and then he went
throughout all Decapolis (the ten cities), and told, wherever
he went, the story of the Saviour's power and love. That is just
what we will all try to do, and what we must do if the love of
Christ has been shed abroad within us. We shall begin by telling
the story to our friends, the members of our own family. We
shall interest them in our account of what we have heard, and
seen, and handled of the Word of life; and when we have done
that, we shall want a wider sphere, and our sphere of service
will widen continually, for we shall keep on seeking fresh
opportunities to publish the name, and fame, and Gospel of
Jesus to others.

VI

CURED AT LAST!

"And a woman having an issue of blood twelve years, which
had spent all her living upon physicians, neither could be healed
of any, came behind him, and touched the border of his garment: and immediately her issue of blood stanched."—
Luke 8: 43, 44.

THOUGH I take Luke's statement as a text, I shall constantly refer to the version of the same story which we
find in Mark 5: 25 to 29.

Here we have one of the Lord's hidden ones: a case not to be
publicly described because of its secret sorrow. We have here
a woman of few words and much shamefacedness. Her malady
subjected her to grievous penalties according to the ceremonial
law. There is a terrible chapter in the Book of Leviticus concerning such a case as hers. She was unclean; everything that
she sat upon, and all who touched it, shared in the defilement.
So that, in addition to her continual weakness, she was made
to feel herself an outcast, under the ban of the law. This
created, no doubt, great loneliness of spirit, and made her wish
to hide herself out of sight. In the narrative before us she said
not a word until the Saviour drew it out of her, for her own
lasting good. She acted very practically and promptly, but she
was a silent seeker: she would have preferred to have remained
in obscurity, if so it could have been. Some here may belong
to the great company of the timid and trembling ones. If
courage before others is needed to secure salvation, matters will
go hard with them, for they shrink from notice, and are ready
to die of shame because of their secret grief. Cowper's hymn
describes their inward feelings, when it says of the woman—

> *Conceal'd amid the gathering throng*
> *She would have shunn'd thy view,*
> *And if her faith was firm and strong,*
> *Had strong misgivings too.*

Such plants grow in the shade, and shrink from the light of the sun. The nature of their sorrows forces them into solitary self-communion. Oh, that the Lord may heal such at this hour!

The immediate cure of this woman is the more remarkable because it was a wayside miracle. The Saviour was on the road to restore the daughter of Jairus; this woman's healing was an extra of grace, a sort of over-splash of the great fountain of mercy. The cup of our Lord's power was full—full to the brim—and he was bearing it to the house of the ruler of the synagogue; this poor creature did but receive a drop which he spilt on the way. The episodes of the Lord Jesus are as beautiful as the main run of his life's poem.

Let us at once speak of this much-afflicted woman, for she is a typical character. While we describe her conduct and *her* cure, I trust she may serve as a looking-glass in which many tremblers may see themselves. We shall carefully note *what she had done*, and then *what came of it*. This will lead us on to see *what she did at last*, and *what we also should do*. May the Holy Spirit make this a very practical discourse by causing you to follow her till you gain the blessing as she did!

Consider, therefore, concerning this woman, WHAT SHE HAD DONE. She had been literally dying for twelve years. What had she been doing? Had she resigned herself to her fate, or treated her malady as a small matter? Far from it. Her conduct is highly instructive.

First, *she had resolved not to die if a cure could be had*. She was evidently a woman of great determination and hopefulness. She knew that this disease of hers would cause her life to ebb away, and bring her to the grave; but she said within herself, "I will have a struggle for it. If there is a possibility of removing this plague it shall be removed, let it cost me what it may of pain or payment." Oh, what a blessing it would be if unsaved ones would say each one for himself, "I am a lost soul; but if a lost soul can be saved, I will be saved. I am guilty; but if guilt can be washed away, mine shall be washed away. I have a hard heart, and I know it; but if a heart of stone can be turned into a heart of flesh, I long to have it so, and I will never rest until this gracious work is wrought in me!" Alas, it is not so with many! Indifference is the rule; indifference about their immortal souls!

Insensibility has seized upon many, and a proud conceit: they are full of sin, and yet they talk of self-righteousness. They are weak, and can do nothing; yet they boast of their ability. They are not conscious of their true condition, and hence they have no mind to seek a cure. May the Holy Spirit show every unregenerate person the fatal nature of his soul's disease; for this, I trust, would lead to the making of a firm resolve to find salvation, if salvation is to be had.

No doubt some are held back from such action by the freezing power of despair. They have reached the conclusion that there is no hope for them. The promises of the Gospel they regard as the voice of God to others, but as having no cheering word for them.

When men have no hope, they soon have no fear. Is not this a dreadful thing? May the Lord save you from such a condition! Despair of God's mercy is an unreasonable thing: if you think you have grounds for it, the lying spirit must have suggested them to you. Holy Scripture contains no justification for hopelessness. Neither the nature of God, nor the Gospel of God, nor the Christ of God, warrant despair. Multitudes of texts encourage hope; but no one Scripture, rightly understood, permits a doubt of the mercy of God. "All manner of sin and blasphemy shall be forgiven unto men." Jesus, the great Healer, is never baffled by any disease of human nature: he can cast out a legion of devils, and raise the dead. Oh that I could whisper hope into the dull ear of yonder mourner! Oh that I could drop a rousing thought into the sullen heart of the self-condemned! How glad should I be!

Alas! many have never come to this gracious resolution, because they cherish a vain hope, and are misled by an idle dream. They fancy that salvation will come to them without their seeking it. Certainly, they have no right to expect such a thing. It is true that our Lord is found of them that sought him not; but that is an act of his own sovereignty and is not a rule for our procedure. The plain directions of the Gospel are, "Seek ye the Lord while he may be found; call ye upon him while he is near" (Isa. 55: 6). How dare they set these gracious words aside? They fancy that they may wake up, one of these fine days, and find themselves saved. Some fancy that in the article of death, they may cry, "God be merciful to me a sinner," and so may leap into salvation. It seems to them a very slight business to be reconciled to God. They imagine that they can be converted just when they will, and so they put it off from day to day, as if it were of no more consequence than going to shop to buy a coat or a gown. Believe me, the Word of God does not set forth the matter in this way. It tells us that even the righteous scarcely are saved, and it arouses us to strive to enter in at the strait gate. God save you from every false confidence which would prevent your being in earnest about the healing of your souls. Spiritually, your case is as desperate as that of the poor woman now before us. May the Lord sweetly constrain you to feel that you must be healed, and that you cannot afford to put off the blessed day!

Let us next note, that *this woman having made her resolve, adopted the likeliest means she could think of*. Physicians are men set apart on purpose to deal with human maladies, therefore she went to the physicians. What better could she do? Though she failed, yet she did what seemed most likely to succeed. Now, when a soul is resolved to find salvation, it is most fit and proper that it should use every likely means for the finding of salvation. Oh, that they were wise enough to hear the Gospel, and to come at once to Jesus; but often they make grave mistakes. This woman went to gentlemen who were supposed to understand the science of medicine. Was it not natural that she should look for help to their superior wisdom? Many, in these days, do the same thing. They hear of the new discoveries of professedly cultured men, and hear their talk about the littleness of sin, and the larger hope, and the non-necessity of the new birth. Poor deceived creatures! They find in the long run that nothing comes of it; for the wisdom of man is nothing but pretentious folly. The world by wisdom knows neither God nor his salvation. We cannot blame the woman that, being a simple soul, and anxious for healing, she went to those first who were thought to know most. Let us not, with Christ so near, go roundabout as she did, but let us touch our Lord at once.

No doubt the sufferer also tried men who had diplomas, or were otherwise authorized to act as physicians. How can you blame her for going to those who were in the succession, and had the official stamp? Alas! it is vain to look to men at all, and foolish to depend on official dignity, or special repute. Some teachers do not know much about their own souls, and therefore know less about the souls of others. Vain is the help of man, be the man who he may. This poor woman is not to be blamed, but to be commended, that she did what seemed best to her, according to her light; but you are warned; go not, therefore, to men.

No doubt she met with some who boasted that they could heal her complaint at once. They began by saying, "You have tried So-and-so, but he is a mere quack; mine is a scientific remedy. You have used a medicine which I could have told you would be worthless; but I have the secret. Put yourself absolutely into my hands, and the thing is done. I have healed many that have been given up by all the faculty. Follow my orders, and you will be restored." Sick persons are so eager to recover that they readily take the bait which is offered them by brazen impudence. Ah, me! "All is not gold that glitters"; and all the professions which are made of helping sin-sick souls are not true professions. Many pretenders to new revelations are abroad, but they are physicians of no value.

There is no medicine beneath the sky that can stay the palpitations of a heart which dreads the judgment to come. No earthly surgery can take away the load of sin from the conscience. No hand of priest or presbyter, prophet or philosopher, can cleanse the leprosy of guilt. The finger of God is wanted here. There is one Heal-all, and only one. Happy is he that hath received this infallible balm from Jehovah Rophi— the Lord that healeth. Yet we marvel not that when souls are pressed down with a sense of guilt, they try anything and everything which offers even a faint hope of relief. I could wish that all my hearers had an intense zeal to find salvation; for even if it led them into passing mistakes, yet, under God's blessing, they would find their way out of them, and end by glorifying the grace of our Lord Jesus Christ, which never fails.

This woman, in the next place, having resolved not to die if cure could be had, and having adopted the likeliest means, *persevered in the use of those means.* No doubt she tried many, and even opposite, remedies. One doctor said, "You had better go to the warm baths of the lake of Tiberias; such bathing will be comforting and helpful." She grew worse at the warm bath, and went to another physician, who said, "You were wrongly treated; you need bracing up in the cold baths of the Jordan."

What perseverance that woman must have had! I am not
going to say anything about our doctors nowadays, no doubt
they are the most learned and skilful that can be: but in earlier
times surgery was murderous, and medicines were poisonous.
Many of the prescriptions of those days are sickening, and yet
ridiculous. I read a prescription, of our Saviour's time, warranted to cure many diseases, which consisted of grasshopper's
eggs. These were supposed to exercise a marvellous influence,
but they are no longer in the list of medicines. The tooth of a
fox was said to possess special powers; but I noticed that one
of the chief drugs of all, the most expensive, but the surest in
its action, was a nail from the finger of a man who had been
hanged. It was important that he should have been hanged:
another finger-nail might have had no efficacy. Poor creatures
were made to suffer most painfully by cruel medicines, which
were far worse than the disease. As for surgical operations, if
they had been designed to kill, they were certainly admirably
arranged for their purpose. The wonder is that for twelve years
poor human nature could stand out, not against the disease,
but against the doctors. The case is much the same spiritually.

How many under their burden of sin go first to one, and then
to another; and still without avail! Travel as fast as you may
in a wrong direction, you will not reach the place you seek.
Vain are all things save Jesus our Lord.

Have you been to Doctor Ceremony? He is, at this time, the
fashionable doctor. Has he told you that you must attend to
forms and rules? Has he prescribed you so many prayers,
and so many services? Ah! many go to him, and they persevere
in a round of religious observances, but these yield no lasting
ease to the conscience. Have you tried Doctor Morality? He
has a large practice, and is a fine old Jewish physician. "Be
good in outward character," says he, "and it will work inwardly,
and cleanse the heart." A great many persons are supposed
to have been cured by him and by his assistant, Doctor Civility,
who is nearly as clever as his master: but I have it on good
evidence that neither of them apart, nor even the two together,
could ever deal with an inward disease. Do what you may,
your own doings will not stanch the wounds of a bleeding heart.
Doctor Mortification has also a select practice; but men are
not saved by denying themselves until they first deny their

self-righteousness. Doctor Excitement has many patients, but his cures seldom outlive the set of sun. Doctor Feeling is much sought after by tender spirits; these try to feel sorrow and remorse; but, indeed, the way of cure does not lie in that quarter. Let everything be done that can be done apart from our blessed Lord Jesus Christ, and the sick soul will be nothing bettered. You may try human remedies for the space of a life-time, but sin will remain in power, guilt will cling to the conscience, and the heart will abide as hard as ever.

But this woman not only tried the most likely means and persevered in the use of them, but *she also spent all her substance over it*. That was perhaps the chief thing in ancient surgery—this golden ointment which did good to the physician, whatever became of the patient. The most important point was to pay the doctor. This woman's living was wasting away as well as her life. She continued to pay, and to pay; but she received no benefit from it all; say, rather, that she suffered more than she would have done had she kept her gold. Thus do men waste their thought, their care, their prayer, their agony over that which is as nothing: they spend their money for that which is not bread. At last she came to her last shekel. In the end there was an end to her means. What would not a man give to be saved? I never wonder that dying men give their estates to priests in the hope that they can save their souls. Health of body, if it could be purchased with gold, would be cheap at any price; but health of soul, holiness of character, acceptance with God, assurance of heaven—these would be cheap if we counted out worlds as poor men pay down their pence for bread. There are men so mean that they would not part with a pound for a place in Paradise; but if these once knew their true condition, they would alter their minds. The price of wisdom is above rubies. If we had mines of gold, we might profitably barter them for the salvation of our souls.

Beloved, you see where this woman was. She was in down-right, desperate earnest to have her mortal malady healed, and so she spared neither her labour nor her living. In this we may wisely imitate her.

We have seen what the woman had done; now let us think of WHAT HAD COME OF IT. We are told that she had suffered many things of many physicians. That was her sole reward for trusting and spending: she had not been relieved, much less healed; but *she had suffered*. She had endured much additional suffering through seeking a cure. That is the case with you who have not come to Christ, but, being under a sense of sin, have sought relief apart from him. All that you do apart from Jesus, in order to win salvation, will only cause you increased suffering. You have tried to save yourself by prayers; your prayers have turned your thoughts upon your sin and its punishment, and thus you have become more wretched than before. You have attended to ceremonies, and if you have used them sincerely, they have wrought in you a solemn sense of the holiness of God, and of your own distance from him; and this, though very proper, has only increased your sorrow. You have been trying to feel good, and to do good, that so you may be good; but the very effort has made you feel how far off you are from the goodness you so much desire. Your self-denial has excited cravings after evil, and your mortifications have given new life to your pride. In the end, I trust this may work for your good, but up till now it has served no healing purpose: you are now at death's door, and all your praying, weeping, church-going, chapel-going, and sacrament-taking, do not help you one bit.

There has been this peculiarly poignant pang about it all, that you are *nothing bettered*. Cheerily did you hope, but cruelly are you disappointed. You cried, "I have it this time," but the bubble vanished as you grasped it. And now, perhaps, this day you are saying, "What can I do? What shall I do?" I will tell you. You can do nothing except what this woman ultimately did, of which I will speak by-and-by. You are now brought to this extremity—that you are without strength, without merit, without power, and you must look out of yourself to another, who has strength and merit, and can save you.

We read of this woman, that though she suffered much, she was nothing better, but *rather grew worse*. No better after twelve years of medicine? She went to the Egyptian doctor, and he promised her health in three months. She was worse. She tried the Syrian doctor: he was a man who had great knowledge of the occult sciences, and was not ashamed to practise enchantments. She was bitterly disappointed to find herself decidedly weaker. Then she heard of a Greek practitioner, who would cure her, heigh presto! in a trice. She paid her remaining money, but she still went backward. She bought disappointment very dearly.

Friend, is this your condition? You are anxious to be right, and, therefore, you are earnest in every effort to save yourself; but still you are nothing bettered. Sad result of so much perseverance! And is not that the case with some of you who are in earnest, but are not enlightened? You are working, and growing poorer as you work. There is not about you so much as there used to be of good feeling, or sincere desire, or prayerfulness, or love for the Bible, or care to hear the Gospel. You are becoming more careless, more dubious than you once were. You have lost much of your former sensitiveness. You are doing certain things now that would have startled you years ago, and you are leaving certain matters undone which once you would have thought essential. Evidently you are caught in the current, and are nearing the cataract. The Lord deliver you!

As a climax of it all, the heroine of our story had now *spent all that she had*. She could not go now to the Egyptian doctor, or to the Syrian doctor, or to the Hebrew doctor, or to the Roman doctor, or to the Greek doctor. No; now she must do without their flattering unction in the future. As for those famous medicines which raised her hopes, she can buy no more of such costly inventions. This was, perhaps, her bitterest grief: but let me whisper it in your ear—this was the best thing that had yet happened to her; and I am praying that it may happen to some of you. At the bottom of your purse I trust you will find wisdom. When we come to the end of self we come to the beginning of Christ. That last shekel binds us to the pretenders, but absolute bankruptcy sets us free to go to him who heals diseases without money and without price. Glad enough am I when I meet with a man who is starved out of self-sufficiency. Now you are ready for Jesus. When all your own virtue has gone out of you, then shall you seek and find that virtue which goeth out of him.

This brings to our notice, in the third place, WHAT THIS WOMAN DID AT LAST. She hears of Jesus of Nazareth, a man sent of God who is healing sick folk of all sorts. She hears attentively; she puts the stories together that she hears; she believes them; they have the likeness of truth about them. "Oh," says she, "there is yet another opportunity for me. I

will get in the crowd, and if I can only touch the bit of blue
which he wears as the border of his garment, I shall be made
whole." Splendid faith! It was thought much of in her own
day, and we may still more highly prize it now that faith has
grown so rare.

Note well *she resolved to trust in Jesus in sheer despair of doing
anything else*. I almost wish I did, that I might come up to you
and say to you personally, "Try Jesus Christ, trust him, and
see whether he will not save you. Every other door is evidently
shut; why not enter by Christ the door? Exercise the courage
which is born of desperation. May God the Holy Spirit help
you now to thrust forth your finger, and get into touch with
Jesus! Say, "Yes, I freely accept Christ. By God's grace,
I will have him to be my only hope. I will have him now."

After all, *this was the simplest and easiest thing that she could do*.
Touch Jesus. Put out thy finger, and touch the hem of his
garment. The prescriptions she had purchased were long; but
this was short enough. The operations performed upon her
had been intricate; but this was simplicity itself. The suffering
she had endured had complicated her case; but this was as plain
as a pikestaff. "Touch with your finger the hem of his garment:
that is all." You have tried many things, great things, and hard
things, and painful things: why not try this simple matter of
faith? Believe in the Lord Jesus Christ, and thou shalt be saved.
Trust Jesus to cleanse you, and he will do it. Put yourself into
your Saviour's hands once for all, and he will save you.

Not only was this the simplest and easiest thing for the poor
afflicted one, but certainly *it was the freest and most gracious*.
There was not a penny to pay. Nobody stood at the door of
the consulting-room to take her guinea; and the good physician
did not even give a hint that he expected a reward. The gifts
of Jesus are free as the air. He healed this believing woman in
the open street, in the midst of the crowd. She had felt that if
she could but get into the throng, she would, by hook or by
crook, get near enough to reach the hem of his garment, and
then she would be healed. Come then, and receive grace freely.
Bring no good works, no good words, no good feelings, no good
resolves, as the price of pardon; come with an empty hand,
and touch the Lord by faith. The good things which you desire,
Jesus will give you as the result of his cure; but they cannot

be the cause or the price of it. Accept his mercy as the gift of his love! Come empty handed, and receive! Come undeserving, and be favoured! Only come into contact with Jesus, who is the fountain of life and health, and you shall be saved.

This was the quietest thing for her to do. She said nothing. She did not cry aloud like the blind men. She did not ask friends to look on, and see her make her venture. She kept her own counsel, and pushed into the press. In absolute silence, she took a stolen touch of the Lord's robe.

You can be saved in silence. You have no need to speak to any person of your acquaintance, not even to mother or father. At this moment, believe and live. Nobody will know that you now are touching the Lord. In after days you will own your faith, but in the act itself you will be alone and unseen. Believe on Jesus. Trust yourself with him.

This is *the only effectual thing.* Touch Jesus, and salvation is yours at once. Simple as faith is, it is never-failing. A touch of the fringe of the Saviour's garment sufficed: in a moment she felt in her body that she was healed of that plague. "It is twelve years ago," she said to herself, "since I felt like a living woman. I have been sinking in a constant death all this while, but now I feel my strength come back to me." Blessed be the name of the great Healer! She was exceeding glad. Tremble she did, lest it should turn out to be too good to be true; but she was most surely healed. Do trust my Lord, for he will surely do for you that which none other can achieve. Leave feeling and working, and try faith in Jesus. May the Holy Spirit lead you to do so at once!

And now, poor convicted sinner! here comes the driving home of the nail. Do THOU AS THIS WOMAN DID. Ask nobody about it, but do it. She did not go to Peter, James, and John, and say, "Good sirs, advise me." She did not beg from them an introduction to Jesus, but she went of her own accord, and tried for herself the virtue of a touch. You have had advising enough; now come to real work. There is too much tendency to console ourselves by conversations with godly men: let us get away from them, and speak to their Master. Talks in the enquiry-room, and chats with Christian neighbours, are all very well; but one touch of Jesus will be infinitely better. I do not blame you for seeking religious advice: this may be a half-way house to call at, but do not make it the terminus. Press on till, by personal faith, you have laid hold on Jesus. Do not tell anybody what you are about to do; wait till it is done. Another day you will be happy to tell the minister and God's people of what the Lord has done for you; but for the present, quietly believe in the Lamb of God which taketh away the sin of the world.

Do not even ask yourself about it. If this poor woman had consulted with herself, she might never have ventured so near the holy One of God. So clearly shut out from society by the law of her people and her God, if she had given the matter a second thought, she might have abandoned the idea. Blessed was the impetuosity which thrust her into the crowd, and kept her head above the throng, and her face towards the Lord in the centre of the press. She did not so much reason as dare. Believe, and have done with it. Stop not to parley with your own unbelief, nor answer your rising doubts and fears; but at once, upon the instant, put out your finger, touch the hem of his garment, and see what will come of it. Do not say, "To-morrow may be more convenient." In this woman's case, there was the Lord before her; she longed to be healed at once, and so, come what may, into the crowd she plunged. She was so enfeebled, that one wonders how she managed to get near Him; but possibly the crowd took her off her feet and carried her onward, as often happens in a rush. However, there was her chance, and she seized it. There was the fringe of the Lord's mantle; out went her finger: it was all done.

You have an opportunity now, by God's great grace. Jesus of Nazareth passeth by at this moment. He who speaks to you is not trying to say pretty things, but he is pining to win your soul for Jesus. Have you believed? You are saved. "He that believeth in him hath everlasting life."

"Oh, but I tremble so!" So did she whom Jesus healed. Her hand shook, but she touched him all the same for that. I think I see her quivering finger. However much the finger of your faith may tremble, if it does but touch the hem of the Lord's garment, virtue will flow from him to you. The power is not in the finger which touches, but in the divine Saviour who is touched. Dear soul, out with your finger! Do not go away till you have touched the Lord by a believing prayer.

VII

THE PHYSICIAN AND HIS PALSIED PATIENT

"And, behold, they brought to him a man sick of the palsy, lying on a bed: and Jesus seeing their faith said unto the sick of the palsy, Son, be of good cheer; thy sins be forgiven thee. And, behold, certain of the scribes said within themselves, This man blasphemeth. And Jesus knowing their thoughts said, Wherefore think ye evil in your hearts? For whether is easier, to say, Thy sins be forgiven thee; or to say, Arise, and walk? But that ye may know that the Son of man hath power on earth to forgive sins, (then saith he to the sick of the palsy,) Arise, take up thy bed, and go unto thine house. And he arose, and departed to his house."—Matt. 9: 2–7.

THE Gospel of Matthew is especially the Gospel of the Kingdom, and of the King. All through Matthew's writing, the title of King constantly occurs in connection with Christ, and his kingliness is prominent from the opening chapter to the close. Here we see the King exercising his royal prerogatives. In this passage we have several instances of Christ acting as he could not have acted if he had not possessed a royal and divine power.

I will go at once to my text, and note, first, that JESUS DEALT WITH THE PALSIED MAN IN A TRULY ROYAL AND DIVINE WAY.

The bearers of the man sick of the palsy had broken through the tiling, whatever that may have been, to get him near the Saviour. They had dropped him down over the heads of the eager throng, and there he lay upon his pallet before Christ, unable to stir hand or foot, but looking up with that gaze of eager expectancy which Christ so well understood.

You will notice that our Lord did not wait for a word to be spoken, he simply looked, and *he saw their faith*. Matthew writes, "Jesus seeing their faith." Who can see faith? It is a thing whose effects can be seen, its signs and tokens are discoverable; and they were eminently so in this case, for breaking up the roof, and putting the man down before Christ in so strange a way, were evidences of their belief that Jesus would cure him. Still, Christ's eyes not only saw the proofs of their faith, but the faith itself. There stood the four men, speaking with their eyes, and saying, "Master, see what we have done! We are persuaded that we have done the right thing, and that thou wilt heal him." There was the man, lying on his bed, looking up, and wondering what the Lord would do, but evidently cheered by the belief that he was now in a position of hope where, in all probability, he would become a man favoured beyond everyone else. Christ not merely saw the looks of this man and his bearers; but he saw their faith.

Ah, friends, *we* cannot see one another's faith; we may see the fruit of it. Sometimes we think that we can discern the lack of it; but to see the faith itself, this needs divine sight, this needs the glance of the eye of the Son of man. Jesus saw their faith; and now, that same eye is looking upon all in this audience, and he sees your faith. Have you any that he can see? "Oh, yes!" some of you can reply, "we have a humble, trembling faith; not such as it ought to be, but such as we are very thankful to possess." Some of you, it may be, are conscious of your sin; and all the faith you have is just a faint hope, a feeble belief that, if he will but speak to you, you shall be forgiven. You believe that he is able to save to the uttermost them that come unto God by him; but you have in the background a fear that you cannot come, or that you may not come in a right way. Still, if it is ever so little faith in him that you have, my Master sees it; and, as in our early days we used to look for a single spark in the tinder that we might get a light on the cold mornings, so does the Lord look for the tiniest gleam of faith in any human heart, that out of it may come a flame of spiritual life. "Jesus seeing their faith." Now then, Christ's eye is looking at you. Whatever faith you have, exert it now; believe in Jesus. He is the Son of God; believe in him as able to save you, for he is able, and he is willing as well as able; and now trust your soul to him, sink or swim. Determine that, if you must die, you will die at the foot of Christ's Cross; but you will go nowhere else for salvation. "Jesus seeing their faith." His royal and divine sight could perceive that which was hidden from all mere mortal men.

But then, when Jesus saw their faith, observe next that *he dealt first with the chief evil which afflicted this man.* He did not begin by curing him of the palsy. That was bad enough; but sin is worse than the palsy, sin in the heart is worse than paralysis of every single muscle. Sin is death, but something worse than death; therefore, Christ, at the very beginning of this miracle, to show his lordship, his royal, his divine power, said to the man, "Son, be of good cheer; thy sins be forgiven thee." This was laying the axe at the root of the man's evil nature. This was hunting the lion, the biggest beast of all the foul creatures that lurked in the densest forest of the man's being. Christ's words drove the unclean animal from his lair, and by his almighty power rent him as though he had been a kid.

Now, at this time, you may have many troubles; and perhaps you are eager to spread them before the Lord. That sick child, your dear husband, who is at home ill, that business which is flagging and likely to fail, that disease of yours which is weakening you, and which makes you scarcely fit to be in the Lord's house. Now, waive all those things, for heavy as they are, they are inconsiderable compared with sin. There is no venom as poisonous as that of sin; this is the wormwood and the gall; this is the deadly fang of the serpent whose sting infects and inflames our whole being. If this evil be removed, then every ill has gone; therefore Christ begins with this, "Thy sins be forgiven thee." Breathe a prayer to him now for the forgiveness of your sin: "Jesus, Master, forgive me! With a word thou canst pardon all my sin; thou hast but to pronounce the absolution, and all my iniquities will be put away at once and for ever. O my Lord, wilt thou not put them away now?"

Notice, also, that *Jesus did absolutely forgive that man:* "Son, be of good cheer; thy sins be forgiven thee." He did not say, "They shall be forgiven," but, "They are forgiven; I absolve thee from them all. Whatever they may have been, thy youthful sins, thy manhood sins, thy sins before the palsy laid hold upon thee, thy sins of murmuring since thou hast been upon that bed, put them all together into one great mass, and though they be multitudinous as the stars of heaven, or as the sands on the seashore, Son, thy sins be forgiven thee." And the man felt that it was so, he believed that it was so, a load was taken from his heart, his whole spirit was lifted up by that gracious word, "Be of good cheer; thy sins be forgiven thee."

Oh, what a dreadful time that is to a man when first he sees his sin! It is the darkest moment of his life; but it is a blessed moment when he sees that Christ has put away his sin, and has said to him, "You shall not die in your iniquities; for they are all forgiven." Everything grows light and bright round about him; he himself is like one who comes up out of a well, or out of a horrible pit, out of the miry clay, yea, out of the very belly of hell. He seems to leap all at once up to the throne of heaven as he sings, "My sins are all forgiven. I am a miracle of grace." Wonder not if the man can scarcely contain himself; marvel not if he runs, and leaps, and dances for very joy.

This is how Christ behaves towards poor, palsied, sin-bound men and women. He sees their faith, and then puts their sin away where it shall be seen no more for ever, for he is a King, he is God, and he is able to forgive and blot out all iniquity. I have heard of one who, having been under a great sense of sin, and being relieved of it, could for a long time only cry out, "He is a great Forgiver." When there were other things to be attended to, he could not see to them, nor speak of any other kind of business but this, "He is a great Forgiver." I do not feel as if I wanted to say anything else to you but this, "He is a great Forgiver. I have found him so; many here have found him so; and all who will trust his great atoning sacrifice shall also know that he is a great Forgiver."

The second division of my subject diverges a little from the first; but it follows the text, and so it is no real divergence. By his royal and divine power, CHRIST READ AND JUDGED MEN'S THOUGHTS.

See those Scribes, those students of the letter of the Word, who know how many letters there are in every Book of the Old Testament, and have counted them so accurately that they can tell which is the middle letter. Wonderfully wise men those! Do you see them? They are very vexed and angry; and they think hard thoughts of Christ. They did not dare to speak out what they thought; the people would not have listened to them just then if they had spoken, so they held their tongues, but they did not hold their hearts, and there was a Thought-reader there—not one who professed the art, but One who possessed it—and he heard where the quickest ear would have failed to detect the faintest sound. Jesus heard the Scribes mentally say, "This." If you look at your Bibles, you will find that the word "*man*" is printed in italics, and that when the Scribes said within themselves, "This," they meant, "fellow"; they meant any black name that you like to put in, "This blasphemer." They would not say what they thought him; they did not like to call him anything but just "This. . . . This offscouring."

Thus, *Christ read their contempt of himself.* They had not uttered it; but he had heard it. It is an awful thing to have a silent contempt of Christ. You may pride yourself on saying, "I have never spoken anything against religion; I have never used a profane expression." No; but if you do not call Jesus your Lord, if you do not own him as your Saviour, he knows what the contemptuous omission means. What you do not say, though you only say "This——," and leave a blank space; he reads it all. If there are any, who have such thoughts of my Lord and Master, I do not wish to know them, and I hope that they will never let any other creature know them; but let them remember that Jesus knows all about them, for he is a King who reads the secrets of all hearts, and in due time he will lay them bare.

But, next, *Jesus marked their charge of blasphemy.* They said in their heart that he blasphemed, for he had taken to himself the prerogative of God. According to Mark's and Luke's accounts, they asked, "Why doth this man thus speak blasphemies? who can forgive sins but God only?" Now, mark you, we who worship Christ as God can never have any fellowship with those who deny his Godhead, nor can they have any fellowship with us; for if he be indeed the Son of God, then they blaspheme him who deny it; and if he be only a man, then we are clearly idolaters and man-worshippers, and he did blaspheme. We are obliged to confess that, and we do confess it; if he was not the Son of God, if he had not power to forgive sins, then they rightly judged that he was a blasphemer. Ah, when thou art afraid that Jesus cannot forgive thy sins, thou art trembling on the very verge of blasphemy! There is such a crime as constructive treason; and there is such a sin as constructive blasphemy. To deny Christ's power to save, is to make him but a man; and if thou puttest him down as only man, thou blasphemest.

Notice, also, how *Jesus judged their thoughts*. He said to them, "Wherefore think ye evil in your hearts?" It was their hearts rather than their thoughts that were evil. Intellectual error generally springs from an unrenewed heart. And what evil had these men thought? They had thought him a blasphemer; they had also thought contemptuously of him; but the greatest evil of all was that they had limited his power; they did not believe that he could forgive. They thought it blasphemy on his part to profess to have the power to forgive the sins of men.

Now I know that you would shrink from openly blaspheming Christ, that is, if you are the person I think you are. Then, however great thy sin at present is, do not make it more by insinuating that he cannot forgive you, for of all sins this must be the most cruel, to think that he is unable to forgive. This stabs at Christ's Saviourship, which is his very heart. If thou sayest, "I am very guilty," say it again, for thou sayest the truth; but if thou sayest, "I am so guilty that he cannot forgive me," I pray thee to withdraw that wicked word, lest thou shouldst limit the Holy One of Israel, and he should have to say to thee, "Wherefore thinkest thou evil in thy heart?" It is thinking evil of Christ to imagine that he cannot forgive.

And observe, once more, that, in dealing with these Scribes, our Lord spoke right royally and divinely to them, for *he revealed the unreasonableness of their thoughts*. He said to them, "Wherefore think ye evil in your hearts?" I ask you if you know any reason why Christ cannot forgive sin? Will anyone who doubts his power to pardon, find a reason for that doubt? If thou believest (and I will assume that thou dost believe) that he is the Son of God, can he not forgive sin? If thou believest that he did heal the lepers, and the paralysed, and even raised the dead, can he not forgive sin? Further, if thou believest that he died for sin, that on the Cross he offered no less a victim than himself, wherefore dost thou think that he cannot forgive? If thou believest that he rose again from the dead—and I know that thou believest this—, if indeed he rose again from the dead for the justification of the ungodly, how is it that he cannot forgive? And if he has gone into glory, and thou knowest that he is at his Father's right hand, and there is making intercession for the transgressors, how canst thou say that he cannot forgive thee?

Now we come back to the palsied man and our Master again, and notice, in the third place, that right royally JESUS OPENLY DECLARED HIS COMMISSION. He seems to me to read the letters patent which his Father gave him when he sent him on his errand of love and mercy: "The Son of man hath power on earth to forgive sins."

First, *Jesus is the Son of man.* He does not conceal that fact. One would have thought that he would have said, "I am the Son of God"; but here he chooses still to hold his Godhead in abeyance, so he says, "The Son of man hath power on earth to forgive sins. I, the Son of Mary, I, the carpenter's Son, I who dwelt at Nazareth thirty years, I who have gone up and down among you, worn with sufferings, pained by your hostility, wearied by labour for you, I, the Son of man, have power to forgive sins." Think of that. He puts himself on his very lowest standing and declares that, as the Son of man, there is bestowed upon him, by reason of his Godhead, the power to forgive sins.

And having thus declared his title, he goes on to say that *he forgives sins as the Son of man on earth.* He was on earth, and he had power on earth; that is, in his earthly life, in his humiliation, when he had made himself for a while to be less than the Father, so that he could say, "My Father is greater than I,"— higher in office just then—, when he had humbled himself, and taken upon himself the form of a servant, he could say, "The Son of man hath power on earth, at his lowest, divested of glory, here as a Man among men, the Son of man hath power on earth to forgive sins." Oh, how I love this word, for if he had power on earth, what power he has in heaven; and if he had power as the Son of man, what power he has as God and Man in one person! Oh, how fully you may trust him! Even the Christ whom they could see, the Son of man, for you know that there was a Christ whom they could not see, that Son of God whom carnal eyes could not behold, who must reveal himself spiritually or be unperceived by mortal sense, even he whom they could see, the Christ whom you poor weeping ones can see, though you cannot see the half of Christ, nay, you cannot see the hundredth part of Christ,—the Christ whom you poor doubters can see, the Christ whom you who are all but blind can only see out of the corners of those eyes of yours when you see men as trees walking,—even that Christ, the Son of man, in his weakness on earth, was able to forgive sins. I do not seem as if I ought to try to preach about this glorious truth; but I feel that I ought to state it, and leave it as a solemn fact for you to reject at your peril if you dare; or to receive with gladdest joy; for, believe me, your only hope lies here. O guilty sons of Adam, here is the way of escape for you! Your father Adam has ruined you; but the Son of man has come to seek and to save you, and he declares that he has power on earth to forgive sins.

Now, notice, in this blessed unrolling of his commission as the Son of man, how *Jesus cheers the sad*. He said to the poor palsied man, "Son, be of good cheer; thy sins be forgiven thee." How this should comfort you who are sad on account of sin! It is the Son of man who can forgive you. You tremble at the greatness of God, you are afraid of his majesty; but this Son of man, your Brother, whose hands were pierced with the nails, and whose feet still wear the nail-prints, whose side has the gash that the spear of the soldier made, he it is who can forgive sins. How tenderly he comes to you! How gently does he deal with you! Here is a hand fit for a surgeon, of whom it is said that he must have an eagle's eye, and a lion's heart, but a lady's hand. Here is a hand of flesh, a dainty, tender hand of love, that brings to you pardon. You have not to encounter God absolutely; but the one Mediator comes in between God and men. He who is bone of your bone, and flesh of your flesh, says to you, "The Son of man hath power on earth to forgive sins."

Beside that, *Jesus assures the forgiven that he has forgiven them.* How I love to think of that blessed fact, that Christ does not forgive us, and keep his forgiveness in the dark, but he says, "Son, thy sins be forgiven thee," giving the assurance of forgiveness to the sinner whom he forgives! The realization of pardon is a delightful feeling. If there is a joy outside of heaven that is higher than all others, it is the joy of a sinful soul when divine forgiveness is granted, making the forgiven one whiter than the driven snow, and fresher than the morning dew. I am a forgiven man, wonder of wonders! God's Son has said it, and his word is sure and steadfast, "Son, thy sins be forgiven thee."

Thus it was that Christ publicly unrolled his divine commission, declaring that he had power on earth to forgive sins. He came here on purpose to forgive human guilt; not to condemn, nay, not even to condemn her who was caught in the act of adultery. "Neither do I condemn thee," said he; "Go, and sin no more." Jesus came not to condemn the thief who was dying on the cross, and confessing that he deserved so to die; nay, but he said to him, "To-day shalt thou be with me in paradise." It is Christ's business to pardon; it is his bliss to pardon; it is his glory to pardon. He came here on purpose that he might pardon the guilty. Oh, that all sinful ones would go to him for forgiveness!

After having thus declared his commission, let us note, in the fourth place, that JESUS EXHIBITED HIS CREDENTIALS.

Since the Scribes disputed his power to pardon, he gave them a practical proof that he could forgive, and I want your special attention to this point. He said to them, in effect, "To forgive sin is a divine act. Now, whether is easier, to say, Thy sins be forgiven thee; or to say, Arise, and walk?" I put it to you, which is the easier of the two? Mark that Jesus does not ask, "Which is the easier, to forgive sin, or to heal the palsy?" No; he said, "Whether is easier, *to say*, Thy sins be forgiven thee; or *to say*, Arise, and walk?"

Well, now, *the first is much the easier*, because there are a great many who can say, "Thy sins be forgiven thee," and you cannot see whether the sins are forgiven or not. Look at the number of those who call themselves priests, who say, after they have heard the penitent's confession, "I absolve thee." It is easy enough to say that; but who is to know whether that person, who has professed penitence, is absolved or not? There is no change apparent to the observer; the poor sinner who is told that he is absolved may credulously derive some delusive comfort from his fellow-sinner's words; but those who look on cannot see any difference in the man or woman coming back from the confessional from what they were when they went there. It is very easy to say, "Thy sins be forgiven thee"; any fool can say it, any knave can say it; but then, if you say, "Arise, and walk," suppose they do not rise and walk, what then? Anybody can stand there, and say to the man sick of the palsy, "Arise, and walk," and the man may make an effort to rise, but fall back as helpless as ever; so that, although both miracles are, in themselves, equally impossible to man, and equally require divine power, yet the saying of the one is easy enough, but the saying of the other is more difficult. Many an impostor would shrink from saying, "Arise, and walk," for he would be mightily afraid that it would be found one thing to say it, and quite another thing for the patient really to rise and walk. Thus Christ said to the Scribes, "I will prove to you that I am divine, and therefore that I have the power to forgive sins, for I will now perform a miracle which you shall see, and which you shall be quite unable to dispute. It shall be wrought before you all, and then you shall know that, as I could do what was evidently the harder thing, that is, say, 'Arise, and walk,' I had the right to say what has become the easier thing, 'Thy sins be forgiven thee.'"

"Then saith he to the sick of the palsy," while he lay there, "Arise, take up thy bed, and go unto thine house." Thus *Jesus marked out the miracle in detail*. It was necessary to pile up the argument to make it complete and overwhelming. First, "Arise, sit up, stand up." The man would not do that if the palsy was still upon him; but at once, "He arose." "Now roll up thy mattress." He stoops down, and you can see him rolling it up; he has it now under his arm, or on his shoulder. "Now," is Christ's next command, "Go unto thine house," and he walks straight away off to his home. For him to go home to his house, was a clearer proof of being cured than for him to remain with Christ, for it might be supposed that, while he was with the Saviour, some strange influence emanating from the great Physician kept him in a state of excitement and up to the mark. So Christ says, "Go home to thine house, to every-day life, just as anybody else might do, go along with you, bed and all"; and off he goes. Every point of detail was necessary to make it clear that this was a real, radical, complete cure, and that the Christ who could work such a miracle was able also to forgive sin.

I remark, next, that *change of nature is the best proof of the pardon of the sinner*. You may come to me now, and say, "Sir, I am forgiven." I am glad to hear it; but how will you behave at home to-night? "I am forgiven," cries one, all of a sudden, under a sermon, as if electrified. Yes, yes; and you want to stop with us, do you, and never go home any more? That will not do, because such a cure as that could not be a perfect, business-like, common-sense cure. Go home to your house. Your moral actions, your temperance, your honesty, your chastity, your obedience to parents, your good conduct as a servant, your generosity as a master, these will not save you; but unless we see them, how are we to know that Christ has wrought a miracle upon you; and if he has not wrought a miracle upon you in raising you up from the palsy of sin, how do we know that he has forgiven you? In fact, we do not know it, and we do not believe that he has, for these two things go together, the one as the evidence of the power that wrought the other. If you have been forgiven, you have been renewed.

You may be forgiven all your sin; but if you are, you will not be to-morrow what you have been to-day. The drunkard's cup will not be lifted to your lips any more; the company of the lascivious will not be pleasant to you again; no oath, no profane speech, no foolish talk will come out of your mouth henceforth. Christ forgives you outright, not because you are cured of your evil habits; but he forgives you while you are still palsied; and the evidence that you are forgiven, the harder thing as the world will always judge it to be, is your taking up your bed, and walking home, quitting all your former sloth, for it will be sloth from this time. The bed which you could not help lying upon once, will become the couch of sloth to you if you lie on it any longer. You will take that up, and you will walk back, and be a man of activity, at your daily labour, in your own house, henceforth as long as you live. Do notice this. We do not preach to you salvation by works; but when you are forgiven, then the good works come.

I think, also, that *the detailed obedience that the Saviour required was the best evidence that he had forgiven the man's sin:* "Arise, take up thy bed, and go unto thine house." Henceforth, to do everything that Christ bids you do, in the order in which he bids you do it, because he bids you do it, to do it at once, to do it joyfully, to do it constantly, to do it prayerfully, to do it thankfully, this shall be the token that he has indeed dealt with you as a pardoning God. I am afraid that there are some, who profess to have been forgiven, who are not as obedient to Christ as they ought to be! I have known them neglect certain duties; I even knew a man once, who would not read some parts of the Word of God because they made him feel uneasy; but be you sure of this, that when you and the Word of God fall out, the Word of God has right on its side. There is something rotten in the state of Denmark when you cannot read a chapter without feeling that you wish that it was not there. If there is any verse that you would like left out of the Bible, that is the verse that ought to stick to you, like a blister, until you really attend to its teaching. There is something wrong with you whenever you quarrel with the Word of God. I say again, that detailed obedience is the surest evidence that the Lord has forgiven your sin. For instance, "He that believeth and is baptized shall be saved." Do not you omit any part of that precept; and if Christ bids you come to his table, and thus remember him, do not live in neglect of that command. At the same time, remember to live soberly, righteously, honestly, godly, in this present evil age; for if you do not, if there is not a detailed obedience, there may be a fear that, after all, the Lord has never said to you, "Thy sins be forgiven thee."

And, last of all, *the best evidence is always seen at home:* "Take up thy bed, and go unto thine house." If there is a place where piety is best seen, and best judged of, it is upon the family altar. What the man is at home, that he really is; what the woman is in her own house, that she is truly. It is very easy, you know, to masquerade in society, to seem to be something very wonderful upon the boards of the world's theatre, and then not to be in reality the king that you seemed to be; but, after all, to be only a very sorry specimen of humanity. "Arise, take up thy bed, and go unto thine house." I remember an old woman, who went to hear a minister of a certain creed that she did not like, though he preached uncommonly well; and when she came out, they asked her how she got on with the preacher. She replied, "Well, he is one of the best of a very bad make." Now, I do not like to have to say that of anybody who professes to be a Christian; and it should not be so. No; and I do not want you to be the worst of a good make, either; though that, perhaps, is better than being the best or the worst of a bad make. We want to be such that we can bear the fullest inspection.

"Ah!" says one, "I came here seeking the pardon of sin, and NOW, sir, you have got off to moral conduct." Quite so; and that is where I want you to get off to. Seek the pardon of sin now; it is to be had, as I have told you, by faith: " Jesus seeing their faith, said unto the sick of the palsy, Son, be of good cheer; thy sins be forgiven thee." But if you want to make sure that Christ is really able to forgive your sin, the very best evidence to you, and the only evidence to the outside Scribes, will be that you take up your bed, and walk.

VIII

THE LORD AND THE LEPER

"And there came a leper to him, beseeching him, and kneeling down to him, and saying unto him, If thou wilt, thou canst make me clean. And Jesus, moved with compassion, put forth his hand, and touched him, and saith unto him, I will; be thou clean. And as soon as he had spoken, immediately the leprosy departed from him, and he was cleansed."—Mark 1: 40–42.

OUR Lord had been engaged in special prayer. He had gone alone on the mountain-side to have communion with God. Simon and the rest search for him, and he comes away in the early morning with the burrs from the hill-side upon his garments, the smell of the field upon him, even of a field that the Lord God had blessed; he comes forth among the people, charged with power which he had received in communion with the Father; and now we may expect to see wonders. And we do see them; for devils fear and fly when he speaks the word; and by-and-by, there comes to him one, an extraordinary being, condemned to live apart from the rest of men, lest he should spread defilement all around. A leper comes to him, and kneels before him, and expresses his confident faith in him, that he can make him whole. Now is the Son of Man glorious in his power to save.

The Lord Jesus Christ at this day has all power in heaven and in earth. To that end it is absolutely needful that we should find a case for his spiritual power to work upon. Is there not one here in whom his grace may prove its omnipotence? Not you, ye good, ye self-righteous! You yield him no space to work in. You that are whole have no need of a physician: in you there is no opportunity for him to display his miraculous force. But yonder are the men we seek for. Forlorn, and lost, full of evil, and self-condemned, you are the characters we seek. You that feel as if you were possessed with evil spirits, and you that are leprous with sin, you are the persons in whom Jesus will find ample room and verge enough for the display of his holy

skill. Of you I might say, as he once said of the man born blind:
you are here that the works of God may be manifest in you.
Be hopeful, then, ye sinful ones! Look up this day for the
Lord's approach, and expect that even in you he will work great
marvels. This leper shall be a picture—yea, I hope a mirror—
in whom you will see yourselves. I do pray that as I go over
the details of this miracle many here may put themselves in the
leper's place, and do just as the leper did, and receive, just as
the leper received, cleansing from the hand of Christ.

I will begin my rehearsal of the Gospel narrative by remark-
ing, first, that THIS LEPER'S FAITH MADE HIM EAGER TO BE
HEALED. He was a leper; but he believed that Jesus could
cleanse him, and his belief stirred him to an anxious desire to
be healed at once.

Alas! we have to deal with spiritual lepers eaten up with the
foul disease of sin; but *some of them do not believe that they ever
can be healed*, and the consequence is that despair makes them
sin most greedily. "I may as well be hanged for a sheep as for
a lamb," is the inward impression of many a sinner when he
fears that there is no mercy and no help for him. Because there
is no hope, therefore they plunge deeper and yet deeper into
the slough of iniquity. Oh, that you might be delivered from
that false idea! Mercy still rules the hour. There is hope while
Jesus sends his Gospel to you, and bids you repent. "I believe
in the forgiveness of sins": this is a sweet sentence of a true
creed. I believe also in the renewal of men's hearts; for the
Lord can give new hearts and right spirits to the evil and
unthankful. I would that you believed it; for if you did, I trust
it would quicken you into seeking that your sins might be forgiven and your minds might be renewed. Do you believe it?
Then come to Jesus and receive the blessings of free grace.

We have a number of lepers who come in among us whose
disease is white upon their brows, and visible to all beholders,
and yet *they are indifferent*: they do not mourn their wickedness,
nor wish to be cleansed from it. They sit among God's people,
and they listen to the doctrine of a new birth, and the news of
pardon, and they hear the teaching as though it had nothing
to do with them. Indifference to spiritual things is the sin of
the age. Men are stolid of heart about eternal realities. An
awful apathy is upon the multitude. The leper in our text was

not so foolish as this. He eagerly desired to be delivered from
his dreadful malady : with heart and soul he pined to be cleansed
from its terrible defilement. Oh that it were so with you! May
the Lord make you feel how depraved your heart is, and how
diseased with sin are all the faculties of your soul! Alas, *there
are some that even love their leprosy!* Is it not a sad thing to have
to speak thus? Surely, madness is in men's hearts. Men do not
wish to be saved from doing evil. They would like to go to
heaven, but they must have their drunken frolics on the road ;
they would very well like to be saved from hell, but not from
the sin which is the cause of it. Their notion of salvation is not
to be saved from the love of evil, and to be made pure and
clean ; but that is God's meaning when he speaks of salvation.
The very name of Jesus tells us *that* : he is called Jesus because
"he shall save his people from their sins." Oh, that He would
come and change their views of things until they were of the
same mind as God towards sin ; and you know he calls it "that
abominable thing which I hate." Oh, if men could see their
love to wrong things to be a disease more sickening than leprosy,
they would fain be saved, and saved at once! Holy Spirit,
convince of sin, that sinners may be eager to be cleansed!

Lepers were obliged to consort together : lepers associated
with lepers, and they must have made up a dreadful confrater-
nity. How glad they would have been to escape from it! But
I know spiritual lepers who *love the company of their fellow
lepers.* Yes, and the more leprous a man becomes, the more do
they admire him. It seems to be the desire of many to know as
much evil as they can. They flock together, and take a dreadful
pleasure in talk and action which is the horror of all pure minds.
Strange lepers, that heap up leprosy as a treasure! Even those
who do not go into gross open sin, yet are pleased with infidel
notions and sceptical opinions, which are a wretched form of
mental leprosy.

Lepers were not allowed to associate with healthy persons
except under severe restrictions. Thus were they separated
from their nearest and dearest friends. What a sorrow! Alas!
I know persons thus separated, who *do not wish to associate
with the godly;* to them holy company is dull and wearisome ;
they do not feel free and easy in such society, and therefore
they avoid it as much as decency allows. How can they hope

to live with saints for ever, when they shun them now as dull and moping acquaintances?

I have come hither this day in the hope that God would bless the word to some poor sinner who feels he is a sinner, and would fain be cleansed. To such I speak at this time with a loving desire for their salvation. I hope my word will come with divine application to some poor heart that is crying, "I wish I might be numbered with the people of God. I wish I were fit to be a door-keeper in the house of the Lord. Oh, that my dreadful sinfulness were conquered, so that I could have fellowship with the godly, and be myself one of them!" I hope my Lord has brought to this place just such lost ones, that he may find them. I am looking out for them with tearful eyes. But my feeble eyes cannot read inward character; and it is well that the loving Saviour, who discerns the secrets of all hearts, and reads all inward desires, is looking from the watch-towers of heaven, that he may discover those who are coming to him, even though as yet they are a great way off. Oh that sinners may now beg and pray to be rescued from their sins! Happy will the preacher be if he finds himself surrounded with penitents who hate their sins, and guilty ones who cry to be forgiven, and to be so changed that they shall go and sin no more.

In the second place, let us remark that THIS LEPER'S FAITH WAS STRONG ENOUGH TO MAKE HIM BELIEVE THAT HE COULD BE HEALED OF HIS HIDEOUS DISEASE. *Leprosy was an unutterably loathsome disease.* As it exists even now, it is described by those who have seen it in such a way that I will not harrow your feelings by repeating all the sickening details. The following quotation may be more than sufficient. Dr. Thomson in his famous work, "The Land and the Book," speaks of lepers in the East, and says, "The hair falls from the head and eye-brows; the nails loosen, decay and drop off; joint after joint of the fingers and toes shrink up and slowly fall away. The gums are absorbed, and the teeth disappear. The nose, the eyes, the tongue and the palate are slowly consumed." This disease turns a man into a mass of loathsomeness, a walking pile of pests. Leprosy is nothing better than a horrible and lingering death. The leper in the narrative before us had sad personal experience of this, and yet he believed that Jesus could cleanse him. Splendid faith! Oh that you who are afflicted with moral

and spiritual leprosy could believe in this fashion! Jesus Christ
of Nazareth can heal even you. Over the horror of leprosy faith
triumphed. Oh that in your case it would overcome the terrible-
ness of sin!

Leprosy was known to be incurable. There was no case of a man
being cured of real leprosy by any medical or surgical treatment.
This made the cure of Naaman in former ages so noteworthy.
Observe, moreover, that our Saviour himself, so far as I can see,
had never healed a leper up to the moment when this poor
wretch appeared upon the scene. Yet this man, putting this
and that together, and understanding something of the nature
and character of the Lord Jesus Christ, believed that he could
cure him of his incurable disease. He felt that even if the great
Lord had not yet healed leprosy, he was assuredly capable
of doing so great a deed, and he determined to apply to him.
Was not this grand faith? Oh that such faith could be found
among my hearers at this hour! Jesus can turn the lion into a
lamb, and he can do it now. He can transform thee where
thou art sitting, saving thee NOW. All things are possible to the
Saviour God; and all things are possible to him that believeth.

This man had a marvellous faith, thus to believe while *he was
personally the victim of that mortal malady.* It is one thing to
trust a doctor when you are well, but quite another to confide
in him when your body is rotting away. For a real, conscious
sinner to trust the Saviour is no mean thing. When you hope
that there is some good thing in you, it is easy to be confident;
but to be conscious of total ruin and yet to believe in the divine
remedy—this is real faith. To see in the sunshine is mere
natural vision; but to see in the dark needs the eye of faith,
to believe that Jesus has saved you when you see the signs of it,
is the result of reason; but to trust him to cleanse you while
you are still defiled with sin—this is the essence of saving
faith.

The leprosy was firmly seated and fully developed in this man.
Luke says that he was "full of leprosy": he had as much of the
poison in him as one poor body could contain, it had come to its
worst stage in him; and yet he believed that Jesus of Nazareth
could make him clean. Glorious confidence! If thou art full
of sin, if thy propensities and habits have become as bad as bad
can be, I pray the Holy Spirit to give thee faith enough to

believe that the Son of God can forgive thee and renew thee, and do it at once. With one word of his mouth Jesus can turn your death into life, your corruption into comeliness. Changes which we cannot work in others, much less in ourselves, Jesus, by his invincible Spirit, can work in the hearts of the ungodly. Of these stones he can raise up children unto Abraham. His moral and spiritual miracles are often wrought upon cases which seem beyond all hope, cases which pity itself endeavours to forget because her efforts have been so long in vain.

I like best about this man's faith the fact that he did not merely believe that Jesus Christ could cleanse a leper, but that he could cleanse *him!* He said, "Lord, if thou wilt, thou canst make *me* clean." It is very easy to believe for other people. The true faith believes for itself first, and then for others. Oh, I know some of you are saying, "I believe that Jesus can save my brother. I believe that he can save the vilest of the vile. If I heard that he had saved the biggest drunkard in Southwark I should not wonder." Canst thou believe all this, and yet fear that he cannot save thee? This is strange inconsistency. If he heals another man's leprosy, can he not heal *thy* leprosy? If one drunkard is saved, why not another? If in one man a passionate temper is subdued, why not in another? If lust, and covetousness, and lying, and pride have been cured in many men, why not in thee? Even if thou art a blasphemer, blasphemy has been cured; why should it not be so in thy case? He can heal thee of that particular form of sin which possesses thee, however high a degree its power may have reached; for nothing is too hard for the Lord. Jesus can change and cleanse thee now. In a moment he can impart a new life and commence a new character. Canst thou believe this? This is the faith which glorified Jesus, and brought healing to this leper; and it is the faith which will save you at once if you now exercise it.

Now, notice, thirdly, that this man's faith WAS FIXED ON JESUS CHRIST ALONE. Let me read the man's words again. He said unto Jesus, "If thou wilt, thou canst make me clean." Throw the emphasis upon the *pronouns*. See him kneeling before the Lord Jesus, and hear him say, "If *thou* wilt, *thou* canst make *me* clean." In himself he had no shade of confidence; every delusion of that kind had been banished by a fierce experience of his disease. He knew that none on earth could deliver him, and that by no innate power of constitution could he throw out the poison; but he confidently believed that the Son of God could by himself effect the cure. This was God-given faith—the faith of God's elect, and Jesus was its sole object.

How came this man to have such faith? I cannot tell you the outward means, but I think we may guess without presumption. Had he not *heard our Lord preach?* Matthew puts this story immediately after the Sermon on the Mount, and says, "When he was come down from the mountain, great multitudes followed him. And, behold, there came a leper and worshipped him, saying, Lord, if thou wilt, thou canst make me clean." Had this man managed to stand at the edge of the crowd and hear Jesus speak, and did those wondrous words convince him that the great Teacher was something more than man? As he noted the style, and manner, and matter of that marvellous sermon, did he say within himself, "Never man spake like this man. Truly he is the Son of God. I believe in him. I trust him. He can cleanse me"? May God bless the preaching of Christ crucified to you!

Perhaps this man had *seen our Lord's miracles.* I feel sure he had. He had seen the devils cast out, and had heard of Peter's wife's mother, who had lain sick of a fever, and had been instantaneously recovered. The leper might very properly argue—To do this requires omnipotence; and once granted that omnipotence is at work, then omnipotence can as well deal with leprosy as with fever. What the Lord has done, he can do again: if in one case he has displayed almighty power, he can display that same power in another case. Thus would the acts of the Lord corroborate his words, and furnish a sure foundation for the leper's hope. Have you not seen Jesus save others? Have you not at least read of his miracles of grace? Believe him, then, for his works' sake, and say to him, "Lord, if thou wilt, thou canst make me clean."

Besides, I think this man may have *heard something of the story of Christ,* and may have been familiar with the Old Testament prophecies concerning the Messiah. We cannot tell but some disciple may have informed him of John's witness concerning the Christ, and of the signs and tokens which supported John's testimony. He may thus have discerned in the

Son of Man the Messiah of God, the Incarnate Deity. Oh cannot you trust the Lord Jesus Christ in this way? Do you not believe—I hope you do—that he is the Son of God; and if so, why not trust him? He that was born of Mary at Bethlehem was God over all, blessed for ever! Do you not believe this? Why, then, do you not rely upon God in our nature? You believe in his consecrated life, his suffering death, his resurrection, his ascension, his sitting in power at the right hand of the Father; why do you not trust him? God hath highly exalted him, and caused all fullness to dwell in him: he is able to save unto the uttermost, why do you not come to him? Believe that he is able, and then with all thy sins before thee, red like scarlet—and with all thy sinful habits, and thy evil propensities before thee, ingrained like the leopard's spots—believe that the Saviour of men can at once make thee whiter than snow as to past guilt, and free from the present and future tyranny of evil. A divine Saviour must be able to cleanse thee from all sin. Say, "Lord, if thou wilt, thou canst make me clean." Faith must be fixed alone on Jesus. None other name is given among men whereby we must be saved. Jesus is God's ultimatum of salvation: the unique hope of guilty men both as to pardon and renewal. Accept him even now.

Now let me go a step further: THIS MAN'S FAITH HAD RESPECT TO A REAL MATTER-OF-FACT CURE. He did not think of the Lord Jesus Christ as a priest who would perform certain ceremonies over him and formally say, "Thou art clean"; for that would not have been true. He wanted really to be delivered from the leprosy. It is easy enough to believe in a mere priestly absolution if you have enough credulity; but we need more than this. It is very easy to believe in Baptismal Regeneration, but what is the good of it? What practical result does it produce? A child remains the same after it has been baptismally regenerated as it was before, and it grows up to prove it. It is easy to believe in Sacramentarianism if you are foolish enough; but there is nothing in it when you believe in it. No sanctifying power comes with outward ceremonials in and of themselves. To believe that the Lord Jesus Christ can make us love the good things which once we despised, and shun those evil things in which we once took pleasure—this is to believe in him indeed and of a truth. Jesus can totally change the nature, and make a sinner into a saint. This is faith of a practical kind; this is a faith worth having.

None of us would imagine that this leper meant that the Lord Jesus could make him feel comfortable in remaining a leper. Some seem to fancy that Jesus came to let us go on in our sins with a quiet conscience; but he did nothing of the kind. His salvation is cleansing from sin, and if we love sin we are not saved from it. We cannot have justification without sanctification. There is no use in quibbling about it; there must be a change, a radical change, a change of heart, or else we are not saved. I put it now to you, Do you desire a moral and a spiritual change, a change of life, thought and motive? This is what Jesus gives. Just as this leper needed a thorough physical change, so do you need an entire renewal of your spiritual nature, so as to become a new creature in Jesus Christ. Oh that many would desire this, for it would be a cheering sign. The man who desires to be pure is beginning to be pure; the man who sincerely longs to conquer sin has struck the first blow already. The power of sin is shaken in that man who looks to Jesus for deliverance from it.

Some sins which have hardened down into habits, yet disappear in a moment when Jesus Christ looks upon a man in love. I have known many instances of persons who, for many years, had never spoken without an oath, or a filthy expression, who, being converted, have never been known to use such language again, and have scarcely ever been tempted in that direction. Others I have known so altered at once that the very propensity which was strongest in them has been the last to annoy them afterwards: they have had such a reversion of the mind's action that, while other sins have worried them for years, and they have had to set a strict watch against them, yet their favourite and dominant sin has never again had the slightest influence over them, except to excite an outburst of horror and deep repentance. Oh, that you had faith in Jesus that he could thus cast down and cast out your reigning sins! Believe in the conquering arm of the Lord Jesus, and he will do it. Conversion is the standing miracle of the church. Where it is genuine, it is as clear a proof of divine power going with the Gospel, as was the casting out of devils, or even the raising of the dead in our Lord's day.

And now we will go another step: THIS MAN'S FAITH WAS
ATTENDED WITH WHAT APPEARS TO BE A HESITANCY. But after
thinking it over a good deal, I am hardly inclined to think it
such a hesitancy as many have judged it to be. He said, "If
thou wilt, thou canst make me clean." There was an "if" in
this speech, and that "if" has aroused the suspicions of many
preachers. Some think it supposes that he doubted our Lord's
willingness. I hardly think that the language justly bears so
harsh a construction. What he meant may have been this—
"Lord, I do not know yet that thou art sent to heal lepers; I
have not seen that thou hast ever done so; but, still, if it be
within the compass of thy commission, I believe thou wilt do it,
and assuredly thou canst if thou wilt. Thou canst heal not only
some lepers, but me in particular; thou canst make me clean."
Now, I think this was a legitimate thing for him to say, as he
had not seen a leper healed—"If it be within the compass of
thy commission, I believe thou canst make me whole."

Moreover, I admire in this text *the deference which the leper
pays to the sovereignty of Christ's will as to the bestowal of his gifts.*
"If thou wilt, thou canst make me clean";—as much as to say,
"I know thou hast a right to distribute these great favours
exactly as thou pleasest. I have no claim upon thee; I cannot
say that thou art bound to make me clean; I appeal to thy pity
and free favour. The matter remains with thy will." The man
had never read the text which saith, "It is not of him that
willeth, nor of him that runneth, but of God that showeth
mercy," for it was not yet written; but he had in his mind the
humble spirit suggested by that grand truth. He owned that
grace must come as a free gift of God's good pleasure when he
said, "Lord, if thou wilt." Beloved, we need never raise a
question as to the Lord's will to give grace when we have the
will to receive it; but still, I would have every sinner feel that
he has no claim upon God for anything.

O sinner, if the Lord should give thee up, as he did the
heathen described in the first chapter of the Epistle to the
Romans, thou deservest it. If he should never look upon thee
with an eye of love, what couldst thou say against his righteous
sentence? Thou hast wilfully sinned, and thou deservest to be
left in thy sin. Confessing all this, we still cling to our firm
belief in the power of grace, and cry, "Lord, if thou wilt, thou

canst." We appeal to our Saviour's pitying love, relying upon his boundless power.

See, also, how the leper, to my mind, *really speaks without any hesitancy*, if you understand him. He does not say, "Lord, if thou puttest out thy hand, thou canst make me clean"; nor, "Lord, if thou speakest, thou canst make me clean"; but only, "Lord, *if thou wilt*, thou canst make me clean"; thy mere will can do it. Oh, splendid faith! If you are inclined to spy a little halting in it, I would have you admire it for running so well with a lame foot. If there was a weakness anywhere in his faith, still it was so strong that the weakness only manifests its strength. Sinner, it is so; and I pray God that thy heart may grasp it—if the Lord wills it he can make thee clean. Believest thou this?

Then, notice that THIS MAN'S FAITH HAD EARNEST ACTION FLOWING OUT OF IT. Believing that, if Jesus willed, he could make him clean, what did the leper do? At once he came to Jesus. I know not from what distance, but he came as near to Jesus as he could. Then he besought him; that is to say, he pleaded, and pleaded, and pleaded again. He cried, "Lord, cleanse me! Lord, heal my leprosy!" Nor was this all; he fell on his knees and worshipped; for we read, "Kneeling down to him." He not only knelt, but knelt to Jesus. He had no difficulty as to paying him divine honour. He worshipped the Lord Christ, paying him reverent homage. He then went on to honour him by an open acknowledgment of his power, his marvellous power, his infinite power, by saying, "Lord, if thou wilt, thou canst make me clean." I should not wonder if some that stood by began to smile at what they thought the poor man's fanatical credulity. They murmured, "What a poor fool this leper is, to think that Jesus of Nazareth can cure him of his leprosy!" Such a confession of faith had seldom been heard. But whatever critics and sceptics might think, this brave man boldly declared, "Lord, this is my confession of faith: I believe that if thou wilt, thou canst make me clean." Now, poor soul, thou that art full of guilt, and hardened in sin, and yet anxious to be healed, look straight away to the Lord Jesus Christ. He is here now. In the preaching of the gospel he is with us always. With the eyes of thy mind behold him, for he beholdeth thee. Thou knowest that he lives, even though thou

seest him not. Believe in this living Jesus; believe for perfect
cleansing. He is very God of very God; bow before him, and
cast thyself upon his mercy. Go home, and on thy knees say,
"Lord, I believe that thou canst make me clean." He will
hear your cry, and will save you. There will be no interval
between your prayer and the gracious reward of faith, of which
I am now to speak.

Lastly, HIS FAITH HAD ITS REWARD. The reward of this man's
faith was, first, that *his very words were treasured up*. Matthew,
Mark, Luke, all three of them record the precise words which
this man used: "Lord, if thou wilt, thou canst make me clean."
They evidently did not see so much to find fault with in them
as some have done; on the contrary, they thought them gems
to be placed in the setting of their gospels. Three times over
are they recorded, because they are such a splendid confession
of faith for a poor diseased leper to have made. I believe that
God is as much glorified by that one sentence of the leper as by
the song of Cherubim and Seraphim, when they continually do
cry, "Holy, holy, holy, Lord God of Sabaoth." A sinner's lips
declaring his confident faith in God's own Son can breathe
sonnets unto God more sweet than those of the angelic choirs.

His next reward was, that *Jesus echoed his words*. He said,
"Lord, if thou wilt, thou canst make me clean"; and Jesus
said, "I will; be thou clean." As an echo answers to the voice,
so did Jesus to his supplicant. If you can only get, then, as
far as this leper's confession, I believe that our Lord Jesus from
his throne above will answer to your prayer.

So potent were the words of this leper that *they moved our Lord
very wonderfully*. Read the forty-first verse: "And Jesus, moved
with compassion." The Greek word here used, if I were to pronounce it in your hearing, would half suggest its own meaning.
It expresses a stirring of the entire manhood, a commotion in
all the inward parts. The Saviour was greatly moved. You
have seen a man moved, have you not? When a strong man is
unable any longer to restrain himself, and is forced to give way
to his feelings, you have seen him tremble all over, and at last
burst out into an evident break-down. It was just so with the
Saviour: his pity moved him, his delight in the leper's faith
mastered him. When he heard the man speak with such
confidence in him, the Saviour was moved with a sacred passion,

which, as it was in sympathy with the leper, is called "compassion." Oh, to think that a poor leper should have such power over the divine Son of God! Yet, in all thy sin and misery, if thou canst believe in Jesus, thou canst move the heart of thy blessed Saviour. Yea, even now his bowels yearn towards thee.

No sooner was our Lord Jesus thus moved than *out went his hand*, and he touched the man and healed him immediately. It did not require a long time for the working of the cure; but the leper's blood was cooled and cleansed in a single second. Our Lord could work this miracle, and make all things new in the man; for "all things were made by him; and without him was not anything made that was made." To make him quite sure that he was cleansed, the Lord Jesus bade him go to the priest, and seek a certificate of health. He was so clean that he might be examined by the appointed sanitary authority, and come off without suspicion. The cure which he had received was a real and radical one, and therefore he might go away at once, and get the certificate of it.

If our converts will not bear practical tests, they are worth nothing; let even our enemies judge whether they are not better men and women when Jesus has renewed them. If Jesus saves a sinner, he does not mind all men testing the change. Jesus does not seek display, but he seeks examination from those able to judge. Our converts will bear the test. Watch him in private life. We can read your verdict. "There is joy in the presence of the angels of God over one sinner that repenteth"; and this proves what you think. It is such a wonderful change. May you be one over whom they rejoice!

If thou believest on Jesus Christ, and if thou wilt trust him, as the sent One of God, fully and entirely with thy soul, he will make thee clean. Behold him on the Cross, and see sin put away. Behold him risen from the dead, and see new life bestowed. Behold him enthroned in power, and see evil conquered. I am ready to be bound for my Lord, to be his surety, that if thou wilt come to him, he will make thee clean. Believe thy Saviour, and thy cure is wrought.

IX

THE CENTURION'S SERVANT

" Jesus saith unto him, I will come and heal him. And Jesus
said unto the centurion, Go thy way; and as thou hast believed,
so be it done unto thee."—Matt. 8: 7, 13.

THE centurion of Capernaum cared for the sick, and was
anxious for the recovery of his palsied servant. He had
done what he could to benefit religiously the people among
whom he dwelt, for the elders of the Jews said, "He loveth our
nation, and he hath built us a synagogue." But he combined
with a desire to benefit the soul a sincere desire for the welfare
of the body; and this was apparent in the interest which he took
in his "boy," his personal servant, or young valet. God has
joined body and soul together, and they ought not to be sun-
dered in our deeds of charity.

This captain's sympathy with his suffering valet was shown
by practical action. He did not say that he felt for him, and
then go off to the guardroom and keep clear of the sick youth;
nor did he merely stand and watch him in his pain, to see how
he would fare, but he aroused himself, he called together the
elders of the city, he summoned his choice friends to him: in
fact, he made the whole circle of his acquaintance feel a
sympathy with him concerning the illness of his body-servant.
Then he sent these elders and friends to the best physician of
the age, and as I think also followed at their heels himself: he
used the surest means within his reach and appealed to him to
whom none ever appealed in vain. From the centurion I gather
that we must not be content with loving our people and building
them synagogues, but we must also build them hospitals and
dispensaries. Find them preachers by all means, but find them
surgeons too. We may not forget the soul, but we must also
remember that the soul dwells in a body liable to many disor-
ders. We may become just a little too spiritual, so spiritual as to

spirit away the very spirit of Christianity. God grant us grace to be as tenderly considerate of suffering humanity as this centurion was, and we probably shall be so if we have as strong faith and as deep humility as he had.

For three years our Lord Himself walked the hospitals: he lived all day long in an infirmary; for all around him at one time they laid the sick in the streets, and at all times physical evil in some form or other came in his way. He put forth his hand, or spake the word, and healed all sorts of maladies, for it was part of his life-work. "I will come and heal him," said he, for he was a physician in constant practice, and would be round at once to see the patient. "He went about doing good," and in all this he would let his people know that he intended not to bless one part of man alone, but the whole of our nature, taking upon himself not only our sins, but our sicknesses. Jesus means to bless the body as well as the soul; and though for this present he hath left our body very much under the power of sickness, for still "the body is dead because of sin, but the spirit is life because of righteousness;" yet every restored limb, and opened eye, and healed wound is a token that Jesus cares for our flesh and blood, and means that the body shall share the benefits of his death by a glorious resurrection.

It will be a very great pity if ever it should be thought that benevolence is divorced from Christianity, for hitherto the crown of the faith of Jesus has been love to men; it is, indeed, the glory of Christianity that wherever it comes it erects buildings altogether unknown to heathenism—hospitals, asylums, and other abodes of charity. The genius of Christianity is pity for the sinful and the suffering. Let the church be a healer like her Lord: at least if she cannot pour forth virtue from the hem of her garment, nor "say in a word" so that sickness may fly, let her be among the most prompt to help in everything that can assuage pain or assist poverty. So ought it to be, for "as Jesus was, so are we also in this world." Did he not tell us, "As the Father hath sent me, even so send I you"? We cannot too diligently study his character, for he has left us an example that we may follow in his steps.

This said, I desire to pass on to my subject, which is of a spiritual kind. I want you to mark the development of the faith of the centurion, and side by side with it the growing manifestation of our Lord's power. Both are seen in the narrative.

The centurion had evidently heard about Christ; perhaps the healing of the ruler's child had satisfied him that Jesus is the Messiah. He had attended at the synagogue. I cannot doubt that a man who had built a synagogue would be sure to go to it; and there he had learned of the Coming One, foretold by prophets and expected by saints. This Anointed One was to work wonders among mankind, and especially wonders of healing. Thus he had gathered that Jesus was the Christ, and he believed in him as having power to heal his sick servant.

The first practical result was that he humbly sent the elders with the urgent request to "come and heal him." He believed that Jesus, if he were present, could restore the dying youth. He had thought it over, and his faith had reached as far as that of Mary and Martha when they said: "Lord, if thou hadst been here, my brother had not died." In effect he said, If thou wilt come here, great Master, my servant will not die. Observe that our Lord's answer was exactly proportioned to the measure of faith in the prayer: "I will come and heal him:" "Thou sayest, come and heal him; I reply, I will come and heal him." So far so good: but the captain's faith is to be seen in a still clearer light. He has been considering the matter still further, and his humility leads him to feel that he ought not to expect Jesus to come to his house. Why should he trouble the Master to leave the crowd and to cease preaching, to come and attend to his servant? He feels himself unfit to entertain one so holy and so great, and therefore he sends off his friends post haste to offer humble apologies, and to beg the Master not to come. He has at the same time advanced in his belief in Christ's power, for he says in effect, "There is no need that thou shouldst come: only will it, merely say the word and the healing is wrought. For I also am a man under authority, deriving authority from being under it, and I have only to say to one soldier go, and to another, come, and my will is done. I have no need to execute my own wishes personally, for my will governs my troop and each man is eager to do my bidding. So, great Master, stay where thou art, go on with thy other work, and only will to bless me and it will be enough; thy desire will be accomplished without fail."

Here was growing faith, and side by side with it was a clearer manifestation of the Master's power. Our Lord Jesus there and then wills that healing power should go forth; he moves no further towards the house where the palsied patient lies, but rather he turns round, and in obedience to the wish of the centurion he walks away; yet the miracle is wrought, the paralytic child has risen from the bed, the captain's heart is gladdened, and those who came to plead stand in the house to praise the Lord. Awe-struck by the finger of God so near and so manifest, what could they do but bless the Lord, who had visited his people?

The first thing I invite you to consider is THE PERFECT READINESS OF OUR LORD JESUS for works of mercy. The centurion was concerned about his servant, just as you and I are, I hope, to-day concerned about certain poor souls which lie paralysed by sin. We mourn over them, and if we could heal them we would gladly suffer any self-denial or suffering. If we could bring our neighbours to Christ, it would be the utmost joy to us. How can we endure to see them die? The mass of working men around us, ay, and the majority of our wealthy neighbours are under the power of the wicked one. To them the things which are seen are the only objects of their thoughts. They will not regard the Gospel of Christ, or eternity, or judgment, or heaven, or hell. The privileges with which our country is so largely endowed are treated as if they were of no value whatever: Sabbaths, Bibles, the Gospel, and the throne of grace are despised. This is mournful indeed!

That willingness we shall see first if we notice that *he did not cavil at the pleas which the Jewish elders urged* on behalf of the centurion, though they must have been very distasteful to his mind. They said, "He is worthy for whom thou shouldst do this": that was not the right style of pleading with him who came to save the lost and bless the undeserving in the freeness of his grace. The elders said, "He loveth our nation, and he hath built us a synagogue," and so on. Poor souls, they were doing their best, and using the kind of argument by which their own hopes were sustained. Our Lord regarded the spirit of their intercession rather than the form in which they offered it; and though the plea, laying so much stress upon human merit, might very well have warranted him in saying, "Hold your peace, for you are damaging rather than helping the case," yet our Lord was so willing that he raised no question. From afar he read the heart of the centurion and he knew that the good man's advocates were altogether misrepresenting his views and feelings. The last thing in the world that the lowly-minded soldier would have pleaded would have been personal worthiness. His own words were, "I am not worthy." But Jesus was so willing to go that he put up with all the blunders of the elders, and responded to their request, "I will come and heal him." Beloved, very likely you and I make quite as great mistakes when we pray: we fancy we pray very correctly, but I wonder what our Lord thinks of our prayers. Surely he has often to pick out the meaning of our hearts from among the errors of our lips; but so willing is he to bless us, that if there be first a willing mind it shall still be accepted, for he rejoiceth to hear every prayer which seeks healing for sin-sick souls.

His willingness is seen, next, in the fact of his so cheerfully *granting the first prayer in the form in which it was put.* They besought him that he would "come and heal" his servant. Now, that was not exactly the best form in which to put it, certainly it was not that which commended itself to the maturer thoughts of the centurion, yet our blessed Master took the prayer just as it was, and he seemed to say, "I see the measure of your faith, and I will give you the blessing as you are able to receive it." The Lord is very generous to come down to our capacities; if he were always to act according to his own divine standard we should be greatly dazzled, but we should be afraid to draw near to him. He condescendingly lays aside the splendour of his majesty to act as well as to speak to us after the manner of men, and then we see the sweet voluntariness of his grace, and the cheerful willingness of his spirit to do us good. If we cannot receive a blessing in any other than a second-class way, we shall have it in the way in which we can take it. Oh what a willing friend we have in Christ.

Notice further, that when the centurion sent a fresh deputation of his choice friends to say to the Master, "Trouble not thyself, I am not worthy that thou shouldst come under my roof," *our Lord did not quarrel with the change of the prayer.* Some people would have said, "What is it that you want? First, I am to come, and when I am almost there I am met with

a request not to come,—what do you mean? This is not respectful, and I will not come." Our gentle Jesus spoke not so. He
thought not of himself, nor his own dignity. Let us imitate his
meek and quiet spirit. When you are trying to do good you will
often be put about by the whims of those whom you would
benefit. You will find that when you do what people ask you
they are not satisfied: many adults are like sick children, who
are always cross and fretful. We must humour these poor
hearts, as our Lord did. He was so willing to bless that he
seemed to give *carte blanche* to those who asked of him: "Yes,
you shall have the blessing which way you like, so that you are
but able to receive it. It shall be given to you according to your
faith."

The Saviour's willingness to bless this centurion's servant
was very manifest from the fact that *he did not impute an ill
motive to the centurion* when he bade him refrain from visiting
the house. There was no mistrust about our Lord. He knew too
much both of man's evil and of the sincerity of those in whom
his grace was placed to suspect and to interpret harshly.
Ignorance and selfishness are mistrustful, but love thinketh
no evil. If there are two ways of understanding a sentence,
and one is better than the other, always read it in the kindest
way, if you can. Never put hard constructions upon words and
actions. You and I might have said in the case before us, "You
see he does not want me in his fine house. He is a centurion
and thinks much of himself, and I am wearing a poor garment,
and therefore he does not want me in his villa to disgrace his
halls. He is a captain, a man in authority, having soldiers under
him, his pride forbids my approach, and therefore I will have
nothing to do with him." But no, it was not in the Master's
heart to think thus bitterly, but as at the first he had said, "I
will come and heal him," so now when genuine humility
requests him not to come, he turns about, but works the
miracle all the same. Our condescending Saviour must be very
willing to bless men, since he takes the true meaning of their
prayers where others would write a harsh interpretation. Be
not afraid to approach him however unworthy you are, for
he will put the best construction upon your broken petitions,
and interpret them always to your gain.

Nor did he demur at all to the comparison which the centurion made. "I also," said the centurion, "am a man under authority." If you were to read that expression with dark spectacles, you might make a great deal of mischief out of it. A caviller might say, "How dare he even for a moment compare himself to the Son of God? How can he draw a parallel of which he is one side and the blessed Lord the other? What impertinence!" Our Lord was no critic. When he has to deal with sincere people, he picks no holes, imputes no motives, and dwells on no mistakes. The centurion did not wish to make his metaphor go on all fours, and our Lord did not treat him as if he did. Many a time have some of us had to suffer from this mode of attack, but never from our Master, nor from those who imitate him. He took the meaning of the centurion's illustration, and he admired it; for indeed it was a grand and beautiful idea, to set forth our Lord Jesus as the great Emperor of the universe to whom all things are under rule, and to whose faintest word each form of force, whether good or evil, is sure to render obedience. He showed that he had rightly estimated Christ, and enthroned him as he should be enthroned in the place of unlimited sovereignty and power.

Secondly, an equally interesting topic is before us in THE CONSCIOUS ABILITY OF OUR LORD. You have seen his perfect willingness, now behold his boundless power. I do not know how it affects your minds, but that sentence from the lip of Jesus, "I will come and heal him," has a strange majesty about it to my soul. It is the word of a king wherein there is power. Perhaps the most majestic word that was ever uttered was "Light be": no sooner was it heard than the eternal darkness fled, and light was: but surely this is scarcely second in grandeur, if second at all; its sound is as much the voice of the Lord as that which scattered the primeval shades: "I will come and heal him." Yet this royal and powerful word was spoken as a matter of course; our Lord Jesus did not deliberate, but the healing word flowed from him as naturally as the perfume from the flowers.

It shows our Lord's conscious ability to deal with all manner of evil, since *he was not at all puzzled by this intricate case.* Almost any other physician would have felt some measure of perplexity. The case is described as that of a man sick of the palsy and yet "grievously tormented." Paralysis can hardly be

connected with acute pain. It brings numbness and so ends
sensation, at least such is my impression. Some interpreters
think the disease must have been a form of tetanus, but there
is no mention of tetanus in either account. It was a palsy, and
yet he was "grievously tormented." I know nothing about it,
but I have read that there is a period in which paralysis may
turn into apoplexy, and the patient may suffer extreme
agony. If so, this may explain the mystery. However, though
the case perplexed many, it did not perplex the Lord Jesus,
for he said, "I will come and heal him." Now, my brother
ministers, have not you and I a great many cases coming in our
way which tax our experience and make us feel at a loss?
Some experiences are a tangled skein, we cannot follow the
thread, and, so far as we do follow it, knots and snarls are our
chief reward. See how Jesus sweeps away all debates with
"I will come and heal him." All the complicated phenomena
of human disease he comprehends, and along the dark labyrinth
of human experience his mighty word makes a way for itself:
undisturbed, and even undelayed, the eternal energy enters the
soul, for Jesus says, "I will come and heal him."

Neither did the extremity of the case at all dishearten him, for
this poor man was ready to die, so Luke tells us, just on the
verge of expiring, yet Jesus says, "I will come and heal him."
It does not matter to Jesus what the stage of the disease may be.
A common physician would shake his head and say, "Ah,
you should have sent for me before. I might have done something at an earlier date, but the sufferer is now beyond all
human help." Poor souls are never beyond the reach of the
Divine Healer, and so he says without a word of doubt, "I
will come and heal him." Ay, had he been dead, Jesus could
have said and could have done the same. "I will come and heal
him" is a word for all emergencies. Beloved, let us never
hesitate to hope in prayer because the persons for whom we
plead are such great and horrible sinners, and so very far gone
in crime. Verily, if we can believe in our great Saviour with
mighty faith, we shall yet hear him say of many a reprobate
and outcast, "I will come and heal him."

As for the method of procedure, our Lord in his conscious
power *treats the modus operandi as a matter of indifference.* He
grants the first petition as it was presented to him, and will

come and heal him; but when he is requested not to come he quite as willingly says, "According to thy faith so be it unto thee." He could heal as well at a distance as near at hand. Present or absent, it was all the same to him. He can save them in their pews, under the preaching which they have heard so constantly, or he can meet with them in their lonely chambers, reading some godly book; or he can wound their hearts by a loving word spoken during a walk with a friend. We have known him call men by his grace right out of the paths of sin, wounding them with secret arrows when they were at ease and secure in the service of the devil. Saul of Tarsus was not on his knees in prayer, but hastening to shed innocent blood, and yet the Lord brought him down and made him seek salvation. Our Lord knows how to reach inaccessible persons; they may shut *us* out, but they cannot shut *him* out. This should much encourage us in pleading for souls which are out of our usual line of action. When we plead with Jesus, let us never bind him down to ways and means of our own choosing, but let us leave to him the method of salvation.

Jesus was so conscious of his power that *you never find him uttering an expression of wonder, or manifesting the slightest surprise when his will is done, and a notable miracle is wrought.* No, but he did wonder at the centurion's faith, and on another occasion he marvelled at the people's unbelief. It is no wonder to Christ that he saves sinners, he is so in the habit of doing it, and he is so able to do it. Virtue goes out of him almost unconsciously, for he is so full of power that he can bless on all sides and scarcely know it. Even as the sun shines north, south, east, and west, and never wonders at its own shining; or as a fountain sendeth forth its sparkling drops, and never stops to admire itself, or to marvel at its own flashing flow, so doth Jesus readily, easily, out of his very nature scatter pardon and salvation on all sides. He marvels at our faith, he marvels oftener at our unbelief, but to him his own power is not a thing of wonder at all. I want you to get fast hold of this thought if you can, and I beg you to hide it away in your hearts, that Jesus Christ is beyond measure able to save. We do not half believe it; we think we do, but we do not even a tithe believe it, for when we meet with a rather hard case we are ready to give it up in despair. Despairing persons we too soon leave in

their gloom; and even melancholy men and women we are shy
of; we wish we had never seen them, instead of believing up
to their point, and believingly interceding until we see them
happy in Christ. If we meet with a horrible blasphemer, or a
foul liver, or a bloated drinker, we feel quite out of our latitude
and in the land of monsters, whereas it is with such cases that
our Lord is much at home, and we ought to pray most about
such persons, and to be most confident that the Gospel was
meant to meet their grievous ills. Is there not a great Saviour
for great sinners?

We shall close by a third equally interesting point, of great
practical value. I have spoken of our Lord's willingness and
power; now we will note THE ABIDING METHOD OF OUR LORD
JESUS.

The first method mentioned here was "Come and heal him."
Jesus then went about doing good, but he does not now vouch-
safe his bodily presence, or give physical tokens of his being
near to anyone. If any say to us, "Lo here," or "Lo there,"
let us not believe them, for Jesus is not now upon the earth;
He hath gone up on high. We do not now pray, "Come and
heal him," in the sense of expecting a vision or revelation of
Christ after the flesh to those whom we love. We hope that he
will come one day a second time, and heal the sicknesses of this
poor world, but till then we know him not after the flesh, neither
do we seek any personal coming. The other and permanent
mode of our Lord's action was that he should speak the word,
and so perform the cure. "Say in a word and my servant shall
be healed." That is the style of our Lord to-day and throughout
the whole of this dispensation. The healing energy of Jesus
is now seen not by his personal presence, but by the power
of his word in answer to the prayer of faith.

When but a little while ago your fields were bare, and your
gardens desolate, if the Lord had suddenly come forth in awful
glory, and caused snow and ice to fly before him, and had then
benignly touched the valleys and the hills, and covered them
with grass and corn, you would have exclaimed, "This is a great
miracle": but in truth it is an equally great display of power
that the deed is done, though by less glaring processes. The
will of the Lord transforms the clods of the valley into an army
of wheat ears and clover balls; his quiet wish reddens the

clusters of the vineyard and ripens the fruit of the garden ; is not this also a marvel of power? What though the Lord has not come forth riding upon cherub wings, nor has he spoken audibly in commanding sentences, yet the secret energy of the eternal word is evermore going forth to give us seedtime and harvest, cold and heat. What diviner form of miracle is to be desired? I believe that when we rise to the possession of a fully developed faith, we shall see ourselves to be daily compassed about with the omnipotence of God, and shall look on every tiny blade of grass, and upon the insect which balances itself thereon, and the dewdrop that decorates it, as being quite as manifestly the finger of God as when Nilus turns to blood, or the dust of Egypt becomes flies. To the believer miracles have not ceased, but the common course of nature teems with them.

The power of the word in answer to the prayer of faith is now our Lord's way of blessing, and this method exactly suits the wish of true *humility*. Humility says, "I am not worthy that God should do anything for me which would attract attention to me or make me seem honoured above others." The lowly soul hears of one who was saved through a dream or a vision, and he feels that he is not worthy to be thus favoured. No, you need not wish for it, the word of the Lord is enough, and that word is nigh you at this moment, in your mouth and in your heart, you have but to hear and your soul shall live.

I am sure that it pleases *faith* better than any other way. Oh that the power of the word might be displayed at this time. Oh my Lord, how I desire of thee that thou wouldst save thousands, and I would be glad if it were done without me, without any of thy servants, if thou wouldst only say in a word and by thy Holy Spirit cause a nation to be born in a day! Certain professors eagerly pine for a great stir: they will not believe that the kingdom of God prospers unless thousands crowd into our assemblies ; and unless great excitement reigns, and all the papers are ringing with the names of famous preachers. They like it all the better if they hear of persons being thrown into fits during the meetings, or read of men and women falling down, or screaming under excitement, and I know not what besides. They can believe in Christ's power if there are signs and wonders, but not else. This is going back to "come and heal him." But we are content to abide by the second mode. Can you not believe that by each one of us making the Gospel of God to have free course, our Lord can effectually save men by his word?

It is perfectly reasonable that we should expect our Lord to display his healing power in this way. What the centurion said was full of forcible argument. He said, "I am a captain of a troop. I do not have to go about from place to place to do everything personally. No, I remain in my quarters and issue orders, and I am sure of their being carried out. I say to this one 'go,' and he goeth, and to my servant 'do this,' and he doeth it." Is it not clear that the far greater Captain of our salvation does not need to come forth bodily in order to save any? His word will suffice. Speak to the powers of darkness, and the captive sinner shall be free. Speak, and the human will must yield to thee, and the human heart must receive thee. Is it not so? We do not believe enough in our Lord. I come back to that; we do not believe enough in what is so perfectly reasonable. If we will but speak our Master's word, and let it go forth, and bear sway, with less and less of our own word to cripple and hinder it, souls must be saved. Do you not believe in the plain preaching of the glad tidings? Remember Jericho, and how by God's own appointed though simple means the huge walls rocked to their fall. Will not the Lord's own means suffice you still? Oh, believers, do you want anything this day except the simple preaching of the gospel? If so, you are departing from the point wherein your faith ought to remain, since still it pleaseth God by the foolishness of preaching to save them that believe. "The world by wisdom knew not God," and never will know God. Trust not philosophy, but stand by the old old story, and pray the Master to work by it as in former ages.

Now, if any one will try in his own case this divine method of healing, it will succeed in his instance as in that of the centurion's servant. If you will believe the power of Christ and trust him to save you, you shall certainly obtain eternal life, and that at once. Can you heartily believe in Jesus as you find him revealed in Scripture? Can you be content without strange feelings, without remarkable terrors, without dreams or visions? Can you be content simply to trust your Saviour?

X

AN ASTOUNDING MIRACLE

"And they went into Capernaum; and straightway on the sabbath day he entered into the synagogue, and taught. And they were astonished at his doctrine: for he taught them as one that had authority, and not as the scribes. And there was in their synagogue a man with an unclean spirit; and he cried out, saying, Let us alone; what have we to do with thee, thou Jesus of Nazareth? art thou come to destroy us? I know thee who thou art, the Holy One of God. And Jesus rebuked him, saying, Hold thy peace, and come out of him. And when the unclean spirit had torn him, and cried with a loud voice, he came out of him. And they were all amazed, insomuch that they questioned among themselves, saying, What thing is this? what new doctrine is this? for with authority commandeth he even the unclean spirits, and they do obey him. And immediately his fame spread abroad throughout all the region round about Galilee."—Mark 1: 21–28.

YOU will find the same narrative in Luke, at the fourth chapter, from the thirty-first to the thirty-seventh verse. These two evangelists commence the narrative by telling us of the singular authority and power which there was about the Saviour's teaching—authority, so that no man dare question his doctrine; power, so that every man felt the force of the truth which he delivered. "They were astonished at his teaching, for his word was with power." Why was it that the Saviour's teaching had such a remarkable power about it? Was it not, first, because he preached the truth? There is no power in falsehood except so far as men choose to yield to it because it flatters them; but there is great force in truth, it makes its own way into the soul. Even though they grow angry their very resistance proves that they recognize the force of what is spoken.

Moreover, the Saviour spoke the truth in a very natural, unaffected manner: the truth was in him, and it flowed freely from him. His manner was truthful as well as his matter. There is a way of speaking truth so as to make it sound like a lie.

Perhaps there is no greater injury done to truth than when it is spoken in a doubtful manner, with none of the accent and emphasis of conviction. Our Saviour spoke as the oracles of God: he spoke truth as truth should be spoken, unaffectedly and naturally: as one who did not preach professionally, but out of the fullness of his heart. There was about his whole conduct and deportment that which made him the fit person to utter the truth, because the truth was incarnate, and embodied, and exemplified in his own person. Truth overflowed at his lips from the deep well of his soul; it was in him and therefore came from him. What he poured forth was his own life, wherewith he was endeavouring to impregnate the lives of others.

That power and authority was seen all the more in contrast with the Scribes; for the Scribes spake hesitatingly; they quoted authority; they begged leave to venture an opinion; quibbling about matters which had no practical importance whatever. They were wonderfully clear upon the tithing of mint and anise; they enlarged most copiously upon the washing of cups and basins; they were profound upon phylacteries and borders of garments. They were at home upon such rubbish, which would neither save a soul, nor slay a sin, nor suggest a virtue. While handling the Scriptures they were mere word-triflers, letter-men, whose chief object was to show their own wisdom. Such attempts at oratory and word-spinning were as far as the poles asunder from the discourses of our Lord. Self-display never entered into the mind of Jesus. He himself was so absorbed in what he had to teach that his hearers did not exclaim, "What a preacher is this!" but, "What a word is this!" and "What new teaching is this!": the word and the teaching with their admirable authority and amazing power subduing men's minds and hearts by the energy of truth.

Now, when they were beginning to perceive this authority in his word, our Lord determined to prove to them that there was real power at the back of his teaching, that he had a right to use such authority, for he was Jesus Christ the Son of God, clothed with divine authority and power. It occurred to him to display before their eyes the fact that as there was power about his speech, there was also power about himself, that he was mighty in deed as well as in word; and hence he wrought the miracle now before us. This truth is much needed at the present moment; for if the Gospel does not still save men, if it is not still "the power of God unto salvation to every one that believeth," then the attacks of scepticism are not easily repelled; but if it be still a thing of power over the minds of men, a power conquering sin and Satan, then they may say what they like, our only answer shall be to lament their doubts and to scorn their scorning.

First, then, to show forth this power and authority, OUR LORD SELECTS A MOST UNHAPPY PERSON ON WHOM TO PROVE HIS POWER.

This person was, first, *one possessed*. A devil dwelt within him. We cannot explain this fact any more than we can explain madness. Many things which happen in the world of mind are quite inexplicable. We accept the recorded fact—an evil spirit entered into this man, and continued in him. He had become like a devil in human form, and so was in a certain manner the opposite of our Lord Jesus. In Jesus dwelt the fullness of the Godhead bodily by an eternal union; in this man the devil dwelt for a while. Is not this an awful picture? But note the fact, the man whom Jesus selects whereon to prove his power and authority was so far gone that the foul fiend controlled his mind, and made a kennel of his body.

I wondered, when thinking this over, whether a person of whom this man is the emblem would come into the congregation to-day; for I have seen such people. I have not dared personally to apply such an epithet to any man, but I have heard it applied: I have heard disgusted friends and indignant neighbours, worn out with the drunken profanity, or horrible filthiness, of some man say, "He does not seem to be a man; he acts like the evil one." Or when it has been a woman, they have said, "All that is womanly is gone; she seems to be a female fiend." Well, the power of Jesus knows no limit. Upon one who was the Devil's Own did our gracious Lord display his authority and power in connection with his gospel teaching; and he is not less able now than then.

This man, further, was *one whose personality was to a great extent merged in the Evil One*. Read the twenty-third verse: "There was in their synagogue a man with an unclean spirit;" the rendering might be equally accurate if we read it, "A man in an unclean spirit." Not only a man *with* an unclean spirit in him, but a man *in* an unclean spirit. The phrase is simple enough; we speak of a man being in drink. For liquor to be in a man does not mean half so much as for a man to be in liquor. To give a more pleasant illustration, we speak of a person's being "in love;" he is absorbed in his affection; we should not express a tenth as much if we said that love is in the man. A man can be in a rage, in a passion; and even so was this man in an evil spirit. The poor creature had no power over himself whatever, and was not himself actually responsible; in all that I say of him I am not condemning *him*, but only using him as a type of human sin. Please do not forget this. As far as the narrative is concerned the man himself scarcely appears; it is the unclean spirit that cries out, "Let us alone; I know thee who thou art." The man was scarcely a man with a will or wish of his own; in fact, you do not notice him till you see him flung down into the midst of the synagogue; you only see the proper man when the Saviour raises him up before them all unharmed and rational.

Have you never seen such men? You say sometimes, and you say truly, "Alas, poor wretch! The drink has the mastery over him; he would never do such things as he does if he was not in drink." We do not mean to excuse him by such an expression, far from it. Or it may be the man is a gambler, and you say, "He is quite besotted by gaming; though he impoverishes his wife and children, yet he is possessed by that spirit so completely that he has not the mind nor the will to resist the temptation." Or it may be that such another person is carried away with unchaste affections, and we say, "How sad! There was something about that man which we used to like; in many points he was admirable, but he is so deluded by his bad passions that he does not seem to be himself." We almost forget the man, and think mainly of the dreadful spirit which has degraded him below the beasts. The type and emblem of such a person as that our Lord selected as the platform whereon to show his power. I wonder whether this voice of mine will reach one of that sort. I sincerely hope that none of you are in such a condition; but if you should be, still there is hope for you in Christ Jesus: he is able to deliver such as are led captive at the will of Satan.

Note further, for we must show you how our Lord selects the worst of cases, it was a man *in whom the evil spirit was at his worst.* Kindly look at the fourth chapter of Luke, verse thirty-three, and you will see that in this man there was "the spirit of an unclean devil." There are glittering sins, and respectable sins, and these will ruin souls; but this poor man had a disreputable demon in him, a spirit of the foulest, coarsest, and most abominable order. I suppose this foul spirit would incite its victim to filthy talk and obscene acts. The evil one delights in sins against the seventh commandment. If he can lead men and women to defile their bodies he takes special delight in such crimes.

If we were to say of such a character as this man pictures, "Let us turn out of the way," who could blame us? If we separated from such sinners, who could censure us? You say, "We could not bear to hear the man speak; the very look of him is offensive;" nor is it strange that you should. There are women so fallen that modesty trembles to be seen in their company; and the feeling that makes you shudder at them is not to be condemned, so long as it does not spring from self-righteousness or lead to contempt. Yet, now, see it and wonder, our blessed Lord and Master fixed his eye of old on the man with the unclean devil in him, and to-day he fixes his eye of mercy on the basest and vilest of mankind, that in their conversion he may show the power and authority of his word.

In this man there did not seem to be anything for the Lord to begin upon. When you are trying to bring a man to the Saviour you look over him to see where you can touch him, what there is in him that you can work upon. Perhaps he is a good husband though he is a drunkard, and you wisely attempt to work upon his domestic affections. If a man has some point of character upon which you can rest your lever, your work is comparatively easy. But with some people you look over them from top to bottom, and you cannot find a spot for hope to rest upon; they seem so utterly gone that there is neither reason, nor conscience, nor will, nor power of thought left in them. Of all this the possessed man in the synagogue is a striking emblem, for when the Lord comes into the synagogue the poor wretch does not begin to pray, "Lord, heal me." No, his first cry is, "Let us alone." He does not seem to resist this cry of the evil spirit in him, though it was so much to his own injury, but he goes on to say, "What have we to do with thee, thou Jesus of Nazareth? Art thou come to destroy us? I know thee who thou art." The possessed man seems wholly lost in the dominating spirit of evil which permeates his entire being.

Now I look upon this, though it be negative, as a very glaring part of the difficulty; for I do not care how far a man has gone in outward sin, if he has some point left in him of common honesty, or love to his family, or generous heartedness, you know where to commence operations, and your work is hopeful; but in those outcasts of whom I am now speaking there is neither lodgment for hope, nor foothold for faith, nor more than a bare ledge for love. As the man in the synagogue was shut up within the demon's influence, so are some men encompassed by their iniquity, blocked up by their depravity. Yet the great Upraiser of the fallen can rescue even these; he is able to save unto the uttermost.

One other matter makes the case still more terrible: *he was a man upon whom religious observances were lost.* He was in the synagogue on the Sabbath, and I do not suppose that this was anything unusual. The worst man of all is one who can attend the means of grace, and yet remain under the full power of evil. Those poor outside sinners who know nothing of the Gospel at all, and never go to the house of God at all, for them there remains at least the hope that the very novelty of the Holy Word may strike them; but as for those who are continually in our synagogues, what shall now be done for them if they remain in sin? It is singular, but true, that Satan will come to a place of worship. "Oh," say you, "surely he will never do that?" He did it so long back as the days of Job, when the sons of God came to present themselves before the Lord, and Satan came also amongst them.

The evil spirit led this unhappy man to the synagogue that morning, and it may be he did so with the idea of disturbing the teaching of the Lord Jesus Christ. I am glad he was there. I wish that all the slaves of sin and Satan would attend upon Sabbath worship. They are then within range of the Gospel gun, and who can tell how many may be reached? Yet how sad it was that the influences of religious worship had altogether failed to rescue this man from his thraldom! They sang in the synagogue, but they could not sing the evil spirit out of him; they read the lessons of the day in the synagogue, but they could not read the foul spirit out of him; they gave addresses from passages of Scripture, but they could not address the unclean spirit out of him; no doubt some of the godly prayed for him, but they could not pray the devil out of him. Nothing can cast out Satan but the word of Jesus himself. His own word, from his own lip, hath power and authority about it, but everything short of that falls to the ground.

Let us now look a little further and observe that OUR LORD ENCOUNTERS A FIRMLY-ENTRENCHED ENEMY.

He had that man so at his command that he brought him to the synagogue that day, and *he compelled him to become a disturber of the worship.* Quietness and order should be in the assemblies of God's people, but this poor soul was egged on to cry out and make horrible noises, so as to raise great tumult in the congregation. The Jews allowed all the liberty they could to persons possessed, and so long as their behaviour was bearable they were tolerated in the synagogues; but this poor mortal broke through the bounds of propriety, and his cries were a terror to all. But see, the Lord Jesus deals with this disturber; this is the very man in whom he will be glorified. So have I seen my Lord convert his most furious enemy and enlist unto his service the most violent of opposers.

The evil one *compelled his victim to beg to be left alone:* as we have it here, "Let us alone." In the Revised Version of Luke the same rendering is put in the margin, but in the text we have "Ah!" While the Lord Jesus was teaching there was suddenly heard a terrible "Ah!" A horrible, hideous outcry startled all, and these words were heard: "Ah! What have we to do with thee?" It was not the voice of supplication; it was distinctly the reverse; it was a prayer not *for* mercy, but *against* mercy.

The translation is however quite good if we read, "Let us alone." Is it not a horrible thing that Satan leads men to say, "Do not trouble us with your Gospel! Do not bother us with religion! Do not come here with your tracts! Let us alone!" They claim the wretched right to perish in their sins, the liberty to destroy their own souls. We know who rules when men speak thus: it is the prince of darkness who makes them hate the light. Do not some of you say, "We do not want to be worried with thoughts of death, and judgment, and eternity; we do not desire to hear about repentance and faith in a Saviour; all we want of religious people is that they will let us alone." This cruel kindness we cannot grant them. How can we stand by and see them perish? Yet how sad the moral condition of one who does not wish to be made pure! You would think it impossible for Jesus to do anything with a man while he is crying out, "Let us alone"; yet it was the evil spirit in this man that our Lord met and overcame. Is there not encouragement for us to deal with those who give us no welcome, but shut the door in our faces?

The foul spirit *made the man renounce all interest in Christ;* he coupled him with himself, and made him say, "What have we to do with thee, thou Jesus of Nazareth?" This was a disclaimer of all connection with the Saviour. He almost resented the Saviour's presence as an intrusion. The voice seems to cry to Jesus, "I have nothing to do with you; go your way and leave me alone; I do not want you; whatever you can do to save or bless me is hereby refused. Only let me alone." Now, when a man deliberately says, "I will have nothing to do with your Jesus; I want no pardon, no salvation, no heaven," I think the most of you would say, "That is a hopeless case; we had better go elsewhere." Yet even when Satan has led a man this length the Lord can drive him out. He is mighty to save.

The unclean spirit did more than that: *he caused this man to dread the Saviour,* and made him cry out, "Ah! Art thou come to destroy us?" Many persons are afraid of the Gospel; to them religion wears a gloomy aspect; they do not care to hear of it for fear it should make them melancholy and rob them of their pleasures. "Oh," say they, "religion would drive me mad." Thus Satan by his detestable falsehoods makes men dread their best friend, and tremble at that which would make them happy for ever.

A further entrenchment Satan has cast up: *he made his victim yield an outward assent to the Gospel.* "I know thee who thou art," said the spirit, speaking with the man's lips, "the Holy One of God." Of all forms of Satan's devices this is one of the worst for workers, when men say, "Yes, yes, what you say is very proper!" You call upon them and talk about Jesus, and they answer, "Yes, sir. It is quite true. I am much obliged to you, sir." You buttonhole them, and speak about the Saviour, and they reply, "It is very kind of you to talk to me so earnestly; I always admire this sort of thing. Zeal is much to be commended in these days." This is one of the strongest of earthworks, for the cannon-balls sink into it, and their force is gone. This makes Satan secure in his hold on the heart. Yet the Saviour dislodged this demon, and therein displayed his power and authority.

We have something more pleasant to think upon as we notice that OUR LORD CONQUERED IN A MOST SIGNAL MANNER.

The conquest *began as soon as the Saviour entered the synagogue,* and was thus under the same roof with the devil. Then the evil one began to fear. That first cry of "Ah," or "Let us alone," shows that the evil spirit knew his Conqueror. Jesus had not said anything to the man. No, but the presence of Christ and his teaching are the terror of fiends. Wherever Jesus Christ comes in Satan knows that he must go out. Jesus has come to destroy the works of the devil, and the evil one is aware of his fate. Now, as soon as ever one of you shall go into a house with the desire to bring the inmates to Christ it will be telegraphed to the bottomless pit directly. Insignificant person as you may think yourself, you are a very dangerous person to Satan's kingdom if you go in the name of Jesus and tell out his Gospel. The Lord Jesus Christ opened the book and read in the synagogue, and soon his explanation and his teaching with authority and power made all the evil spirits feel that their kingdom was shaken. "I beheld," said our Lord at another time, "Satan fall like lightning from heaven;" and that fall was commencing in this "beginning of the Gospel of Jesus Christ the Son of God." The first token of our Lord's triumph was the evident alarm which caused the evil spirit to cry out.

The next sign was *that the devil began to offer terms to Christ,* for I take it that is the reason why he said, "I know thee who thou art, the Holy One of God." He did not confront our Lord with the hostile doubt, "If thou be the Son of God;" but with the complaisant compliment, "I know thee who thou art." "Yes," the false spirit said, "I will allow this man to say his creed, and avow himself one of the orthodox, and then perhaps I shall be let alone. The man is sound in his views, and so my living in him cannot be a bad thing after all. I am quite willing to admit all the claims of Jesus, so long as he will not interfere with my rule over the man." The evil one had read his Bible, and knew how Daniel had called Jesus "the Most Holy," and so he calls him "The Holy One of God."

When Jesus comes in his power, and men hear his word, this deceitful compromise is often proposed and attempted. The sinner says, "I believe it all. I deny nothing. I am no infidel; but I mean to keep my sin; and I do not intend to feel the power of the Gospel so as to repent and have my sin chased out of me. I will agree to the Gospel, but I will not allow it to control my life." However, this coming to terms shows that the fallen spirit knows his Destroyer. He would fain be let down easily. He is willing to crouch, to cringe, to fawn, and even to bear testimony to the truth, if he may but be allowed to keep in his den—that den a human soul.

Then came our Lord's real work on this man. *He gave the evil spirit short and sharp orders.* "Silence! Come out!" "Jesus rebuked him." The word implies that he spoke sharply to him. How else could he speak to one who was maliciously tormenting a man who had done him no harm? The Greek word might be read, "Be muzzled." It is a harsh word; such as an unclean tormenting spirit deserves. "Silence! Come out." That is exactly what Jesus means that the devil shall do when he delivers men from him. He says to him, "Come out of the man; I do not want pious talk and orthodox professing; hold your peace and come out of him." It is not for evil spirits, nor yet for ungodly men, to try to honour Christ by their words. Traitors bring no honour to those they praise. Liars cannot bear witness to the truth; or if they do they damage its cause. "Be still," says Jesus; and then, "Come out." "Oh," says the unclean spirit, "let me stay, and the man shall go to church; he shall even go to the sacrament." "No," says the Lord, "Come out of him. You have no right within him; he is mine, and not yours. Come out of him!" O sinners, sin must quit you or it will ruin you for ever; are you not eager to be rid of it?

Now see the conquest of Christ over the unclean spirit. *The fiend did not dare to utter another word*, though he went as near it as he could. He "cried with a loud voice". He made an inarticulate howling as he left the man. As he came out he tried to do his victim some further injury, but in that also he failed. He tore at him, and threw him down in the midst of the synagogue, but Luke adds, "He came out of him, having done him no hurt." From the moment when Jesus bade him "come out," his power to harm was gone; he came out like a whipped cur. See how Jesus triumphs. As he did this literally in the man in the synagogue, so he does it spiritually in thousands of cases. The last act of the fiend was malicious, but fruitless. I have seen a poor creature rolled in the dust of despair by the departing enemy, but he has soon risen to joy and peace. Have you not seen him in the enquiry-room, weeping in the dismay of his spirit? But that has caused him no real harm, it has even been a benefit to him, by causing him to feel a deeper sense of sin, and by driving him quite out of himself to the Saviour.

Lastly, THE SAVIOUR RAISES BY WHAT HE DID A GREAT WONDERMENT. The people that saw this were more astonished than they generally were at the Saviour's miracles, for they said, "What thing is this? What new teaching is this? for with authority commandeth he even the unclean spirits, and they do obey him." The wonder lay in this: here *was man at his very lowest*; he could not be worse. I have shown you the impossibility of anybody being worse than this poor creature was. Now, under the preaching of the Gospel the worst man that lives may be saved. While he is listening to the Gospel a power goes with it which can touch the hardest heart, subdue the proudest will, change the most perverted affections, and bring the most unwilling spirit to the feet of Jesus. I speak now what I do know, because I have seen it in hundreds of cases, that the least likely persons, about whom there seemed to be nothing whatever helpful to the work of grace or preparatory for it, have nevertheless been turned from the power of Satan unto God. Such have been struck down by the preaching of the Gospel, and the devil has been made to come out of them, and they have become new creatures in Christ Jesus. This creates a great wonderment, and causes great staggering among the ungodly: they cannot understand it; but they ask, "What thing is this? and what new doctrine is this?"

Notice, in this case, that *Jesus worked entirely and altogether alone*. In most of his other miracles he required faith. In order to have salvation there must be faith; but this miracle before us is not a parable of man's experience so much as of Christ's working, and that working is not dependent upon anything in man.

The miracle seems to me to teach just this, that the power of Christ to save from sin does not lie in the person saved; it lies wholly in Jesus himself; and, further, I learn that though the person to be saved be so far gone that you could scarcely expect faith of him, yet the Gospel coming to him can bring faith with itself, and do its own work from the very beginning. What if I say that the Gospel is a seed that makes its own soil! It is a spark that carries its own fuel with it; a life which can implant itself within the ribs of death, ay, between the jaws of destruction. The Eternal Spirit comes with his own light and life and creates men in Christ Jesus to the praise of the glory of his grace. Oh, the marvel of this miracle!

Oh, you that preach Christ, preach him boldly! No coward lips must proclaim his invincible Gospel! Oh, you that preach Christ, never choose your place of labour; never turn your back on the worst of mankind! If the Lord should send you to the borders of perdition, go there and preach him with full assurance that it shall not be in vain. Oh, you that would win souls, have no preference as to which they shall be; or, if you have a choice, select the very worst! Remember, my Master's Gospel is not merely for the moralist, in his respectable dwelling, but for the abandoned and fallen in the filthy dens of the outcast. The name of Jesus is high over all, in heaven, and earth, and sky, therefore let us preach it with authority and confidence; not as though it were an invention of men. He has said he will be with us, and therefore nothing is impossible. The Word of the Lord Jesus cannot fall to the ground; the gates of hell cannot prevail against it.

XI

FEVER, AND ITS CURE

"And he arose out of the synagogue, and entered into Simon's house. And Simon's wife's mother was taken with a great fever; and they besought him for her. And he stood over her, and rebuked the fever; and it left her: and immediately she arose and ministered unto them."—Luke 4: 38, 39.

PETER was of Bethsaida; but yet he had a house at Capernaum. Is it not highly probable that he had moved there to be near our Lord's headquarters, to hear everything that he said, to see all his miracles, and to yield him constant attendance and service? I think it was so. This is what we should expect from the Lord's true-hearted followers; and I am sad when I remember how many professed disciples of Jesus nowadays act on another principle. When they are removing they do not consider whether they shall be near the house of prayer or the place of usefulness. Though their souls have been fed, and they have declared intense love to the church and the pastor, they nevertheless go away with a light heart to places where there are no means of grace. Should these things be so? In choosing our residence, we should have large respect to its relation to our soul's work and welfare. We should ask, "Shall we be where we can honour our Lord?"

In his house, Simon willingly entertained his wife's mother, which is presumptive evidence that he was a good man, willing out of love to run risk of discomfort. We have evidence that his wife's mother was a good woman; for the moment that she was healed, she arose and ministered unto them; whereas, in too many cases, an invalid and aged person would demand to be waited upon. She was a blessing to any house, for she evidently lent all the strength she had to the work of the family. I know just such women, whose very life is to minister to others. Happy Peter to have such a mother-in-law! Happy mother-in-law to have such a son!

Good as the tenants were, sickness came to the house. Capernaum was situated, like several other towns, in that low, marshy district which surrounds the northern part of the sea of Galilee, near the spot where the Jordan runs into it. There was always a great deal of ague about; and that ague, putting on its very worst form, had come to Peter's house as "a great fever," and had laid low his excellent mother-in-law, much to the grief of all. However dear you may be to the heart of God, and however near you live to him, you will be liable to sorrow. "Although affliction cometh not forth of the dust, neither doth trouble spring out of the ground; yet man is born unto trouble, as the sparks fly upward." None of us can hope for entire exemption from affliction: I am not sure that we should wish for it.

But then, it so happened—and it so happens always—that just when the trial came, Jesus came too. It is very beautiful to see the Lord of life close on the track of the fever, ready to deliver his chosen one. As our tribulations abound, so do our consolations. I have often noticed that when we are exceeding glad, some ill news will hurry up to calm our excitement. On the other hand, when we are exceeding sorrowful, the Lord, by his Holy Spirit, causes a sense of peace and rest to steal over us, and sustain us. How often have I found the divine presence more consciously revealed, and more sweetly sustaining in the hour of trouble than at any other season! I would not invite the fever to my house; but if Jesus would come with it, I would not be alarmed at its approach.

When Jesus came, they told him of her. Make a practice of telling the Lord about all your family concerns. Bring sicknesses and other troubles to your best friend. Do it at family prayer, but do it also at your bedside alone. If Jesus has come to stay with you, he will not hold himself aloof from your anxieties. He comes with his great sympathetic heart to be afflicted in your afflictions. Keep no secret from him, since he keeps none from you; for, "The secret of the Lord is with them that fear him." So Peter and the rest told Jesus of the good woman who was bedridden with fever, and at once the Lord Jesus went into the room, and brought his divine power to bear upon the disease, that she might be at once restored. He stood over her; he rebuked the fever; he took her by the hand and lifted her up, and in a moment the fever was gone, and she was not only well, but strong.

It is a very singular thing that, as far as I know, in the whole range of homiletics there is not one in which this cure of the fever is treated as the other healing miracles have been. The other miraculous cures have been legitimately regarded by preachers of the Word as types of the removal of certain forms of sin. When we preach about the leper, we talk to you concerning great sin, and grievous defilement. When we consider the story of Lazarus, who had been dead, we perceive that every point of his resurrection bristles with spiritual teaching. If it is so in other miracles, why not in this?

Let me, first, remind you, that SPIRITUAL FEVERS ARE VERY COMMON. *A fever begins with a kind of restlessness.* The patient cannot be quiet, nor be at ease in any position. He cannot help it; he is tossed to and fro, and is like the troubled sea. He suspects everybody, and has confidence in nothing. Are there not many who are in that condition with regard to spiritual things? Their religion is a question, rather than a doctrine; an experiment, and not an experience. Their own interest in Christ is a grave anxiety, rather than an assured delight. They believe the promise, but cannot grasp it for themselves, so as to feel sure and happy. No promise, no truth, no heavenly gift, can yield them repose: they are tossed up and down like the locust.

This restlessness affects them with regard to temporal things too: they are always anxious, doubtful, timorous. There is that excellent woman Martha. She has had a task to tear herself away from the washing and mending; and while she has been sitting here she has been wondering all the while whether she put the guard before the fire when she came out. She has felt three or four times in her pocket for her keys. She is half afraid that an accident will happen to the baby before she gets back. She is anxious about everything she can think of, and anxious about some things she has not thought of. Will her husband be home before she gets back? How will he be? Will he like his supper? Will the children all be well to-morrow? Evidently she has the domestic fever upon her, and rest is out of the question.

I know what it is as a minister to feel very feverish about

the characters and proceedings of the members of the church. I have been told that farmers are very liable to the weather-fever. It is either too wet or too dry. There may be good times for the root-crops; but then, it is bad for the corn. Merchants have the speculative fever, and workmen the strike fever. Some of you tradesfolk are wonderfully feverish in reference to your shop and your stocktaking. Will you, after all, have a good season, and make a fair profit? When a man falls into that state, although we do not call in a doctor, there is great need to call in the heavenly Physician. A Christian in good, sound, spiritual health, is calm, quiet, peaceful, happy, full of repose; for he is obedient to that sweet verse of the psalm, "Rest in the Lord, and wait patiently for him."

Some folks with this fever are troubled with the *burning heat of irritability*. They take offence where none is intended. Members of churches who get into this irritable state are always imagining that they have enemies all around them: everybody has not been quite respectful to their royal highnesses; they treasure up little slights, and feel highly indignant. I know more people with this fever than I should like to mention. It is a happy thing to live with a brother who is spiritually and mentally sound; for then you may speak freely, and you need not be afraid of being misunderstood; but feverish folk make you an offender for a word, or a look. They are grieved because you did not see them, or did see them: either way you are wrong. He cannot help it, poor man! It is not the man so much as it is the fever that is on him.

The influence of fever is seen in other ways. It is *intermittent*, and makes the patient *change from hot to cold*. Feverish persons love a religion of excitement. They are eager and impatient, omit repentance, and leap into a false security. Their zeal is not according to knowledge; and so it is fierce as the blaze of thorns under a pot, and it dies out as soon. What haste they make! Everything must be done immediately; the patient waiting of faith is too slow for them. They are determined to drive the church before them, and drag the world after them; but to plod on in Scriptural ways they cannot endure. We like to see the healthy heat of earnestness; but theirs is the burning heat of passion. This fever heat soon turns to a chill; and they shiver with dislike of the very thing they cried up so loudly. They are as cold as they were hot; and again they turn to be as hot as they were cold. A strange fever is upon them, and you know not where to find them. The steady warmth of vital principle, intelligent faith, true love to Christ, and zeal for the conversion of souls, has little in common with the fever of fanaticism. May God grant that we may always have the warmth of healthy life, but may we be saved from being delirious one day and lethargic the next!

A worse kind of fever, perhaps, is that which shows itself in *thirst* of different kinds. Some suffer from the yellow fever of avarice: they thirst for gold-water, and the more they drink the more the thirst consumes them. They rise up early, they sit up late, they eat the bread of carefulness, and all they long for is to gain and hoard; but the love of Jesus is not near their hearts. They are all hack and hurry, toil and turmoil, woe and worry. The deadly yellow fever is upon them—they must lay up much goods for many years, and add field to field till they are left alone in the earth. God save his people from even a touch of this fever!

Some are smitten with the scarlet fever of ambition. They must be everybody. Some would be great, greater, greatest, and then greater still, always sighing for the pre-eminence, like Diotrephes. Ambition, kept in due check, may be right enough; but when it rises to fever heat, it is a great sin. The man does not enjoy what he has because he is lusting for more; and meanwhile he treads down his brethren and becomes high-minded, and unkind. While anyone is still a little higher than himself, he is envious and malicious.

Alas, I have to mention one other fever, which is a kind of gastric fever, *a fever of the stomach!* It comes to men who have degraded themselves below the brutes by intoxication. When they seek to abstain and quit the cup, a drink-fever hinders them. Some imagine that it is an easy thing to escape from drunkenness; but it is not so. Those who are now true children of God have given us an awful description of the hankering which came upon them months after they had given up the drink. Often it seemed to them nothing but a miracle that they kept clear of the temptation: they felt as if they must drink or die. Have great pity upon the drunkard in his struggle to escape. Help him all you can by words of encouragement, and especially by the grand encouragement of your own example; for, believe me, it is a horrible fever, and happy is he who has never felt it.

Yet one more fever I would mention. There is one which I may well call *brain-fever*—a very common disease nowadays. Persons cannot be satisfied with the old doctrines of the Gospel; they must have something new. They do not know that in theology nothing new is true, and nothing true is new. God has given us a faith which he once for all delivered unto the saints, with no intent that it should ever be changed. Do you think that revelation is imperfect, and that we are to improve upon it? After all, then, it is not God's revelation that we are to believe, but our own deductions therefrom, and our own improvements thereupon. God forbid that we should fall under such a delusion! Very many young men—and I dare say young women, too, though I do not so often meet with them—have begun to feel that they must *think*; which, also, we should be glad for them to do. But they dream that they must think their own thoughts, and they will not submit their thoughts to the instruction of the Spirit of God. This is a vain thought. They claim that they may think as they please; and so it comes to pass that their thoughts are not God's thoughts. They diverge more and more from the eternal truth of God, till they wander among the dark mountains of error, and perish in utter infidelity. God keep us from this. If this fever is upon any one of you, may the cooling hand of the Holy Spirit, and the sobering influence of a divine experience, bring you back to spiritual and mental health again.

Secondly, THESE FEVERS ARISE FROM MANY CAUSES.

Peter's wife's mother may have been smitten with fever through the undrained and boggy spots around the sea of Galilee, especially where the Jordan makes a marsh. *She dwelt in a low spot*, where the air was full of malaria, and the fever pounced upon her. Ah, Christian people, if you live below your privileges, if you live in the marshland of worldliness, if prayer is neglected, if the Bible is not read, if the great truths of the Gospel do not fill your meditations, if you sojourn much among ungodly folk, and make them your companions, you are living in a low situation, where you will get one or other of these fevers before long. If you climb the mountains of confidence in God, and dwell near to God, and rest your souls upon him, the fever will soon vanish. The sunlight of his countenance is a sure cure for the fever of anxiety. Abide with him, and the heat of anxiety will depart, and your irritability will disappear, and you will be calm and joyful.

A second great cause of spiritual fever is *allowing things to stagnate*. The moment the sanitary authorities cut drains, and let the waters run out of the land, and carry away the filth, the fever begins to abate. When the waters are no longer putrid, but have free course, then the source of fever is taken away. How many people get into a feverish state through having everything stagnant! You do not teach in the Sunday School: your teaching power is stagnant. You never go out to the village station to preach: your talking power is stagnant. You have nobody to pray for: your intercessory power is stagnant. Everything about you is still and stale. You have nothing to live for, nothing to do; and therefore your whole being is shut up within itself, and this breeds mischief. Spiritual fever soon disappears before holy, unselfish activity.

Fevers, again, come on through excessive heat. In countries where the temperature rises high, fever is more common and fatal than with us. The white man dies, and even the black man finds it hard to live in parts of Africa. I fear that life in London is growing very much like the tropical regions. Our forefathers took things rather more coolly than we do. In Cromwell's time, a writer tells us that he walked all down Cheapside in the early morning, and found all the blinds down, because at every house they were having family prayer. Where will you go to find such a state of things in this burning age? You are up in the morning, and at it; and all day long you are at it. Little rest is given to our minds; and yet we want holy rest. We need to sit at Jesus' feet with Mary, and because we do not do so, the burden and heat of the day are telling upon our spiritual constitutions.

But, worst of all, *fever is often born of filth*. There is nothing more putrid in the natural world than sin is in the moral world. Flee from sin as you would from a reeking dunghill of rottenness. I charge you, children of God, be clean in yourselves and your surroundings. "Be ye clean that bear the vessels of the Lord." It is hard to avoid contact with evil in these days; but yet we must aim at it. Our public walls disgust us with indecencies of the most staring kind: they make us blush for the times. We can, however, keep ourselves from the resorts of the frivolous, the vicious, and the drunken; and I beseech you, as you love the Lord, and as you desire to be healthy in his sight, stand not in the way of sinners, nor sit in the seat of the scorners. Run not with the multitude to do evil. Come ye out from among them: be ye separate: touch not the unclean thing, for then God will be a Father unto you, and ye shall be his sons and daughters.

Fever also comes of overcrowding. Where people are closely packed together in their sleeping places, breathing exhausted air, there disease lurks as in its chosen lair. I am afraid that we most of us get too crowded by fellowship with men; conversing with them from morning to night, working with them, dealing with them in business; and thus learning their ways and catching their spirit. Oh, to get into the purer atmosphere of heaven, and to be alone with God!

I would remind you also that *fevers are often caused by poor diet.* Persons have not enough to eat, and the fever germs fructify in their weakness. With many Christians the rule seems to be one spiritual meal a week. Your very respectable Christian person goes out to worship on Sunday morning; but at no other time. What does he do on Sunday afternoon or on Sunday evening? He is at home taking his ease. At a Prayer Meeting, some time ago, one brother prayed that the Lord would bless those who were at home " on beds of sickness *and on sofas of wellness.*" The last words were unexpected, but very needful.

They live on one meal a week. Would any of you, who are doing this, oblige me with a trial of this regimen in reference to your bodies? Will you only eat on a Sunday morning? You shall take what you please at that one meal, and consume as much as you can of it; but you must have only that one meal till next week. Do you decline the experiment? I pray you, do not carry out the experiment of spiritual starvation, lest you die in the operation.

Alas! many have poor spiritual diet. Spiritual meals nowadays, when they are taken, do not amount to much. In many a place where Christ was preached by the good old man, who is now in heaven, you will find that anything else is held forth except the Lord Jesus. Your cultured gentleman sickens at the idea of preaching about the precious blood. He calls the cardinal doctrine of the atonement "the theology of the shambles." He is ashamed to speak of original sin, or the new birth, or to tell men that if they are not saved, they will be cast into hell. He is too refined to speak plain truth. You may eat a thousand meals of his sort of meat before you will know that you have had a mouthful; for it is all light as air, and unsubstantial as froth.

Some become fevered, not so much by what they do themselves, as by being in *contact with others who are full of the disease;* for it is exceedingly contagious. I can bear witness to that. It has been my lot to deal with the fevers of doubt, depression, anxiety, and despair, and it is hard to deal with these without catching them. I remember that one day I saw several mournful cases of depression. I will not say that the patients ought to have been in an asylum; but I am sure that many in those places are as reasonable as those I conversed with. They were sadly doubting, fearing, trembling, and dreading; and it was no light work to treat their unhappy cases. I tried to comfort them, and I hope that I succeeded in a measure; but by the time that I had borne the burdens of a half dozen of them, I needed comfort myself. It is not easy to lift others up without finding yourself exhausted.

What must you do? Run away from these sorrowful ones? By no means. You must seek more grace, that, instead of being dragged down by them, you may draw them upward to God and brighter things. Be filled with spiritual life, and then you will survive your contact with the feeble and diseased.

Now thirdly, THIS FEVER, IN ANY OF ITS FORMS, IS MISCHIEVOUS. What does it do? Well, fever *puts you altogether out of order.* You cannot precisely say where a fever begins or ends, or in what organ it operates most powerfully; for it puts the whole system out of gear. Nothing is right. You feel as if you could not sit, or lie, or be quiet in any position. You cannot do anything, and yet you must be doing. Now, when a soul gets into the fever of unbelief, and fear, and anxiety, it is in general disorder. The prayer is fevered; the song languishes; the patience fails; the service drags. The mind is like a harp whose strings are out of tune. It is a mischievous thing, this fever—mischievous to every faculty.

And then *it brings pain and misery*. In the commencement of
a fever, pain is usually felt in the joints and other parts of the
body. If I am fearful and anxious, I am in mental pain. If I am
doubting and dreading, I am in pain. If I am fretty, irritable,
petulant, murmuring, I must have pain ; and hence it is an evil
thing to be overtaken by a spiritual fever.

Mental fever *takes away his beauty* from the Christian. A man
who has a fever has his features pinched and drawn. Are there
not some Christians who do not look as they used to look?
For they are ill-humoured, or timid, or fretful, or hasty, and all
through the inward fever. Their voice has lost the joyful note
it used to have, and their whole deportment is dreary. The Lord
would have his people beautiful and gladsome. He made them
that they might show forth his praise.

This mental heat brings with it *languor and weakness*. The
man is a Christian, but he is not much of a Christian. He lives,
but he does not grow, nor exhibit strength. We want, in these
days, Christian men with stamina in them. What work healthy
souls will do! But when they catch fever in their souls, what
painful and futile efforts they make!

It is to be feared that *those who give way to fever may drift
into delirium* by-and-by ; for fevers often lead to that. My good
friend who begins complaining just a little, does not know that
he will grow to be one of the most obstinate grumblers in the
world. My good sister, who is only a little nervous and fretty,
does not know into what an abyss of unbelief she will yet
plunge. Oh, that we could be silent before him, in holy calm
and peace! We should then escape that delirium of rebellious
dread into which so many are hurried.

I must also remind you of one thing more: *this disease*, as I
have said, *is catching*. If some of you could fret, and trouble,
and worry yourselves, and did not at the same time injure
others, it might not so much matter ; but the sad fact is, there
are some Christians who drag others down into their own
wretchedness. You spoil the joys of the saints. They are willing
to comfort you, but you ought not to be so ready to cause them
disquietude. It is a dreadful waste of time and thought—this
looking after the fevered ones. When an army has to carry half
its number in ambulances, it takes well-nigh the other half to
carry them, and no fighting can be done. The cruelties of war

are great; but I am told that the aim is now to be, not to kill the opposite party, but to wound them. If you kill a man, he counts one as a loss to the other side; but if you wound a man, and another man is called out to look after him, that counts as a loss of two from the fight. This is the sort of craft whereby Satan injures the host of God. He does not kill off some of you by leading you into gross sin, but he wounds you, so that you need more than one to look after you; and thus the strength of the army of salvation is greatly diminished. I am content to be a nurse, but I had rather be winning souls.

Lastly, THERE IS ONE WHO CAN CURE THE FEVER. I am afraid that I have given rather a sad description, and I am sorry that some of you have been obliged to say, "However sad, it is true of us." But observe the cure, which is not wrought by medicine, or surgery, or any profound system of the doctors. The cure lies here. The poor patient lies flat in her bed. We read, "She was laid, and sick of a fever." She could not therefore sit up, much less rise from the bed. When she opened her eyes, and looked up, she saw the Lord Jesus Christ *standing over her*. O fevered soul, open thine eyes now, and see Jesus standing over thee! With tender love and infinite compassion he looks down upon thee; he shields thee, thinks of thee, and watches over thee for good. He will help thee; therefore, fear not.

Then, next, to her great surprise, *the Lord touched her*. Dear Master, touch the fevered ones now. Oh, to feel that he is a real man like yourself, your brother, very near to you! This is the touch which will drive out the fever. I love the old verse:

> *A man there was, a real man,*
> *Who once on Calvary died;*
> *That same dear man exalted sits*
> *High at his Father's side.*

The Lord Jesus is a real Man, and so he touches you in your feeble and suffering nature, and he seems to say, "In all your afflictions I am afflicted." When saints are in the furnace, one like unto the Son of God is there with them. They are sufferers, but he is "the Man of sorrows, and acquainted with grief." The Lord give you to feel the touch of the true humanity of Christ!

We read that, when our Lord had touched her, *he rebuked the fever*. Your feverishness deserves his rebuke. Oh, that he would bid it begone! Oh, that he would say, "Begone unbelief! Begone anxiety! Begone fretfulness! Begone doubt and fear"! Oh, that Jesus would come now, and speak to your feverishness, and you shall be as happy as the birds of paradise.

This morning I had a great joy, which I will tell to you. It is this note: "Dear Sir,—I feel so happy to tell you that the Lord has pardoned a poor outcast of society. I got into your place in a crowd, hoping nobody would see me. I had been out all night, and was miserable. While you were preaching about the leper, my whole life of sin rose up before me. I saw myself worse than the leper; cast away by everybody. There is not a sin I was not guilty of. *As you went on I looked straight away to Jesus.* A gracious answer came, 'Thy sins, which are many, are forgiven.' I never heard any more of your sermon. I felt such joy to think that Jesus died even for a poor harlot. Long ere you get this letter I trust to be on the way to my dear home I ran away from. Do please pray for me, that I may be kept by God's almighty power. I can never thank you enough for bringing me to Jesus"—and so on. If it had not been for that bit about going home, I might have had some doubt about it; but when a fallen girl goes home to her father and mother, it is a safe case. This gives me joy: do you wonder? To see souls saved is heaven to me.

The next thing Jesus did was to raise her up. You must have felt, when lying very ill, as if you were buried in the bed. So the Saviour gave his hand to her, and *he lifted her up*. She did not think that she could rise, but with his aid she sat up. Then he gave her an instant cure, and at the same time renewed her strength. No trace of fever remained. She was perfectly well. Her instinct, as a matronly woman and head of the household, was to rise at once to prepare a meal for her Benefactor and his disciples. Oh, that you doubting ones, you fevered ones, might at once be cured and lifted up, so that you would immediately set about serving the Lord, and ministering to those around you! Come, let us be as happy as ever we can be, and as useful as it lies in our power to be, and may the fever never visit any one of us again!

XII

GRACE AND OBEDIENCE

"He that made me whole, the same said unto me, Take up thy bed and walk."—John 5 : 11.

JUST a few observations upon the narrative itself. It was a feast day, and Jesus Christ came up to Jerusalem to find opportunities for doing good among the crowds of his countrymen. I see all the city glad; I hear the voice of rejoicing in every house as they hold high festival and eat the fat and drink the sweet. But where does Jesus keep the feast? How does he spend his holiday? He walks among the poor, whom he loves so well. Behold him in the hospital. There was one notable Bethesda or house of mercy in Jerusalem : it was a poor provision for the city's abounding sickness, but such as it was it was greatly prized. There was a pool which every now and then was stirred by an angel's wing, and wrought an occasional cure, and around it charitable persons had built five porches, and there on the cold stone steps a number of blind and halt and withered folk were lying, each one upon his own wretched pallet, waiting for the moving of the waters.

Our Lord was at home amid this mercy, for here was room for his tender heart and powerful hand. He feasted his soul by doing good. Let us learn this lesson, that in the times of our brightest joys we should remember the sorrowful, and find a still higher joy in doing them good. Let us keep the feast by sending portions to those for whom nothing is prepared, for else the famishing may bring a curse upon our feasting. When we are prospered in business let us set aside a portion for the poor. Blessed shall they be who, like the Lord Jesus, visit the sick and care for them.

Coming into the hospital our Lord noticed a certain man whose case was a very sad one. There were many painful cases there, but he singled out this man, and it would seem that the reason for his choice was that the poor creature was in the worst plight of all. If misery has a claim on pity, then the greater the sufferer the more is mercy attracted towards him. This poor victim of rheumatism or paralysis had been thirty-eight years bound by his infirmity. Let us hope there was no worse case in all Bethesda's porches! Thirty-eight years is more than half the appointed period of human life. We may well pity the man who endures the pangs of rheumatism even for an hour, but how shall we sufficiently pity him who has not been free from it for hard on forty years? Even if the case was not one of pain, but of paralysis, the inability to work and the consequent poverty of so many years were by no means a small evil. Our Lord, then, selects the worst case to be dealt with by his curing hand, as a type of what he often does in the kingdom of grace, and as a lesson of prudence to us, instructing us to give our first aid to those who are first in point of need.

The man whom Jesus healed was by no means an attractive character. Our Saviour said to him when he was healed, "Sin no more, lest a worse thing come unto thee," from which it is not an improbable inference that his first infirmity had come upon him by some deed of vice or course of excess. In some way or other he had been guilty of that which brought upon his body the suffering which he was enduring. Now, it is considered generally to be a point beyond all dispute that we should help the worthy but should refuse the worthless, that when a man brings a calamity upon himself by wrong doing we are justified in letting him suffer, that he may reap what he has sown. This cold Pharisaic idea is very congenial to minds which are bent upon saving their coin.

Now, I venture to say that our Saviour never taught us to confine our alms to the deserving. He would never have bestowed the grand alms of grace on any one of us if he had carried out that rule; and if you and I had received no more at the hands of God than we deserved, we should not have been in this house of prayer. We cannot afford to cramp our charity into a sort of petty justice, and sour our almsgiving into a miniature assizes. When a man is suffering let us pity him, however the suffering has come. When a man had been in misery so long as thirty-eight years, it was time that his infirmity should be more considered than his iniquity, and that his present sorrow should be thought upon more than his former folly. So Jesus thought, and therefore he came to the sinner, not with reproach, but with restoration; he saw his disease rather than his depravity, and gave him pity instead of punishment. Our God is kind to the unthankful and to the evil; be ye therefore merciful, as your Father also is merciful. Remember how our Lord said, "Pray for them that despitefully use you . . . that ye may be the children of your Father which is in heaven; for he maketh his sun to rise on the evil and on the good, and sendeth rain on the just and on the unjust" (Matt. 5: 44, 45).

In addition to the supposition that this man had at some time been grossly guilty, it seems pretty clear from the text that he was a poor, shiftless, discouraged, inanimate, stupid sort of body. He had never managed to get into the pool, though others had done so who were as infirm as himself. He had never been able to win a friend or secure a helper, though from the extreme length of his infirmity one would have thought that at some period or another he might have found a man to place him in the pool when the angel gave it the mystic stir. The Saviour's asking him, "Wilt thou be made whole?" leads us to think that he had fallen into such a listless, despairing, heartsick condition, that though he came daily to the edge of the pool as a matter of habit, he had not only ceased to hope, but had almost ceased to wish. Our Lord touched the chord which was most likely to respond, namely, his will and desire to be made whole, but the response was a very feeble one. His answer shows what a poor creature he was, for there is not a beam of hope in it, or even of desire: "I have no man, when the water is troubled, to put me into the pool: but while I am coming, another steppeth down before me." But the utter imbecility and want of brain of the poor creature is most seen in the fact that like a simpleton he went to Christ's enemies and told them that it was Jesus that had made him whole. I am sure there was no malice in his thus informing our Lord's enemies, for if there had been he would have said, "It was Jesus who bade me take up my bed," whereas he worded it thus, "It was Jesus which had made him whole."

Our Lord did not, therefore, require much of him; he did not ask even for a distinct avowal of faith from him, but only for that small measure of it which might be implied in his answering the question, "Wilt thou be made whole?" This poor man evinced none of the shrewdness of the man born blind, who answered the Pharisees so keenly; he was of quite another type, and could do no more than state his own case to Jesus. Thank God, even that was enough for our Lord to work with. The Lord Jesus saves people of all sorts. He hath among his disciples men of quick and ready wit, who can baffle their opponents, but quite as often:

> He takes the fool and makes him know
>   The wonders of his dying love:
> To bring aspiring wisdom low,
>   And all its pride reprove.

Note well that this man's mind, though there was not much of it, was all engrossed and filled up with the fact that he had been made whole. Of the person of Jesus he knew next to nothing, for he had only seen him for an instant, and then he wist not that it was Jesus: his one idea of Jesus was, "He that made me whole." Now this was natural in his case, and it will be equally natural in our own. Even when the saved ones are more intelligent, and of larger mind than this poor paralytic, they must still chiefly think of the Son of God as their Saviour, as he that made them whole. If I do not know much about the Lord, yet I do know that he has saved me. I was burdened with guilt and full of woes, and could not rest day nor night until he gave me peace; yet I can say "one thing I know, whereas I was blinded by error, now I see; whereas I was paralysed by sin, I am now able to stand upright and walk in his ways." This poor soul knew the Lord experimentally, and that is the best way of knowing him.

As for the cavilling Pharisees, you observe that they took no notice of the glorious fact of the man's cure; they wilfully ignored what Christ had done, but they fell full swoop upon that little, insignificant circumstance that it had been done on the Sabbath-day, and then they spent all their thoughts and emotions upon that side issue. They say nothing of the man's being restored, but they rage because he carried his bed on the Sabbath-day. It is much the same with the men of the world at this day. They habitually ignore the fact of conversion; if they do not deny it they look upon it as being a trifle, a matter

not worth caring about. What though they see the harlot made
chaste, and the thief made honest, and the profane made
devout, and the despairing made joyful, and other moral and
spiritual changes of the utmost practical value, they forget all
this, and they attack some peculiar point of doctrine, or mode of
speech, or diversity of manner, and raise a storm concerning
these. Is it because the facts themselves, if fairly looked at,
would establish what they do not care to believe? The fact that
Christianity is doing marvels in the world, such as nothing
else ever did, they persistently forget, but that fact is just
what you and I must as persistently remember. We must dwell
upon what Christ has by his Holy Spirit wrought within our
nature by renewing us in the spirit of our minds, and we must
make this work of grace a fountain of argument which shall
establish our faith and justify our conduct.

First, then, this is our JUSTIFICATION for what we do when we
obey Christ. This poor man could not defend the action of
taking up his bed and walking, for his enemies were learned in
the law and he was not. You and I could defend it very easily,
for it seems to us a very proper thing to do under the circumstances. The weight of his bed was not much more than that
of an ordinary great-coat, it was a simple rug or mat upon
which he was lying; there really was no violation of God's law
of the Sabbath, and therefore there was nothing to excuse.
This poor man stood in awe of the scribes and doctors. These
learned pharisees and priests were too much reverenced for this
poor creature to answer them in their own manner; but he
did what you and I must always do when we are at all puzzled;
he hid behind the Lord Jesus, and pleaded, "He that made me
whole, the same said unto me, take up thy bed." That was quite
enough for him, and he quoted it as if he felt that it ought to be
enough for those who questioned him. Truly it ought to have
been so. I may not be able to find in my own knowledge and
ability an authority equal to the authority of learned unbelievers, but my personal experience of the power of grace will
stand me in as good a stead as this man's cure was to him. He
argued that there must be in the man who made him whole
enough authority to match the greatest possible rabbi that ever
lived. Even his poor, feeble mind could grasp that, and surely
you and I may do the same, we can defend ourselves behind the

breastwork of our Saviour's gracious work, and the consequent authority which belongs to him.

Over against all objections we set the divine authority of Jesus. He by whose blood we are cleansed, and by whose Spirit we are renewed, is Lord and lawgiver to us. His precept is our sufficient warrant. If we go to the communion table, and revilers say, "What is the use of eating a piece of bread and drinking a drop of wine? Why think so solemnly of so small a matter?" We reply, He that made us whole, the same said, "Do this in remembrance of me." We abjure what he has not ordained, but we cling to his statutes. If he had commanded a rite still more trivial, or a ceremony still more open to objection in the eyes of carnal man, we would make no further apology than this: He who has created us anew, and given us a hope of heaven, and led us to seek after perfect holiness; he has bidden us do it. This is our final reply, and although we could find other justifications they would be superfluous.

The same apology applies to all *the doctrines of the Gospel.* I say again, ungodly men will not admit, or if they admit it they ignore it, that the Gospel works a marvellous change in men's hearts. If they want proof we can find them instances by thousands, of the reclaiming, elevating, and purifying power of the Gospel of Jesus Christ. The Gospel is daily working spiritual miracles, but this they forget, and they go on to find fault with its peculiar doctrines. Justification by faith they frequently quarrel with. "Well now," they say, "that is a shocking doctrine: if you teach men that they are to be saved by faith alone, and not by their works, of course they will lead loose lives; if you continually declare that salvation is of grace alone, and not of merit, the inevitable result will be that men will sin that grace may abound." We find a complete answer to this calumny in the fact that believers in justification by faith and in the doctrines of grace are among the best and purest of men, and that as a fact these truths work holiness; but we do not care to argue thus; we prefer to remind our adversaries that he who has caused us to be regenerate men himself taught us that whosoever believeth in him shall be saved, and expressly declared that he that believeth in him hath everlasting life. By the mouth of his servant Paul he has said that by grace are men saved through faith, and that not of themselves, it is the gift of God. He hath also told us that by the works of the law shall no flesh be justified, and he has bidden us declare that "the just shall live by faith." If this Gospel does not make men better, and change their evil natures, you may question it if you like, and we do not wonder that you should; but while it continues its purifying work we shall not blush or stammer when we declare the doctrines which are its essence and life. Our regeneration proves to us our Lord's authority, and upon that we are prepared to base our creed.

The same applies also to all *the precepts* which the Christian is called upon to obey. For instance, if he is true to his colours, he keeps himself aloof from all the sinful pleasures, practices, and policies of the world, in which others take delight, and consequently the ungodly world says that he is singular, precise, and self-opinionated. This is the answer for all Christians— "He that made us whole, the same said to us, ye are not of the world, even as I am not of the world. Come ye out from among them and be ye separate, touch not the unclean thing, and I will receive you." If you follow the precepts of the Lord Jesus Christ, you may meet all charges of singularity by urging the supremacy of the Saviour, whose power has made you a new creature. Where his word is, there is a power to which we bow at once. It is not ours to question our Saviour, but to obey him. We are cleansed by his blood, we are redeemed by his death, and we live by his life, and therefore are not ashamed to take up his Cross and follow him.

This apology ought to suffice even those who oppose us, for if they felt as grateful as we do they would obey also. They ought at any rate to say, "We cannot blame these men for doing as Jesus bids them, because he has done so much for them." Surely the poor man who had been thirty-eight years paralysed could not be blamed for obeying the command of one who in a moment restored him to health and strength. If he became his servant for life, who would censure him? Should not such a benefactor exert a boundless influence over him? What could be more natural and proper?

Now, you unconverted people must excuse us, if we, in obedience to our Lord Jesus, do many things which to you seem very singular, for though we would not needlessly offend, we cannot please you at the risk of displeasing our Lord. We do not owe so much to you as we owe to him, in fact, truth to tell, we do not feel that we owe anything to the world. Like the shipmen who put out to sea against Paul's advice, our only gain has been loss and damage. In serving the world we found the labour weariness and the wages death; but as for our Lord Jesus, we owe him everything, and so you must excuse us if we try to follow him in everything. It seems to us that this is an excuse which you ought to accept from us as covering the whole ground, but if you refuse it we are not at all dismayed, for it quite suffices *us*, yea, more than suffices us, it makes us glory in what we do. Does Jesus command? Then it is ours to obey. This satisfies our conscience now, and it will do so amid the solemnities of death.

Instead of admitting that this is not an ample justification, let us go further still in the strength of it. If the world has accounted us vile for obeying our Lord, let us be viler still; and inasmuch as he that made us whole said, "Go ye into all the world and preach the Gospel to every creature," let us endeavour to spread abroad everywhere the savour of his name, consecrating ourselves body, soul, and spirit to the extension of his Kingdom. He who made us whole will make the world whole yet by his own wondrous power.

And now, secondly, the cure brought forth AN OBLIGATION:— "He that made me whole, the same said unto me, Take up thy bed, and walk." The argument takes this form: first, if he made me whole he is divine, or he could not do this miracle; or, to say the least, he must be divinely authorised: and if he be divine, or divinely authorised, I must be bound to obey the orders which he issues. Is not that a plain argument which even the poor, simple mind of the paralytic man was able to grasp and wield? Let us try and feel the force of that argument ourselves. Jesus who has saved us is our God; shall we not obey him? Since he is clothed with divine power, and majesty, shall we not scrupulously endeavour to know his will, and zealously endeavour to carry it out in every point, as his Spirit shall enable us?

In addition to the divine character which the miracle proved and displayed, there was the goodness which shone in the deed of power and touched the poor man's heart. His argument was—"I *must* do what my great Deliverer bids me. How can you think otherwise? Did he not make me whole? Would you have *me*, whom he has thus graciously restored, refuse to fulfil his desire? Must I not take up my bed the moment he gives me strength to do it? Do you not see that I am under an obligation which it would be shameful to deny? He restores these limbs, and I am bound to do with them what he orders me do with them. He says 'walk,' and since these once withered feet have been restored, shall I not walk? He bids me roll up my bed, and since I could not have used my hands till just now his word gave them life, shall I not use them to roll up the bedrug at his bidding?" There was no answering such reasoning.

If you have been saved by the grace of God, your salvation has put you under obligation henceforth to do what Jesus bids you. Are you redeemed? Then ye are not your own, ye are bought with a price. Have you been adopted into the divine family? Then it clearly follows that, because you are sons, you should be obedient to the law of the household; for is not this a first element of sonship, that you should reverence the great Father of the family? The Lord has been pleased to put away your sin, you are forgiven: but does not pardon demand amendment? Shall we go back to the old sins from which we have been cleansed? Shall we live in the iniquities from which we have been washed by the blood of our Lord Jesus? That were horrible to think of. It would be nothing less than devilish for a man to say, "I have been forgiven, and therefore I will sin again."

Brethren and sisters upon whom Christ has wrought his great work, you have experienced the love of God, and therefore, if God has so loved you, you are bound to love him in return. If God has so loved you, you must also love your brother man. Do not love to God and love to man spring up as a sure consequence of the love of God shed abroad in the heart? But love is the mother of obedience: thus everything connected with our Lord lays us under obligation to obey him. There is not a single blessing of the covenant but what necessarily entails its corresponding duty; and here I scarcely like to say *duty*, for these blessings of the covenant make duty to be our privilege and holiness to be our delight. He that made you whole has commanded this and that to be done by you: I counsel you to keep the King's commandment. As Mary said to the waiters at the wedding at Cana so say I to you—"Whatsoever he saith unto you, do it." Doth he bid you pray? Then pray without ceasing. Doth he bid you watch as well as pray? Then guard every act, and thought, and word. Doth he bid you love your brethren? Then love them with a pure heart fervently. Doth he bid you serve them and humble yourself for his sake? Then do so, and become the servant of all. Hath he said, "Be ye holy, for I am holy"? Then aim at this by his Holy Spirit. Hath he said, "Be ye perfect, even as your Father which is in heaven is perfect?" Then strive after perfection, for he that made you whole has a right to direct your way, and it will be both your safety and your happiness to submit yourselves to his commands.

Now we call your attention, in the third place, to the text under the sense of CONSTRAINT—"He that made me whole, the same said unto me, take up thy bed and walk." He made him whole by saying, "Rise, take up thy bed." The carrying of the bed was part and parcel of the cure. The first part of the healing word was "rise," but the second was "take up thy bed." Now, it was not an ordinary word which Jesus spoke to that man—a mere word of advice, warning, or command; but it was a word full of power, like that which created light out of darkness. When the Lord said to the poor man, "Rise," he did rise. A thrill went through him; those stagnant blood vessels felt the life-blood stir and flow, those dormant nerves were aroused to sensations of health, for omnipotence had visited the impotent man and restored him.

It was all done by the power of the one thrilling sentence, which tarried not to be questioned, but accomplished the end for which the Lord had sent it. Not unwillingly did the restored man carry his bed, yet he did it of constraint, for the same power which made him whole made him obedient. Before the divine energy had touched him, he seemed scarcely to have any will at all, and the Lord had to hunt to find a will in him, saying, "Wilt thou be made whole?" But now he cheerfully wills obedience to his benefactor, and in the force of the command he carried out the Lord's behest. I say that his taking up his bed, and walking, was done by Christ's enabling, and done by Christ's constraining, and I pray that you may know by experience what this means. What I want you to feel is this— "I cannot help obeying Christ, for by his Holy Spirit he has

spoken me into a life which will never die and never be van-
quished. He thrills me through and through continually. I
can no more help seeking to obey Christ than this man could
help carrying his bed when the Lord, by a word of power, had
bidden him do so."

My last word is a practical lesson. The church of God on earth
at this present time anxiously desires to spread her influence
over the world. For Christ's sake we wish to have the truths
we preach acknowledged, and the precepts which we deliver
obeyed. But mark, no church will ever have power over the
masses of this or any other land, except in proportion as she
does them good. The day has long since passed in which any
church may hope to prevail on the plea of history. "Look at
what we were," is a vain appeal: men only care for what we are.
The sect which glorifies itself with the faded laurels of past
centuries, and is content to be inactive to-day, is near to its
inglorious end. In the race of usefulness men nowadays care
less about the pedigree of the horse and more about the rate
at which it can run. The history of a congregation or a sect is of
small account compared with the practical good which it is
doing. Now, if any church under heaven can show that it is
making men honest, temperate, pure, moral, holy, that it is
seeking out the ignorant and instructing them, that it is seeking
out the fallen and reclaiming them, that in fact it is turning
moral wastes into gardens, and taking the weeds and briars
of the wilderness and transforming them into precious fruit-
bearing trees, then the world will be ready to hear its claims
and consider them.

If you have a church that is devout, that is holy, that is
living unto God, that does good in its neighbourhood, that by
the lives of its members spreads holiness and righteousness; in
a word, if you have a church that is really making the world
whole in the name of Jesus, you shall in the long run find that
even the most carnal and thoughtless will say, "The church
which is doing this good is worthy of respect, therefore let us
hear what it has to say." Living usefulness will not screen us
from persecution, but it will save us from contempt. A holy
church goes with authority to the world in the name of Jesus
Christ its Lord, and this force the Holy Spirit uses to bring
human hearts into subjection to the truth.

XIII

THE LAD'S LOAVES IN THE LORD'S HANDS

" Jesus took the loaves."—John 6: 11.

LOOK, there are the people! Five thousand of them, as hungry as hunters, and they all need to have food given to them, for they cannot any of them travel to buy it! And here is the provision! Five thin wafers—and those of barley, more fit for horses than for men—and two little anchovies, by way of a relish! Five thousand people and five little biscuits wherewith to feed them! The disproportion is enormous: if each one should have only the tiniest crumb, there would not be sufficient. In like manner, there are millions of people in London, and only a handful of whole-hearted Christians earnestly desiring to see the city converted to Christ; there are more than a thousand millions of men in this round world, and oh, so few missionaries breaking to them the bread of life; almost as few for the millions, as were these five barley cakes for those five thousand! The problem is a very difficult one. The contrast between the supply and the demand would have struck us much more vividly if we had been there, in that crowd at Bethsaida.

But the Lord Jesus was equal to the emergency: none of the people went away without sharing in his bounty; they were all filled. Our blessed Master, now that he has ascended into the heavens, has more rather than less power. Have faith in God, who is in Christ Jesus; have faith in the compassion of the Great Mediator: he will not desert the people in their spiritual need, any more than he failed that hungry throng, in their temporal need, long ago.

We will now look at these biscuits and sardines, which seem to be truly an insufficient stock-in-trade to begin with, a very small capital indeed on which to conduct the business of feeding five thousand persons.

We will begin by saying that THESE LOAVES AND FISHES HAD A
PREVIOUS HISTORY. Andrew said to Jesus, "There is a lad here,
which hath five barley loaves, and two small fishes."

Notice, first, then, *the providence of God in bringing the lad
there.* We do not know his name; we are not told anything
concerning his parentage. Was he a little pedlar, who thought
that he could make some money by selling a few loaves and
fishes, and had he nearly sold out? Or was he a boy that the
apostles had employed to carry this slender provision for the
use of Jesus and his friends? We do not know much about
him; but he was the right boy in the right place that day.
Christ never is in need but he has somebody at hand to supply
that need. Have faith in the providence of God. What made
the boy bring the loaves and fishes, I do not know. Boys often
do unaccountable things; but bring the loaves and fishes he
did; and God, who understands the ideas and motives of lads,
and takes account even of barley loaves and fishes, had appointed that boy to be there.

Mr. Stanley tells us that, when he came out of that long
journey of his through the forest (I think after a hundred and
sixty days of walking in darkness,) and found himself at last
where he could see the sun, he felt that there was a special
providence of God that had taken care of him. I am very glad
that Mr. Stanley felt that it was the hand of God that had
brought him out of the noisome shade; but I do not need to go
to Africa to learn that we are beset behind and before by his
goodness. Many of us have felt a special providence of God in
our own bed-chambers; we have met with his hand in connection with our own children. Yea, every day we are surrounded
by tokens of his care. "Whoso is wise, and will observe these
things, even they shall understand the loving-kindness of the
Lord." "I am sure God took care of me," said one; "for as I
was going along a certain street, I slipped on a piece of orange-peel,
and had what might have been a serious fall; yet I was not hurt
in the least." To which his friend replied, "I am sure God has
taken care of *me;* for I have walked along that street hundreds of
times, and have never slipped on a piece of orange-peel, or on
anything else." Full often God draws near to us in common life.

Let us also believe in his providence with regard to the church
of Christ: he will never desert his people; he will find men when

he wants them. Thus it has ever been in the history of the
saints, and thus it shall ever be. Before the Reformation there
were many learned men who knew something of Christ's
Gospel; but they said that it was a pity to make a noise, and
so they communed with one another and with Christ very
quietly. What was wanted was some rough bull-headed fellow
who would blurt the Gospel out, and upset the old state of
things. Where could he be found? There was a monk named
Luther, who, while he was reading his Bible, suddenly stumbled
on the doctrine of justification by faith; he was the man: yet
when he went to a dear brother in the Lord, and told him how he
felt, his friend said to him, "Go back to thy cell, and pray and
commune with God, and hold thy tongue." But then, you see,
he had a tongue that he could not hold, and that nobody else
could hold, and he began to speak with it the truth that had
made a new man of him. The God that made Luther, knew
what he was at when he made him; he put within him a great
burning fire that could not be restrained, and it burst forth,
and set the nations on a blaze. Never despair about providence.
God never yet did come to a point of distress as to his truth but
what suddenly one came forward, a David with a sling and a
stone, or a Samson with a jawbone, or a Shamgar with an ox-
goad, who put to rout the adversaries of the Lord. "There is a
lad here." The providence of God had sent him.

Next, *this lad with his loaves was brought into notice.* When
they were searching for all the provisions in the company, this
obscure boy, that never would have been heard of else, was
brought to the front, because he had his little basket of biscuits.
Andrew found him out, and he came and said to Jesus, "There
is a lad here, which hath five barley loaves, and two small
fishes." So, rest assured, that if you have the Bread of Life
about you, and you are willing to serve God, you need not be
afraid that obscurity will ever prevent your doing it. "Nobody
knows me," says one. Well, it is not a very desirable thing that
anybody should know you: those of us who are known to
everybody would be very glad if we were not; there is no very
great comfort in it. He that can work away for his Master, with
nobody to see him but his Master, is the happiest of men. "I
have only one hundred people to preach to," said a country
pastor to me; and I replied, "If you give a good account of

those hundred, you have quite enough to do." If all you have is very little—just that pennyworth of loaves and fishes—use that properly, and you will do your Master service; and in due time, when God wants you, he knows where to find you. You need not put an advertisement in the paper; he knows the street you live in, and the number on the door. You need not go and push yourself to the front; the Lord will bring you to the front when he wants you; and I hope that you do not want to get there if he does not want you. Depend upon it, should you push forward when you are not required, he will put you back again. Oh, for grace to work on unobserved, to have your one talent, your five loaves and two fishes, and only to be noticed when the hour suggests the need, and the need makes a loud call for you.

When brought into notice, the loaves and fishes did not fare very well; *they were judged insufficient for the purpose*; for Andrew said, "What are they among so many?" The boy's candle seemed to be quite snuffed out: so small a stock—what could be the use of that? Now, I dare say, that some of you have had Satan saying to you, "What is the use of your trying to do anything?" To you, dear mother, with a family of children, he has whispered, "You cannot serve God." He knows very well that, by sustaining grace, you can; and he is afraid of how well you can serve God if you bring up those dear children in his fear. He says to the colporteur over yonder, "You have not much ability; what can you do?" Ah, dear friend! he is afraid of what you can do, and if you will only do what you can do, God will, by-and-by, help you to do what now you cannot do. But the devil is afraid of even the little that you can do now; and many a child of God seems to side with Satan in despising the day of small things. "What are they among so many?" So few, so poor, so devoid of talent, what can any of us hope to do? Disdained, even by the disciples, it is small wonder if we are held in contempt by the world. The things that God will honour, man must first despise. You run the gauntlet of the derision of men, and afterwards you come out to be used of God.

Though seemingly inadequate to feed the multitude, these loaves and fishes would have been quite enough for the boy's supper, yet *he appears to have been quite willing to part with them*. The disciples would not have taken them from him by force; the Master would not have allowed it: the lad willingly gave them up to be the commencement of the great feast. Somebody might have said, "John, you know that you will soon be able to eat those five cakes and those two little fishes; keep them; get away into a corner: every man for himself." Is it not a good rule, "Take care of number one"? Yes, but the boy whom God uses will not be selfish. Am I speaking to some young Christian to whom Satan says, "Make money first, and serve God by-and-by; stick to business, and get on; then, after that, you can act like a Christian, and give some money away," and so on? Let such a one remember the barley loaves and the fishes. But now that he brings them to Christ, all those thousands of people are fed, and he gets as much himself as he would have had if he had eaten his own stock. And then, in addition, he gets a share out of the twelve baskets full of fragments that remain. Anything that you take away from self and give to Christ is well invested; it will often bring in ten thousand per cent. The Lord knows how to give such a reward to an unselfish man, that he will feel that he that saves his life loses it, but he that is willing even to lose his life, and the bread that sustains it, is the man who, after all, gets truly saved.

This, then, is the history of these loaves. He would yield it to his Lord. Now, do you see what I am driving at? I want to get a hold of some of the lads, and some young men and young women—I will not trouble about your age, you shall be lads if you are under seventy—I want to get hold of you who think that you have very little ability, and say to you, "Come, and bring it to Jesus." We want you. Times are hard. The people are famishing. Though nobody seems to need you, yet make bold to come out; and who knows but that, like Queen Esther, you may have come to the kingdom for such a time as this? God may have brought you where you are to make use of you for the converting of thousands; but you must be converted yourself first. Christ will not use you unless you are first his own.

But now I want to show you that THESE BARLEY CAKES GOT INTO A GRAND POSITION. The text says, "Jesus took the loaves." He took them into his own hands, which one day would bear the nail-prints. This may teach us several lessons.

First, *they were now associated with Jesus Christ*. Henceforth

those loaves do not so much suggest the thought of the lad's
sacrifice as of the Saviour's power. Is it not a wonderful thing
that Christ, the living God, should associate himself with our
feebleness, with our want of talent, with our ignorance, with
our little faith? And yet he does so. If we are not associated
with him, we can do nothing; but when we come into living
touch with him, we can do all things. Those barley loaves in
Christ's hands become pregnant with food for all the throng.
Have you that love the Lord Jesus Christ thought of *this*, of
bringing all that you possess to him, that it may be associated
with him? There is that brain of yours; it can be associated
with the teachings of his Spirit: there is that heart of yours;
it can be warmed with the love of God: there is that tongue of
yours; it can be touched with the live coal from off the altar:
there is that manhood of yours; it can be perfectly consecrated
by association with Christ. Hear the tender command of the
Lord, "Bring them hither to me," and your whole life will be
transformed. I know that you have been praying, and saying,
"I have not this, and I cannot do that." Stay not to number
your deficiencies; bring what you have, and let all that you
are, body, soul, and spirit, be associated with Christ. Although
he will not bestow upon you new faculties, the faculties you
have will have new power.

But, further, *they were transferred to Christ*. A moment ago,
they belonged to this lad, but now they belong to Christ.
"Jesus took the loaves." He has taken possession of them;
they are his property. Oh, Christian people, do you mean what
you say when you declare that you have given yourselves to
Christ? If you have made a full transfer, therein will lie great
power for usefulness. But do not people often say, "If I might
make some reserve"? "What meaneth then this bleating of
the sheep in mine ears, and the lowing of the oxen which I
hear?" What about that odd thousand that you put in the
funds the other day? What about the money saved up for a
new bonnet? You sometimes sing—

> *Yet if I might make some reserve,*
> *And duty did not call,*
> *I love my God with zeal so great,*
> *That I should give him all.*

Ah, well! when you have really yielded all, you may sing that again; but I am afraid that there are but few who can sing it truly. Oh, that we had more real putting of the loaves into Christ's hands! The time that you have not used for self, but given to Christ; the knowledge that you have not stored, as in a reservoir, but given to Christ; this is the way in which London's need will be met, and the world's hunger will be satisfied.

What is better still, as these loaves were given to Jesus, so *they were accepted by Jesus.* They were not only dedicated, they were also consecrated. Jesus took the five barley loaves, and the two little fishes, and in doing so he seemed to say, "These will do for me." As the Revised Version has it, " Jesus *therefore* took the loaves." Was there any reason why he should? Yes, because they were brought to him; they were willingly presented to him; there was a need of them, and he could work with them, "therefore" he took the loaves. Children of God, if Christ has ever made use of you, you have often stood and wondered however the Lord could accept you; but there was a "therefore" in it. He saw that you were willing to win souls : he saw the souls needed winning, and he used you, even *you.* Am I not now speaking to some who might be of great service if they yielded themselves unto Christ, and Christ accepted them, and they became accepted in the Beloved? Let us join one now in heaven, who on earth brought her all, and pray—

> *Oh, use me, Lord, use even me,*
> *Just as thou wilt, and when, and where:*
> *Until thy blessed face I see,*
> *Thy rest, thy joy, thy glory share!*

But, what is better still, *these loaves and fishes were blessed by Christ* as he lifted up his eyes, and gave thanks to the Father for them. Think of it. For five little cakes and two sprats Christ gave thanks to the Father; apparently a meagre cause for praise, but Jesus knew what he could make of them, and therefore gave thanks for what they would presently accomplish. "God loves us," says Augustine, "for what we are becoming." Christ gave thanks for these trifles because he saw whereunto they would grow. Do you not think that, having thanked the Father, he also thanked the boy? And in after years these words of gratitude would be ample recompense for such a tiny deed. Like the woman who cast in the two mites to the treasury, he gave his all, and doubtless was commended for the gift. Though high in glory to-day, Christ is still grateful when such offerings are made to him; still he thanks his Father when, with timid, trembling hands, we offer to him our best, our all, however small; still is his heart gladdened when we bring him our scanty store that it may be touched by his dear hand, and blessed by his gracious lips.

And when the loaves had been blessed, the next thing was, *they were increased by Christ.* Peter takes one, begins to break it, and as he breaks it, he has always as much in his hand as he started with. When he has done, he has his hands just as full of fish and as full of bread as ever. If you serve God you will never run dry. He who gives you something to say one Sunday will give you something to say another Sunday.

But, mark once more: when Jesus took the loaves, it was not only to multiply, but also to dispose of them. *They were distributed by Christ.* He did not believe in multiplication, unless it was attended by division. Christ's additions mean subtraction; and Christ's subtractions mean additions. He gives that we may give away. He multiplied as soon as ever the disciples began to distribute; and when the distribution ended, the multiplication ended. Oh, for grace to go on distributing! If you have received the truth from Christ, tell it out!

Putting all this together, if we all would bring our loaves and fishes to the Lord Jesus Christ, he would take them, and make them wholly his own. Then, when he should have blessed them, he would multiply them, and he would bid us distribute them, and we could yet meet the needs of London, and the needs of the whole world even to the last man. A Christ who could feed five thousand can feed five millions. There is no limit. If you can believe that Christ can feed fifty, then you can believe that he can feed five hundred, five thousand, five millions, five hundred millions, if so it pleases him.

But now, thirdly, and to conclude, THESE LOAVES AND FISHES HAD AN AFTER-HISTORY. They got into Christ's hands. What was the result?

First, *a great deal of misery was removed* by the lad's basketful of barley cakes. Those poor people were famished; they had been with Christ all day, and had had nothing to eat; and had they been dispersed as they were, tired and hungry, many of them would have fainted by the way; perhaps some would even have died. Oh, what would we give if we might but alleviate the misery of this world! I remember the Earl of Shaftesbury saying, "I should like to live longer. I cannot bear to go out of the world while there is so much misery in it." And you know how that dear saint of God laid himself out to look after the poor, and the helpless, and the needy, all his days. Perhaps I speak to some who never woke up yet to the idea that, if they were to bring their little all to Christ, he could make use of it in alleviating the misery of many a wounded conscience, and that awful misery which will come upon men if they die unforgiven, and stand before the judgment bar of God without a Saviour.

Yes, young man, God can make you the spiritual father of many. As I look back upon my own history, little did I dream when first I opened my mouth for Christ, in a very humble way, that I should have the honour of bringing thousands to Jesus. Blessed, blessed be his name! He has the glory of it. But I cannot help thinking that there must be some other lad here, such a one as I was, whom he may call by his grace to do service for him. When I had a letter sent to me by the deacons of the church at New Park Street, to come up to London to preach, I sent it back by the next post, telling them that they had made a mistake, that I was a lad of nineteen years of age, happy among a very poor and lowly people in Cambridgeshire, who loved me, and that I did not imagine that they could mean that I was to preach in London. But they returned it to me, and said that they knew all about it, and I must come. Ah, what a story it has been since then, of the goodness and loving-kindness of the Lord!

You must not think that God picks out all the very choice and particularly fine persons. It is not so in the Bible; some of those that he took were very rough people: even the first apostles were mostly fishermen. Paul was an educated man, but he was like a lot out of the catalogue, one born out of due time; the rest of them were not so, but God used them; and it still pleases God, by the base things and things that are not, to bring to nought the things that are. I do not want you to think highly of yourself; your cakes are only five, and they are barley, and poor barley at that; and your fish are very small, and there are only two of them. I do not want you to think much of them, but think much of Christ, and believe that, whoever you may be, if he thought it worth his while to buy you with his blood, and is willing to make some use of you, it is surely worth your while to come and bring yourself, and all that you have, to him who is thus graciously ready to accept you. Put everything into his hands, and let it be said of you this day, "And Jesus took the loaves."

And next, *Jesus was glorified;* for the people said, "He is a prophet." The miracle of the loaves carried them back to the wilderness, and to the miracle of the manna; they remembered that Moses had said, "The Lord thy God will raise up unto thee a Prophet from the midst of thee, of thy brethren, like unto me" (Deut. 18: 15). For this Deliverer they longed, and as the bread increased so grew their wonder, until in the swelling cakes they saw the finger of God, and said, "This is of a truth that Prophet that should come into the world." That little lad became, by his loaves and fishes, the revealer of Christ to all the multitude; and who can tell, if you give your loaves to Christ, whether thousands may not recognize him as the Saviour because of it? Christ is still known in the breaking of bread. But the people went further with reference to Christ, after they had been fed by the loaves and fishes: they concluded that he was a prophet, and they began whispering among themselves, "Let us make him a king." Now, in a better sense than the text implies, I would to God that you and I, though humbly and feebly, might serve Christ till people said, "Christ is a Prophet. Let us make him a King." This sermon I offer my Master, if he will be pleased to accept it, though it is but a barley cake, and I pray that by it some may take Jesus Christ to be their King. Oh, that he had a throne in the hearts of many whom he shall feed at this time with the bread of heaven!

When the feast was finished, *there were fragments to be gathered.* This is a part of the history of the loaves—they were not lost; they were eaten, but they were there; people were filled with them, but yet there was more of them left than when the feast began. Each disciple had a basketful to carry back to his Master's feet. Give yourself to Christ, and when you have used yourself for his glory, you will be more able to serve him than you are now; you shall find your little stock grow as you spend it. Remember Bunyan's picture of the man who had a roll of cloth. He unrolled it, and he cut off so much for the poor. Then he unrolled it, and cut off some more, and the more he cut it, the longer it grew. Upon which Bunyan remarks—

> *There was a man, and some did count him mad;*
> *The more he gave away, the more he had.*

It is certainly so with talent and ability, and with grace in the heart. The more you use it, the more there is of it; and if you continue to draw on your strength, your strength will get to be more mighty through God. The more you do, the more you may do, by the grace of the Ever-blessed One!

Last of all, it came to pass, that *these loaves had a record made about them*. There is many a loaf that has gone to a king's table and yet never been chronicled; but this boy's five cakes and two little fishes have got into the Bible. To make quite sure that we should never forget how much God can do with little things, this story is told four times over, and it is the only one of Christ's miracles which has such an abundant record.

And now, as a practical issue, let us put it to the test. You young people who have lately joined the Church, do not be long before you try to do something for Christ. You that have for a long time been trusting Christ, and have never yet begun to work, arouse yourselves to attempt some service for his sake. Aged friends and sick friends can still find something to do. Perhaps, at the last, it will be found that the persons whom we might have excused on account of illness, or weakness, or poverty, are the people who have done the most. I find that, if there is a really good work done, it is usually done by an invalid, or by somebody who might very properly have said, "I pray thee, have me excused." How is it that so many able-bodied and gifted Christians seem to be so slow in the Master's service? If there is a political meeting, you are all there, every bit of you, over your politics, which are not worth a penny a year; but when it comes to souls being saved, many of you are mute as fishes.

One of our friends gave a good answer to a brother who said to him, "I have been a member of a church now for forty years.

I am a father in Israel." He asked him, "How many children have you? How many have you brought to Christ?" "Well," the man said, "I do not know that I ever brought anybody to Christ." Upon which our friend retorted, "Call yourself a father in Israel, and yet you have no children! I think you had better wait until you have earned the title."

Again I cannot help reminding those who are not Christ's, that while I have not directly preached to them, I have tried, by a side wind, to be preaching to them all the time. Either you are the Lord's, or you are not. If you are Christ's servant, take a sheet of paper, and write down, "Lord, I bring my loaves and fishes to thee;" and if you are not Christ's, confess the awful truth to yourself and face it. I wish that you would make a record of it in black and white, putting down both name and date, "*I am not Christ's.*" Take a good look at it, try and grasp what it means, to withhold yourself from him who loves you, and waits to save; then ask yourself why you are not his. I remember a woman, not long ago, who said that at her work it came across her mind, "I am not saved." She was sweeping the room, and when she finished that, she said to herself, "I have to cook the dinner, but I am not saved." She went into the kitchen, and had her fire all ready, and her food; but all the while she was putting things in the pot she kept saying to herself, "I am not saved"; and so it was when she was busy all the afternoon; and when her husband came home, she could not help blurting it out to him, "Oh, husband, I am not saved!" But he was; and he pointed her to Christ; they knelt together, and oh, how he prayed with her! She found that which she so earnestly sought, and it was not very many days before she could say, "Oh, husband, I am saved!" May that be the case with you!

XIV

GOOD CHEER FROM CHRIST'S PRESENCE

"And straightway he constrained his disciples to get into the ship, and to go to the other side before unto Bethsaida, while he sent away the people. And when he had sent them away, he departed into a mountain to pray. And when even was come, the ship was in the midst of the sea, and he alone on the land. And he saw them toiling in rowing; for the wind was contrary unto them: and about the fourth watch of the night he cometh unto them, walking upon the sea, and would have passed by them. But when they saw him walking upon the sea, they supposed it had been a spirit, and cried out: for they all saw him, and were troubled. And immediately he talked with them, and saith unto them, Be of good cheer: it is I; be not afraid. And he went up unto them into the ship; and the wind ceased: and they were sore amazed in themselves beyond measure, and wondered. For they considered not the miracle of the loaves: for their heart was hardened."—Mark 6 : 45–52.

WE have here a word of comfort given to a ship-load of believers *who were where their Lord had sent them*. They had been unwilling to put out to sea, though it was probably calm enough at the time, but they did not wish to leave the Lord Jesus. He constrained them to go, and thus their sailing was not merely under his sanction, but by his express command. They were in their right place, and yet they met with a terrible storm.

The little inland sea upon which they sailed lies in a deep hollow, and from the shore there pours a sudden downdraft of tremendous wind for which it is not possible to be prepared. By one of these whirlwinds the whole sea was stirred up to boiling, as only those little lakes can be. So, though they were where Jesus bade them go, they were in desperate peril, and you must not think that you are in a wrong position because you are in trouble. Do not consider that adverse circumstances are a proof that you have missed your road; for they may even be an evidence that you are in the good old way, since the path of believers is seldom without trial. You did well to embark, and to leave the shore; but remember, though your Lord has insured the vessel, and guaranteed that you shall reach your haven, he has not promised that you shall sail over a sea of glass; on the contrary, he has told you that "in the world you shall have tribulation," and you may all the more confidently believe in him because you find his warning to be true.

Their Lord had bidden his disciples make for the other side, and therefore they did their best, and continued rowing all night, but making no progress whatever because the wind was dead against them. It was with difficulty that they could keep what little way they had made, and not be blown back again to the starting-place. Probably you have heard it said that, if a Christian man does not go forward, he goes backward; that is not altogether true, for there are times of spiritual trial when, if a man does not go backward, he is really going forward. The Christian man may make little or no headway, and yet it may be no fault of his, for the wind is contrary. Our good Lord will take the will for the deed, and reckon our progress, not by our apparent advance, but by the hearty intent with which we tug at the oars.

Often, when a believer groans in prayer, and cannot pray, he has offered the best prayer; and when he tries to win men's hearts and does not win them, his zeal is as acceptable as if it convinced a nation; and when he would do good and finds evil present with him, there is good in the desire. If he threw up the oars, and drifted with the wind, that would be another thing; but if our Lord sees him "toiling in rowing," albeit no progress is made, he has never a word to say against his servant, but he will bid him "be of good cheer."

It does not appear, from the narrative, that the disciples had any fear about the storm, except such as might naturally arise even in the minds of fishermen when they were dreadfully tossed upon the sea. They probably said to one another, "Did not our Master constrain us to set forth on this voyage? Though we meet with this storm, we are not to be blamed." Certain believers, who have lately been brought to know the Lord, have been great losers in temporal things by becoming Christians. What then? Let them not be terrified by this fact; even

Christ's ship is tossed with tempest. Let them row on against the wind; and even if the storm increases in fury, let them not lose heart. One who knew the seas right well exclaimed, "Though he slay me, yet will I trust in him"; and in so doing he glorified God, and ere long found himself in a great calm. Does Jesus bid us make for the shore? Then let us row on, even if we cannot make headway, for Jesus knows all about it, and orders all things well.

Why, then, did our Saviour, when he came to this ship-load of apostles who had been toiling and rowing, say to them, "Be of good cheer"? They were bold, brave men and were not at all afraid of the sea. What, then, did they fear? He would not have so spoken unless they had been afraid of something; and on looking at the text we see, to our astonishment, that *they were afraid of Jesus himself.* They were not afraid of wind and storms and waves and tempests, but they were afraid of their best Friend. That is the point which he aimed at by saying, "Be of good cheer: *it is I;* be not afraid."

First, then, consider with me THE CAUSE OF THEIR FEAR.

If we had not sailed over the same lake—I mean, if we had not suffered the same experience—, it might have surprised us that they were afraid of their Lord. He was appearing for them and coming to their rescue. He was about to still the tempest for them, yet they were afraid *of him*, of him whom they loved and trusted. So holden were their eyes, so hardened were their hearts, that they were afraid of their Lord, and afraid of him when he was giving them the best reasons for trusting him. Before their eyes he was displaying himself as Lord over all, Master of wind and wave, and yet they were afraid of him. The greatness of his power would have comforted them had they understood the truth; but they did not consider the miracle of the loaves, and therefore they were in a state of perplexity, and were sore afraid.

Jesus was acting meanwhile in great gentleness to them; he was displaying his power, but it was not in a dazzling and over-whelming manner. Admire the sacred gentleness which made him move as though he would have passed by them. If he had suddenly appeared in brilliant light in the middle of the ship, he might well have astounded them, and driven them to fright. If, in a moment, he had shone forth just at the stern, or alighted from the heavens upon the deck, they would have been petrified with alarm; but he began by showing himself away there on the crest of the billow, and one cried to his fellow, "See you that strange light yonder?" They watch, and Jesus comes nearer! They can discern a figure; they can see a man step from wave to wave with majestic tread. In tenderness he will not flash upon them all at once. As when the morning breaketh by slow increase of light, so Jesus came to his timid followers. Even then, he moved as though he would pass by them, that they might not be alarmed by his appearing to bear down upon them as an adversary. Even thus he manifests himself to us in the riches of his grace in all wisdom and prudence.

The fears of the trembling crew were sufficiently aroused by even seeing him at a distance; they were so afraid that they cried out thinking that they saw a ghost. What would they have done had he not, in gentleness to their weakness, manifested himself gradually to them, and set himself in a sidelight? Take what way the Master might, his disciples were still afraid, and we are not much wiser nor much more courageous than they were. The manifestation of the Christ of God to us in all his glory will have to be by degrees as long as we are in this body; and, mayhap, even in heaven, it may not be at the very first that we shall be able to endure the fullness of its joy: even there, he may have to lead us to fountains of water which at the first we did not discover, and guide us into more and more of that superlative knowledge which will utterly eclipse all acquaintance that we have of him now, as the sunlight puts out the stars.

The Lord, after all, was doing nothing more than they knew he could do. Twenty-four hours had not passed since they had seen him perform a work of creation, for he had taken bread and fish, and multiplied them so as to make a festival for five thousand men, beside women and children, and to leave far more, when all had eaten, than had been in store when first the loaves and fishes had been counted. After this miracle, they ought not to have been surprised that he should traverse the sea. To walk the waters is to suspend a law, but to make loaves and fishes is to exercise the supreme power of creation, which must for ever remain with God himself: knowing this, they ought not to have been astonished,—not so soon, at any rate.

The memory of that festival ought not to have vanished quite so quickly from the most forgetful minds. Yet when they saw him only doing what they knew he could do, only doing something not a jot more difficult than he was accustomed to do, they cried out for fear.

Was it not because *they dreaded contact with the spiritual, the mysterious, and the supernatural?* Although we are talking now about them, and perhaps half saying in our minds, "If we had been there, we should not have been afraid of Jesus, and have cried out"; we do not know what we say; it takes very little of the supernatural to make a man's flesh creep, let the man be who he may. When Belshazzar saw the handwriting upon the wall, he trembled most because of the mystery involved in a moving hand with which no visible body was connected. The unseen is the birthplace of fear. Imagination exaggerates, and conscience whispers that some great ill will befall us. We are nearing the confines of the mysterious world where God and spirits dwell, and hence we tremble. Yet, beloved, the spirit-world is the last thing which Christians should tremble at, for there can be nothing in the supernatural world which we have cause to dread. If there be such a thing as a ghost walking the earth, I, for one, should like to meet it, either at dead of night or noon of day.

I have not the least particle of faith in rambling spirits. Those who are in heaven will not care to be wandering in these foggy regions; and those in hell cannot leave their dread abode. Whence, then, shall they come? Are they devils? Even so, and what then? A devil is no new personage; we have fought with devils full often, and are prepared to resist them again, and make them fly. The Lord will tread Satan, who is the master of evil spirits, under our feet shortly; why, then, should we be afraid of his underlings? Nothing supernatural should cause any Christian man the slightest alarm. We are expressly forbidden to fear the fear of the heathen, and that is one of their greatest horrors, their dread of witchcraft and necromancy, and other supposed manifestations of evil spirits. We who believe in Jesus are to be ashamed of such superstitions, lest a lie should have dominion over us.

If saintly spirits and holy angels can appear among men, what then? It would be a joy and a privilege to meet them.

We are come to an innumerable company of angels; they bear us up in their hands lest we dash our feet against a stone.

Let us consider, secondly, THE METHOD BY WHICH OUR MASTER CHEERED HIS FOLLOWERS WHEN THEY WERE AFRAID OF THE SUPERNATURAL.

First of all, *he assured them that he was not a disembodied spirit.* He said, "It is I," and that "I" was a Man who did eat and drink with them, a man of flesh and blood, whom they had seen and heard and touched. They were comforted when they knew that it was really no disembodied spirit, but a Man in flesh and blood.

I beg you always to remember, concerning our Lord Jesus Christ, that he is not to be regarded as an unclothed spirit, for he wears a body like our own. It would greatly detract from our comfort if we doubted the real personality of Christ, and the truth of his Resurrection. Our Lord has taken into heaven our human nature in its entirety, body as well as soul, and he ever liveth, not as a spirit, but as a man like ourselves, all sin excepted, and he lives there as the pledge that we shall be there too in the completeness of our manhood, when the trumpet of the Resurrection sounds.

As a real man Jesus reigns above; he is no phantom, no ghost, no spirit, but a risen Man, touched with the feeling of our infirmities, who pities us, and loves us, and feels for us; and in that capacity he speaks to us out of the glory of heaven, and he saith, "It is I; be not afraid."

Another thought lies on the surface of the passage, *Jesus comforted them by the assurance that it was really himself.* They were not looking upon a fiction, they were looking upon Christ himself.

Be sure of the reality of the Christ you trust in. It is very easy to use the name of Jesus, but not quite so easy to know his person; it is common to talk about what he did, and not to feel that he lives just as truly as we do, and that he is a Person to be loved, and to be trusted in, just as much as our own brother, or father, or friend. We want a real, living, personal Christ! A phantom Christ will not cheer us in a storm; it is rather the cause of fright than hope: but a real Christ is a real consolation in a real tempest. May every one of you truly know the personal Saviour to whom you can speak with as much certainty as if you could touch his hand!

But the pith of the comfort lay in this, he said, "It is I; be not afraid," which being interpreted means, *it is Jesus*, be not afraid. When our Lord met Paul on the road to Damascus, he said to him, "I am Jesus." But when he spoke to those who knew his voice, and were familiar with him, he did not quote his name, but said, "It is I." They were sheep that had been long enough with the Shepherd to know his voice, and they had only to hear him speak, and without a name being mentioned they perceived that it was the Lord. To this conclusion they should have come at first. But as they blundered, and said, "It is a spirit," the loving Master corrected them by saying, "It is I,—it is Jesus." It is not possible for me to convey to you what richness of consolation lies in the thought that Jesus is Jesus, which is, being interpreted, a Saviour. That one character and office is cheering, but the same is true of all the names he wears. All the glorious titles and the blessed emblems under which he is set forth are rich in good cheer.

It is Jesus who walks the water of your trouble, and comes to you, Jesus the Son of God, the Alpha and the Omega, the Head over all things to his Church, the All-in-all of all his people.

When Jesus wished to encourage John, in the first chapter of the Revelation, the comfort he gave to him was, "I am the first and the last." The comfort of the Lord's people lies in the Person and Character of Jesus. Here is their solace, "IT IS I." But what a big "I" it is. Compound in one all that is conceivable of goodness, and mercy, and grace, and faithfulness, and love; add perfect humanity, and infinite Godhead, and all the sovereign rights, powers, and possessions of the Highest, and these are all contained in the one little letter "I" when Jesus says, "It is I; be not afraid."

You have not reached the bottom of it yet. The Greek is "ἐγώ εἰμι," "*I am*." Literally rendered, the word which Jesus said was not "It is I," but "I am." When he would cheer his ancient people, the Lord bade Moses comfort Israel by saying, "I AM hath sent me unto you." The self-existence of their God was to be the joy of the tribes. When Jesus said to those who came to take him in the garden, "I am," they fell backward, such was the power of that word; but when he said to these his cowering disciples, "I am," they were drawn towards him, and yet they lost not the awe which must ever go with that incommunicable name "I AM."

Believer, Jesus saith to you, "I am." Is your wife dead? Is your child to be buried? Have your possessions failed? Is your health departing? Are your joys declining? Alas! it is a dying, fleeting world, but there is One who is always the same, for Jesus says to you, "I am; and because I live, you shall live also." Be comforted; whatever else is gone, wherever else the arrows of death may fly, your Jesus still lives. "I am"; blessed word of rich comfort to be heard amid the darkness of the night by weary mariners whose spirits had been sinking within them.

The glory of it all was brought out by the fact that "Jesus went up unto them into the ship"; and as he stood amid them, the stillness all around proved that the "I am" was there. Had he not moved upon the face of the deep, as once the Spirit moved there, and did there not come order out of the tempest's chaos even as at the beginning? Where the great "I AM" is present, the winds and the waves perceive their Ruler, and obey him.

Our third point for consideration is this, THERE ARE TIMES WHEN WE SHALL BE LIKELY TO NEED SUCH COMFORT AS THIS.

Jesus spoke this message to believers, tossed with tempest, and we need it *when we are depressed by the surroundings of these evil times.* In seasons of depressed trade, great sickness, terrible wars, and public disasters, it is balm to the spirit to know that Jesus is still the same. Sin may abound yet more, the light of the Gospel may burn low, and the prince of darkness may widely sway his destroying sceptre; but, nevertheless, this truth standeth sure, that Jesus is the "I AM." At certain periods, diabolical influence seems paramount; the reins of nations appear to be taken out of the hand of the great Governor: and yet it is not so. Look through the darkness, and you shall see your Lord amid the hurricane, walking the waters of politics, ruling national convulsions, governing, over-ruling, arranging all, making even the wrath of man to praise him, and restraining it according to his wisdom. Above the howling of the blast I hear his voice announcing, "It is I." When men's hearts sink for fear, and the rowers feel their oars ready to snap by the strain of useless toil, I hear that word which is the soul of music, "It is I; be not afraid. I am ruling all things. I am coming to the rescue of the barque, my Church; she shall yet float on smooth waters, and reach her desired haven."

Another time of need will surely be *when we reach the swellings of Jordan*. As we shall get near the spirit-world, and the soul will begin to strip off her material garment to enter on a new form of life, how shall we feel as we enter the unknown world? Shall we cry out, "It is a Spirit!" as we salute the first who meets us? It may be so; but then a sweet voice will destroy death's terror, and end all our alarms, and this shall be its utterance, "It is I; be not afraid." This new world is not new to Jesus; our pains and dying throes are not unknown to him! The disembodied state, wherein the spirit sojourns for a while unclothed, he knows it all, for he died, and entered into the spirit-land, and can sympathize with us in every step of the way. In what sweet company shall we pass through the valley of death-shade! Surely its gloom will turn to brightness, as when a cavern, wrapt in blackness, is lit up with a hundred torches, and myriads of gems sparkle from roof and walls. Passing through the sepulchre, its damp darkness shall flash and glow with unexpected joys and marvellous revelations of the Ever-blessed, because Jesus will be with us, and "the Lamb is the light." If, in that dread hour, we shall feel the least trembling at our Lord as the Judge of all the earth, that dread shall vanish as he cries, "It is I."

This comfort may serve us *when we suffer great tribulation*. May you be spared this trial if God so wills; but should it come, you will all the better understand me. They that "do business in great waters" know that our troubles are, at times, so pressing that we lose our heads and are not able to cope with our trials. Forebodings fill the air, and our sinking spirits chill the very marrow of our life. We become like men distraught; or, as David put it, we reel to and fro, and stagger like a drunken man, and are at our wits' end. Then, ah then, the voices of our comrades in the ship are of little value, and even the echoes of former words from the Lord are of small account; nothing will serve but the present and sure consolations of the Lord Jesus.

We shall need this same word of comfort *whenever the Lord*

graciously reveals himself to us. His glory is such that we are not able to bear much of it. Its very sweetness overpowers the heart. Saints have had to ask for a staying of the intense delight which seemed to overbear their natural faculties. Those who have enjoyed those transporting manifestations can quite understand why John has written, "When I saw him, I fell at his feet as dead" (Rev. 1: 17). An awful delight—or shall I say a delightful awe?—throws the man upon his face. John had laid in Jesus' bosom, and yet, when he had a clear manifestation of his glorified Saviour, he could not bear it till his tender Friend laid his hand upon him, and said, "Fear not." So will it be with each of us when we are favoured with the visits of the Well-beloved, we shall greatly need that he should say to us, "It is I, your Brother, your Friend, your Saviour, your Husband; be not afraid. Great as I am, tremble not in my presence, for I am Jesus, the Lover of your soul."

Once more, there is a day coming *when the Son of man will be revealed in the clouds of heaven.* We know not when it will be, but we are solemnly warned that when men look not for him he will suddenly appear. He will come as a thief in the night to the mass of men; but as for believers, they are not in darkness that that day should come upon them as a thief: to them he comes as a long-expected friend. When he cometh, there will be seen tokens, signs in the heavens above and in the earth beneath, which we shall recognize. We may then, perhaps, be distressed by these supernatural portents, and begin to tremble. What, then, will be our delight when we hear him say, "It is I; be not afraid!" Lift up your heads, ye saints, for the coming of the Lord draweth nigh, and to you it is not darkness, but day; to you it is not judgment and condemnation, but honour and reward. What bliss it will be to catch the first glimpse of our Lord on the throne! Sinners will wring their hands, and weep and wail because of him; but we shall know his voice, and welcome his appearing. When the last trumpet rings out clear and loud, happy shall we be to hear that gladsome sound, "It is I; be not afraid." Rolling earth and crumbling mountains, darkened sun and blackened moon, flames of fire and shocks of earthquake, gathering angels and chariots of God, none of these things shall amaze us while Jesus whispers to our soul, "I am," and yet again, "It is I; BE NOT AFRAID."

XV

SIMPLE BUT SOUND

"One thing I know, that, whereas I was blind, now I see."
—John 9: 25.

DID it ever strike you how wonderfully calm and collected our Lord must have been at this time? He had been preaching in the temple, talking to a multitude of Jews. They grew furious with him; a number of stones which were used in repairing the temple were lying about on the floor, and they took up these stones to cast at him. He, by some means, forced a passage, and escaped out of the midst of them; and when he came to the gate of the temple with his disciples—who seem to have followed him in the lane which he was able to make through the throng of his foes,—he saw this blind man; and as if there had been no bloodthirsty foes at his heels, he stopped —stopped as calmly as if an attentive audience had been waiting upon his lips—to look at the blind man. The disciples stopped too, but they paused to ask questions. How like ourselves! We are always ready to talk. How unlike the Master! He was always ready to act. The disciples wanted to know how the man came to be blind, but the Master meant to deliver the man from his blindness. We are very apt to be entering into speculative theories about the origin of sin or the cause of certain strange providences; but Christ is ever seeking out, not the cause, but the remedy; not the reason of the disease, but the way by which the disease can be cured.

The blind man is brought to him. Christ asks him no questions; but, spitting upon the dust, he stoops down, and works the dust into mortar, and when he has done this, taking it up in his hands, he applies it to what Bishop Hall calls the eye-holes of the man (for there were no eyes there), and plasters them up, so that the spectators look on, and see a man with clay upon his eyes. "Go," said Christ, "to the pool of Siloam, and wash." Some kind friends led the man, who was only too glad to go. Unlike Naaman, who made an objection to wash in Jordan, and be clean, the blind man was glad enough to avail himself of the divine remedy. He went, he washed the clay from his eyes, and he received his sight, a blessing he had never known before. With what rapture he gazed upon the trees! With what delight he lifted up his face to the blue sky! With what pleasure he beheld the costly, stately fabric of the temple; and methinks, afterwards, with what interest and pleasure he would look into the face of Jesus, the Man who had given him his sight.

It is not my object to expound this miracle now, but well it setteth forth, in sacred emblem, the state of human nature. Man is blind. Father Adam put out our eyes. We cannot see spiritual things. We have not the spiritual optic; that has gone, gone for ever. Christ comes into this world, and his Gospel is despicable in men's esteem even as spittle; the thought of it disgusts most men. He puts the Gospel on the blind eye—a Gospel which, like clay, seems as if it would make men more blind than before, but it is through "the foolishness of preaching" that Christ saves them that believe. The Holy Spirit is like Siloam's pool. We go to him, or rather he comes to us; the convictions of sin produced by the Gospel are washed away by the cleansing influences of the Divine Comforter; and, behold we, who were once so blind that we could see no beauty in divine things, and no excellence in the crown jewels of God, begin to see things in a clear and heavenly light, and rejoice exceedingly before the Lord.

The man no sooner sees than he is brought before adversaries, and our text is a part of his testimony in defence of the "Prophet" who had wrought the miracle upon him, whom not as yet did he understand to be the Messias. "One thing I know, that, whereas I was blind, now I see."

We have before us, in these words, AN UNANSWERABLE ARGUMENT.

Every now and then, you and I are called into a little debate. Persons do not take things for granted in this age, and it is quite as well that they should not. There have been ages in which any impostor could lead the public by the nose. Men would believe anything, and any crazy maniac, man or woman, who might stand up and pretend to be the Messiah, would be sure to have some followers. I think this age, with all its faults, is not so credulous as that which has gone by. There is a great deal of questioning. You know that there is some questioning where there should not be any. Men, who stand high in official positions, and who ought long ago to have had their faith established, or to have renounced their position, have ventured to question the very things they have sworn to defend. There is questioning everywhere, but to my mind it seems that we need not be afraid. If the Gospel of God be true, it can stand any quantity of questioning. I am more afraid of the deadness and lethargy of the public mind about religion than any sort of enquiry or controversy about it. As silver tried in the furnace is purified seven times, so is the Word of God; and the more it is put into the furnace, the more it will be purified, and the more beauteously the pure ore of revelation will glitter in the sight of the faithful. Never be afraid of a debate. Never go into it unless you are well armed; and if you do go into it, mind that you take with you the weapon I am giving you. Though you may be unarmed in every other respect, if you know how to wield this, you may, through grace, come off more than a conqueror. The argument which this man used was this, "Whereas I was blind, now I see."

It is forcible, because it is *a personal argument*. I heard a person, the other day, use a similar argument. I had been laughing at a certain system of medicine—and really it seems to me pardonable to laugh at all the systems, for I believe they are all almost equally as good or bad as the others. The person in question said, "Well, I can't laugh at it." "Why?" I asked. "Because," said he, "it cured me." Of course, I had no further answer. If this person had really been cured by such-and-such a remedy, it was to him an unanswerable argument. The fact is, the personality of the thing gives it power. People tell us that, in the pulpit, the minister should always say "We," as editors do in writing. We should lose all our power if we did. The minister of God is to use the first person singular, and constantly to say, "I bear eye-witness for God that, in my case, such-and-such a thing has been true." I will not blush nor stammer to say, "I bear my personal witness to the truth of Christ's Gospel in my own case." Lifted up from sin, delivered from bondage, from doubt, from fear, from despair, from an agony intolerable—lifted up to joys unspeakable, and into the service of my God,—I bear my own testimony; and I believe, Christians, that your force in the world will be mightily increased if you constantly make your witness for Christ a personal one.

I daresay my neighbour, over there, can tell what grace has done for him. Yes; but to me, to my own soul, what grace has done for me will be more of an establishment to me for my faith than what Christ has done for him. And if I stand up, and talk of what God's grace has done for this or that brother, it may do very well; but if I can say, "I myself have proved it," here is an argument which drives in the nail, ay, and clinches it, too. "I believed, therefore have I spoken," said the psalmist. Luther was a man of strong faith, and therefore he kindled faith in others. That man will never move the world who lets the world move him; but the man who stands firm, and says, "I *know* such-and-such a thing, because it is burnt into my own inner consciousness," such a man's very appearance becomes an argument to convince others.

Moreover, this man's argument was *an appeal to men's senses*, and hardly anything can be supposed more forcible than that. "I was blind," said he; "you saw that I was; some of you noticed me at the gate of the temple; I *was* blind, now I see. You can all see that I can look at you; you perceive at once that I have eyes, or else I could not see you in the way I do." He appealed to their senses. The argument which our holy religion needs, at the present moment, is a new appeal to the senses of men. You will ask me, "What is that?" The holy living of Christians. The change which the Gospel works in men must be the Gospel's best argument against all opposers. When first the Gospel was preached in the Island of Jamaica, some of the planters objected grievously to it. They thought it an ill thing to teach the negroes, but a missionary said, "What has been the effect of your negro servant Jack hearing the Gospel?" and the planter said, "Well, he was constantly drunk before, but he is sober now. I could not trust him, he was a great thief; but he is honest now. He swore like a trooper before, but now I hear nothing objectionable come from his mouth." "Well," said the missionary, "then I ask you if a

Gospel, that has made such a change as that in the man, must not be of God, and whether you ought not rather to put your influence into its scale than to work against it." When we can bring forward the harlot who has been made chaste, when we can also show the drunkard who has been made sober, or, better still, when we can bring the careless, thoughtless man who has been made sedate and steady; the man who cared not for God, nor Christ, who has been made to worship God with his whole heart, and has put his confidence in Jesus, we think we have then presented to the world an argument which they will not soon answer.

We bring you forward proofs. I hope there are scores and hundreds who are yourselves the proofs of what the living Gospel can do. Many and many a story could I tell of a man who was a fiend in human shape, a man who, when he came home from work, made it an hour of peril, for his wife and children fled to hide from him; and that man now, see him when he goes home, how he is welcomed by his wife, how the children ran down to meet him; you shall hear him sing more loudly now than ever he cursed before, and he who was once a ringleader in the army of Satan has now become a ringleader in the army of Christ.

The Lord's is the glory of it. That is the argument, "Whereas I was blind, now I see." Do we not know of some who, when they came to make their profession before the church, said, "If anyone had told me, three months ago, that I should be here, I should have knocked him down. If any man had said I should make a profession of faith in Jesus, I should have called him all the names in the world. I become a canting Methodist! Not I!" But yet grace has changed the man; his whole life is different now. Those who hate the change cannot help observing it. They hate religion, they say; but if religion does such things as these, the more of it the better. Now we want in the dark lanes and alleys of London, ay! and in our great wide streets, too, where there are large shops and places of business, we want to give the grovelling world this argument, against which there is no disputing, that, whereas there were some men blind, now they see; whereas they were sinful, now they are virtuous; whereas they despised God, now they fear him; we believe this is the best answer for an infidel age.

What a deal of writing there·has been lately about and against Dr. Colenso! You need not think of reading the replies to his books, for most of them would be the best means of sending people to sleep that have ever been invented; and, after all, they don't answer the man; most of them leave the objections untouched, for there is a speciousness in the objection which is not very easily got over. I think we should be doing much better if, instead of running after this heathenish bishop, we should be running after poor sinners; if, instead of writing books of argument, and entering into discussions, we keep on each, in our sphere, endeavouring to convert souls, imploring the Spirit of God to come down upon us, and make us spiritual fathers in Israel. Then we may say to the devil, "Well, sir, you have stolen a bishop, you have taken away a clergyman or so, you have robbed us of a leader or two; but, by the help of God, we have razed your territories, we have stolen away whole bands; here they are, tens of thousands of men and women who have been reclaimed from the paths of vice, rescued from the destroyer, and made servants of the Lord." These are your best arguments; living personal witnesses of what divine grace can do.

We will change our view of the subject now. Our text presents us with A SATISFACTORY PIECE OF KNOWLEDGE: "One thing I know, that, whereas I was blind, now I see."

An affectation of knowledge is not uncommon. The desire for knowledge is almost universal; the attainment of it, however, is rare. But if a man shall attain the knowledge of Christ, he may take a high degree in the Gospel, a satisfactory degree, a degree which shall land him safe into heaven, put the palm-branch in his hand, and the eternal song in his mouth; which is more than any worldly degrees will ever do. "One thing I *know*." The sceptic will sometimes overwhelm you with his knowledge. You simple minds, that have read but little, and whose business occupations take up so much of your time that you probably never will be very profound students, are often in danger of being attacked by men who can use long words, who profess to have read very great books, and to be very learned in sciences, the names of which you have scarcely ever heard. Meet them, but be sure you meet them with a knowledge that is better than theirs. Don't attempt to meet them on their own ground; meet them with this knowledge. "Well," you can say, "I know that you understand more than I do; I am only a poor unlettered Christian, but I have a something in here that answers all your arguments, whatever they may be. I do not know what geology saith; I may not understand all about history; I may not comprehend all the strange things that are daily coming to light; but one thing I know—it is a matter of absolute consciousness to me,—that I, who was once blind, have been made to see." Then just state the difference that the Gospel made in you; say that, once, when you looked at the Bible, it was a dull, dry book; that when you thought of prayer, it was a dreary piece of work; say that, now, the Bible seems to you a honeycomb full of honey, and that prayer is your vital breath. Say that, once, you tried to get away from God, and could see no excellence in the divine Character, but that now you are striving and struggling to get nearer to God. Say that, once, you despised the Cross of Christ, and thought it a vain thing for you to fly to; but that, now, you love it, and would sacrifice your all for it. And this undoubted change in your own consciousness, this supernatural work in your own innermost spirit, shall stand you in the stead of all the arguments that can be drawn from all the sciences; your one thing shall overthrow their thousand things, if you can say, "Whereas I was blind, now I see."

Says one, "I don't know how that can be." Let me suppose that someone has just discovered galvanism, and I have had a galvanic shock. Now, twenty people come and say, "There is no such thing as galvanism; we do not believe in it for a moment," and there is one gentleman proves by Latin that there cannot be such a thing as galvanism, and another proves it mathematically to demonstration, and twenty others prove it in their different ways. I should say, "Well, I cannot answer you in Latin, I cannot overthrow you in logic, I cannot contradict that syllogism of yours; but one thing I know—I have had a shock of it,—that I *do* know"; and I take it that my personal consciousness of having experienced a galvanic shock will be a better answer than all their learned sayings. And so, if you have ever felt the Spirit of God come into contact with you (and that is something quite as much within the reach of our consciousness as even the shock of electricity and galvanism), and if you can say of that, "One thing I know, which cannot be beaten out of me, which cannot be hammered out of my own consciousness, that, whereas I was blind, now I see"; —it will be quite sufficient reply to all that the sceptic may bring against you.

How often are you assailed, not only by the sceptic, but by our very profound doctrinal brethren! I know some very great doctrinal friends, who, because our experience may not tally with theirs, will sit down and say, "Ah! you don't know the power of vital godliness"; and they will write very severe things against us, and say that we don't know the great secret and don't understand the inner life. You never need trouble yourself about these braggarts; let them talk on till they have done. But if you do want to answer them, do it humbly by saying, "Well, you may be right, and I may be mistaken; but yet I think I can say, 'One thing I know, that, whereas I was blind, now I see.'" And you young Christians sometimes meet with older believers, very good people too, but very wise, and they will put you into their sieves. Some of our brethren always carry a sieve with them; and if they meet a young brother, they will try to sift him, and they will often do it very unkindly, ask him knotty questions. I always compare this to a man's trying a newborn child's health by putting nuts into his mouth, and if he cannot crack them, saying, "He is not healthy." Well, I have known very difficult questions asked about such things as sublapsarianism, or supralapsarianism, or about the exact difference between justification and sanctification, or something of that sort. Now, I advise you to get all that sort of knowledge you can; but, putting all of it together, it is not nearly equal in value to this small bit of knowledge, "One thing I know, that, whereas I was blind, now I see." And even now, though I have no doubt about my own acceptance in Christ, and my having been brought to see, yet, compared with this piece of knowledge, I do count all the excellency of human knowledge,—ay, and all the rest of divine knowledge, too,—to be but dross and dung, for this is the one thing needful, the one soul-saving piece of knowledge, "One thing I know, that, whereas I was blind, now I see."

Do you see a beauty in Christ? Do you see a loveliness in the Gospel? Do you perceive an excellence in God your Father?

Can you read your title clear to mansions in the skies? You could not do this once. Once, you were a stranger to these things; your soul was dark as the darkest night without a star, without a ray of knowledge or of comfort; but now you see. Seek after more knowledge; but, still, if you cannot attain it, and if you tremble because you cannot grow as you would, remember this is enough to know for all practical purposes, "One thing I know, that, whereas I was blind, now I see."

We will again change our view of the subject. This is A MODEL CONFESSION OF FAITH.

This blind man did not do as some of you would have done. When he found his eyes, he did not use them to go and hunt out a quiet corner so that he might hide himself in it; but he came out boldly before his neighbours, and then before Christ's enemies, and said, "One thing I know, that, whereas I was blind, now I see." Why, there are some of you who, I hope, have grace in your heart, but you have not courage to confess it; you have not put on your regimentals. I suppose you call yourselves members of the Church Militant, but you are not dressed in the true scarlet; you do not come forward, and wear the Master's badge, and openly fight under his banner. I think it is very unkind of you, and very dishonouring to your Master. There are not many who speak for him, and it is a shame that you should hold your tongue. If he has given you eyes, I am sure you ought to give him your tongue. If he has taught you to see things in a new light, I am sure you ought not to be unwilling to confess him before men. After so much kindness in the past, it is cruel ingratitude to be ashamed to confess him. You do not know how much you would comfort the minister. Converts are our sheaves, and you, who are not added to the church, do as it were rob us of our reward. No doubt you will be gathered into God's garner, but then we do not know anything about that; we want to see you gathered into God's garner here; we want to hear you boldly say, "Whereas I was blind, now I see."

You cannot tell, besides, how much good you might do to others. Your example would move your neighbours, your confession would be valuable to saints, and might be a help to sinners. Your taking the decisive step might lead others to take it. Your example might be just the last grain cast into the scale, and might lead others to decide for the Lord. I am ashamed of you, who were once blind, yet now see, but do not like to say so. I pray you lay the matter to heart; and, ere long, come out, and say, "Yes, I cannot withhold it any longer. Whereas I was once blind, now I see."

"Well," says one, "I have often thought of joining the church, but I can't be perfect." Now this man did not say, "I was once imperfect, and now I am perfect." Oh, no! If you were perfect, we would not receive you into church-fellowship; because we are all imperfect ourselves, and we should fall out with you if we did take you in. We don't want those perfect gentlemen; let them go to heaven; that is the place for perfect ones, not here.

"Well," says someone else, "I have not grown in religion as I should like to do; I am afraid I am not as saintly as I would desire to be." Well, strive after a high degree of holiness, but remember that a high degree of holiness is not necessary to a profession of your faith. You are to make a profession as soon as you have any holiness, and the high degree of it is to come afterwards.

"Ah!" says another, "but I could not say much." Nobody asked you to say much. If you can say, "Whereas I was blind, now I see," that is all we want. If you can but let us know that there is a change in you, that you are a new man, that you see things in a different light, that what was once your joy is now your sorrow, and what was once a sorrow to you is now your joy, if you can say, "All things have become new"; if you can say, "I feel a new life heaving within my bosom; there is a new light shining in my eyes. I go to God's house now in a different spirit. I read the Bible, and engage in private prayer, after quite a different fashion. And I hope my life is different, I hope my language is not what it used to be. I try to curb my temper. I do endeavour to provide things honest in the sight of all men. My nature is different; I could no more live in sin as I once did than a fish could live on dry land, or a man could live in the depths of the sea,"—this is what we want of you.

Suppose now a person getting up in the Church Meeting, and saying, "Brethren, I come to unite with you. I know the Greek Testament; I have also read a good deal in Latin; I understand the Vulgate; I can now, if you please, give you the 1st chapter of Mark in Greek, or the 2nd chapter of Exodus in Hebrew, if you like. I have also, from my youth up, given myself to the study of the natural and applied sciences. I think I am master of rhetoric, and I am able to reason logically." Suppose he went on then to say what he knew about business, what a skilful tradesman he had been; and after going through that should say, "I have a great deal of theological knowledge; I have read the Fathers; I have studied Augustine; I could talk about all the ponderous tomes that were written in the ancient times; I am acquainted with all the writers on the Reformation, and I have studied the Puritans through and through; I know the points of difference between the great Reformed teachers, and I know the distinction between Zwingli and Calvin,"—I am sure, if a man were to say all that, before I put it to the vote whether he should be admitted to Church membership, I should say, "This dear brother has not any idea of what he came here for. He came here to make a confession that he was a living man in Christ Jesus, and he has been only trying to prove to us that he is a learned man. That is not what we want"; and I should begin to put to him some pointed questions, something like this, "Did you ever feel yourself a sinner? Did you ever feel that Christ was a precious Saviour, and are you putting your trust in him?" and you would some of you say, "Why, that's just what he asked poor Mary, the servant girl, when she was in the meeting five minutes ago!" All that learned lumber is good enough in its place; I do not depreciate it; I wish you were all scholars; I love to see you great servants in the Master's cause; but the whole of that put together is not worth a straw, compared with this, "One thing I know, that, whereas I was blind, now I see."

And this is all we ask of you; we only ask you, if you wish to join the church, to be able to confess that you are a changed character, that you are a new man, that you are willing to be obedient to Christ and to his ordinances, and then we are only too glad to receive you into our midst. Come out, I pray you, ye that are hiding among the trees of the wood, come forth. Whosoever is on the Lord's side, let him come forth. It is a day of blasphemy and rebuke. He that is not with Christ is against him, and he that gathereth not with him scattereth abroad.

And now, to conclude, my text may be used in a further way; for it sets before us A VERY CLEAR AND MANIFEST DISTINCTION.

You cannot every one of you say, "One thing I know, that, whereas I was blind, now I see." Solemnly, as in the sight of God, I speak to you; lend me your ears, and may these few words of truth sink into your hearts! *Are there not some of you who cannot even say, "I was blind"?* You do not know your own blindness; you have the conceit to imagine that you are as good as most people, and that if you have some faults, yet certainly you are not irretrievably lost. You have no idea that you are depraved, utterly depraved, saturated through and through, and rotten at the core. If I were to describe you in Scriptural language, and say, "Thou art the man," you would be shocked at me for giving you so bad a character. You are amiable, your outward carriage has always been decorous, you have been generous and benevolent, and, therefore, you think there is no need for you to be born again, no necessity for you to repent of sin. You think that the Gospel is very suitable for those who have gone into foul, open sin; but you are too good rather than too bad! You are stone-blind, and the proof that you are so is this, that you do not know your blindness! A man who is born blind does not know what it is to lose sight; the bright beams of the sun never made glad his heart, and, therefore, he does not know his misery.

And such is your state. You do not understand what it is that you have lost; what it is that you need. I pray God to do for you what you cannot do for yourselves, make you feel now, once for all, that you are blind. There is hope for the man who knows his blindness, there is some light in the man who says he is all darkness—there is some good thing in the man who says he is all foul. If you can say, "Vile and full of sin I am," God has begun a good work in you. You know that, when the leper was afflicted with leprosy from head to foot, the priest looked at him, and, if there was a single spot where there was no leprosy, he was unclean; but the moment the leprosy covered him everywhere, then he was made clean; and so you, if you know your sin so as to feel your utterly ruined, lost estate, God has begun a good work in you; and he will put away your sin, and save your soul. Alas! there are many who do not know that they are blind.

And yet I know, to my sorrow, there are many of you who know that you are blind, but *you don't see yet*. I hope you may.

To know your blindness is well, but it is not enough. It would be a dreadful thing for you to go from an awakened conscience on earth to a tormenting conscience in hell. There have been some, who have begun to find out that they are lost here, and then have discovered that they are lost hereafter as well. I pray you, do not tarry long in this state. If God hath convinced you of sin, I pray you do not linger. The way of salvation—oh, how many times I have preached this! and how many times more will it be necessary to tell you over and over again the same thing?—the way of salvation is simply this, trust Christ, and you are saved; just as you are, rely upon him, and you are saved. With no other dependence, with no other shadow of a hope, sinner, venture on him, venture wholly, venture now. I hear the wheels of the Judge's chariot behind thee. He comes! He comes! Fly, sinner, fly! I see God's bow in his awful hand, and he has drawn the arrow to its very head. Fly, sinner, fly, while yet the wounds of Christ stand open; hide thyself there as in the cleft of the Rock of Ages. Thou hast not a lease of thy life, thou canst not tell that thou shalt ever see another Sabbath-day to spend in pleasure; no more warnings may ever ring in your ears. Sinner, turn! God puts this alternative before some of you now—turn or burn. "Turn ye, turn ye from your evil ways; for why will ye die?" One of the two it must be—die or turn. Believe in Christ, or perish with a great destruction. "He that being often reproved hardeneth his neck, shall suddenly be destroyed, and that without remedy."

And you who are aroused and convinced, I pray you to trust Christ, and live. The whole matter is very simple, "Whereas I was blind, now I see." Dost thou see that Christ can save thee? Dost thou believe that he will save thee if thou wilt trust him? Then trust him, and you are saved. The moment you believe, you are saved, whether you feel the comfort of it or not;—ay, and the thought arising from the full belief that you are saved will yield you the comfort which you will never find elsewhere. Have I trust in Christ, O my soul? Thou knowest, O Lord, I have; thou knowest I have.

> *Other refuge have I none,*
> *Hangs my helpless soul on thee.*

It is written, "He that believeth on him is not condemned." Then I am not condemned. Perhaps I feel at this present moment no joy, but then the thought that I am not condemned will also make me feel joy by-and-by; yet I must not build on my joy, I must not build on my feelings, but simply on this, that God has said, "He that believeth and is baptized shall be saved." I, believing in Christ, am saved. And that is true of you also. Well, then, you are saved, your sin is blotted out, your iniquity is forgiven, you are a child of God, the Lord accepts you,—if you have really trusted Christ,—you are an heir of heaven. Go and sin no more; go and rejoice in pardoning love.

XVI

THE WITHERED HAND

"And, behold, there was a man which had his hand withered. . . . Then saith he to the man, Stretch forth thine hand. And he stretched it forth; and it was restored whole, like as the other."—Matt. 12: 10, 13.

NOTE well the expression. Jesus "went into their synagogue; and, *behold*, there was a man which had his hand withered." A mark is set, as it were, in the margin, as if it were a notable fact. That word "*behold*" is a sort of note of exclamation to draw attention to it. "Behold, there was a man which had his hand withered." In many congregations, if there should step in some one of the great and mighty of the land, people would say, "Behold, there was a duke, an earl, or a bishop there." But although there were some great ones occasionally in our Saviour's congregation, I find no notes of admiration about their presence, no "beholds" inserted by the evangelists as if to call attention to their appearance. No doubt if there were in a congregation some person of known intelligence and great learning, who had earned to himself a high degree, there are persons who would say, "Do you know that Professor Science or Doctor Classic was present at the service?" There would be a "behold" put to that in the memories of many. Yet in the synagogue there was a poor man whose hand had been withered, and we are called upon to note the fact.

It was his *right* hand which was withered, the worse of the two for him, for he could scarcely follow his handicraft or earn his bread. I have no doubt he was a very humble, obscure, insignificant individual, probably very badly off and in great poverty, because he could not work as his fellow craftsmen could, but not a man of any rank, or learning, or special intelligence. His being in the assembly was in itself nothing very remarkable. I suppose he had been accustomed to go to the synagogue as others of his townsmen did; yet the Holy Spirit takes care to mark that he was present, and to have the word "behold" hung out like a signal, that it might be regarded as a special subject for consideration that the crippled man was there.

And it matters very little to the preacher or to the congregation that *you* are here, if you are some person of note or consequence; for we make no note of dignitaries here, and attach no special consequence to any one in this place, where the rich and the poor meet together. But if you happen to be here as a needy soul wanting a Saviour, if you happen to be here with a spiritually withered hand so that you cannot do the things that you would, and you are wanting to have that hand restored to you, there shall be a *"behold"* put to that, and especially shall it be doubly emphatic if the Master shall say to you, "Stretch out thy withered hand," and if the divine power shall restore that hand and a deed of grace shall be accomplished. What our Lord wanted on that particular Sabbath morning was somebody to work upon, somebody whom he might heal, and so defy the traditional legality of the Pharisees who said that it was wrong to heal on the Sabbath day. Christ did not want their health that morning: he looked out for their sickness that he might illustrate his healing power. He did not want any greatness in anybody there; but he did want some poor needy one in whom he could display his power to heal. If you are rich and increased in goods and have need of nothing, my Master does not want you. He is a physician, and those who practise the healing art look out for sickness as their sphere of operation. If we were to tell a wise physician of a town where nobody was sick, but everybody enjoyed perfect health, he would not settle there, unless he wished to retire from practice. My Master does not come into the assemblies where all feel themselves quite content with themselves, where there are no blind eyes, no deaf ears, no broken hearts, no withered hands; for what do such folks need with a Saviour? He looks around and his eye fixes itself upon pain, upon necessity, upon incapacity, upon sinfulness, upon everything to which he can do good; for what he wants in us mortals is the opportunity to do us good and not a pretence on our part that we can do him good.

I do not know that our crippled friend when he went to the synagogue that morning expected to get his withered hand healed. Being, perhaps, a devout man, he went there to worship, but he got more than he went for. And it may be that some of you whom God means to bless do not know what you have come here for. You came because you somehow love the ordinances of God's house, and you feel happy in hearing the Gospel preached. You have never yet laid hold of the Gospel for yourselves, never enjoyed its privileges and blessings as your own, but still you have a hankering after the best things. What if to-night the hour has come, the hour which sovereign grace has marked with a red letter in the calendar of love, in which your withered hand shall be made strong, and your sin shall be forgiven!

First, we will say a little about THE PERSON TO WHOM THE COMMAND IN OUR TEXT IS ADDRESSED. "Then said Jesus to the man, stretch forth thine hand."

This command was addressed, then, to *a man who was hopelessly incapable of obeying*. "Stretch forth thine hand." I do not know whether his arm was paralysed, or only his hand. As a general rule when a thorough paralysis, not a partial one, takes place in the hand it seizes the entire member, and both hand and arm are paralysed. We usually speak of this man as if the entire limb had been dried up, and yet I do not see either in Matthew, Mark, or Luke, any express declaration that the whole arm was withered. It seems to me to have been a case in which the hand only was affected. We used to have, not far from here, I remember, at Kennington Gate, a lad who would frequently get on the step of the omnibus and exhibit his hands, which hung down as if his wrists were broken, and he would cry, "Poor boy! poor boy!" and appeal to our compassion. I fancy that his case was a picture of the one before us. We cannot decide positively that the arm was still unwithered, but we may notice that our Lord did not say, "Stretch out thine arm," but "thine hand," so that he points to the hand as the place where the paralysis lay. It was not a sham disease. He had not made a pretence of being paralysed, but he was really incapable. The hand had lost the moisture of life. The spirits which gave it strength had been dried out of it, and there it was a withered, wilted, useless thing, with which he could do nothing ; and yet it was to such a man that Jesus said, "Stretch forth thine hand."

This is very important for us to notice, because some of you under a burden of sin think that Christ does not save real sinners—that those people whom he does save are, in some respects, not quite so bad as you—that there is not such an intensity of sin about them as about your case, or if an intensity of sin, yet not such an utter hopelessness and helplessness as there is about you. You feel quite dried up, and utterly without strength. It is exactly to such as you that the Lord Jesus Christ directs the commands of the Gospel. We are bidden to preach to you, saying, "Believe," or at other times, "Repent, and be baptized, every one of you;" "Believe in the Lord Jesus Christ, and thou shalt be saved"—commandments not addressed, as some say they are, to sensible sinners, but to insensible sinners, to stupid sinners, to sinners who cannot, so far as moral ability is concerned, obey the command at all. Such are bidden so to do by him, who in this case bade the man do what he, naturally in and of himself, was quite incapable of doing; because you see if he could stretch out his hand himself, there was no miracle wanted, for the man's hand was not withered at all. But it is clear that he could not move his hand, and yet the Saviour addressed him as if he could do it; in which I see a symbol of the Gospel way of speaking to the sinner; for the Gospel cries to him in all his misery and in-capacity, "To thee, even to thee, is the word of this salvation sent." This very incapacity and inability of thine is but the space in which the divine power may be displayed, and because thou art thus incapable, and because thou art thus unable, therefore to thee does the Gospel come, that the excellency of the power may be seen to dwell in the Gospel, and in the Saviour himself, and not at all in the person who is saved.

But, mark you, it came to *one who was perfectly willing*, for this man was quite prepared to do whatever Jesus bade him do. If you had questioned him you would have found no desire to retain that withered hand—no wish that his fingers should remain lifeless and useless. But the worst of many uncon-verted people is that they do not want to be healed—do not want to be restored. As soon as a man truly longs for salvation, then has salvation already come to him; but most of you do not wish to be saved. "Oh," say you, "we truly wish to be saved." I do not think so, for what do you mean by being

saved? Do you mean being saved from going down to hell?
Everybody, of course, wishes that. Did you ever meet a thief
that would not like to be saved from going to prison or being
locked up by the policeman? But when we talk about salvation, we mean being saved from the habit of wrong-doing;
being saved from the power of evil, the love of sin, the practice
of folly, and the very power to find pleasure in transgression.
Do you wish to be saved from pleasurable and gainful sins?
Find me the drunkard who sincerely prays to be delivered
from drunkenness. Bring me an unchaste man who pines to be
pure. Find me one who is an habitual liar and yet longs to
speak the truth. Bring me one who has been selfish and who
in his very heart hates himself for it, and longs to be full of
love and to be made Christlike. Why, half the battle is won in
such cases. The initial step is taken. The parallel holds good
in the spiritual world. The character I have in my mind's eye
is the case of a soul desiring to be what it cannot be, and to do
what it cannot do, and yet desiring it. I mean the man who
cries in agony, "To will is present with me, but how to perform
that which is good I find not." "I would, but cannot, repent.
My heart feels like a stone. I would love Christ, but, alas, I
feel that I am fettered to the world. I would be holy, but, alas,
sin comes violently upon me, and carries me away." It is to
such people that Jesus Christ's Gospel comes with the force of a
command. Wilt thou be made whole, my friend? Dost thou
desire to be saved from sin? Dost thou wish to be emancipated
from the bondage of corruption? Thou mayest be. And this
is the way in which thou mayest be saved,—"Believe in the
Lord Jesus Christ, and thou shalt be saved": his name is called
Jesus, for he shall save his people from their sins. He has come
on purpose to do this to real sinners, and not to mere pretenders,
for it is clear that he cannot save men from sins if they have
none. He cannot heal withered hands if there are no withered
hands to be healed. Even to you is this glorious word of the
good news proclaimed; God grant you grace to hear it believingly and to feel its power!

Secondly, I want to speak a little upon THE PERSON WHO GAVE
THE COMMAND. It was *Jesus* who gave it. *He* said, "Stretch
forth thine hand."

Did our Lord speak this in ignorance, supposing that the

man could do so? By no means, for in him is abundant knowledge. He had just read the hearts of the Pharisees, and you may
be sure that he who could read those subtle spirits could certainly see the outward condition of this patient. He knew that
the man's hand was withered, and yet he said, "Stretch forth
thine hand." When I read in Scripture the command, "Believe
in the Lord Jesus Christ," I am sure that Jesus Christ knows
what he is saying. "Go ye," said he, "into all the world, and
preach the Gospel to every creature." Yes, to every creature.
I have heard some of Christ's professed servants say that to
bid dead sinners live is of no more use than to shake a handkerchief over the graves in which the dead are buried; and my
reply to them has been, "You are quite right. Do not do it,
for it is evident you are not called to it. Go home and go to
bed. The Lord never sent you to do anything of the kind, for
you own you have no faith in it." But if my Master sent *me* as
the herald of Resurrection, and bade me shake a handkerchief
over the graves of the dead, I would do it, and I should expect
that this poor handkerchief, if *he* commanded it to be shaken,
would raise the dead, for Jesus Christ knows what he is doing
when he sends his servants. If he does not send us, it is a fool's
errand indeed to go and say, "Ye dead men, live"; but his
commission makes all the difference.

We are to say to the dead, "Awake, and Christ shall give you
life." What, wake first, and then get life afterwards? I shall
not try to explain it, but that is the order of the Scripture:
"Awake, thou that sleepest, and arise from the dead, and
Christ shall give thee life." If my Master puts it so, I am quite
satisfied to quote his words. I cannot explain it, but I delight
to take him in his own way, and blindly follow his every step,
and believe his every word. If he bids me say, "Arise from the
dead," I will gladly do it now. In the name of Jesus, ye dead
ones, live. Break, ye hard hearts. Dissolve, ye hearts of steel.
Believe, ye unbelievers. Lay hold on Christ, ye ungodly ones.
If he speak by his ministers, that word shall be with power; if
he speak not by us, it is little matter how we speak. Well may
the judicious brother say that there would be no use in *his*
bidding the dead arise, for he confesses that his Master is not
with him. Yet it is the Lord Jesus Christ who says to this man
with the withered hand, "Stretch forth thine hand."

To me it is a sweet thought that he is able to give power to do what he gives the command to do. When you are bidden to believe, and you stand with tears in your eyes and say, "Sir, I cannot understand, and I cannot believe," dost thou not know that he who bids thee believe can give thee power to believe? When *he* speaks through his servants, or through his word, or directly by his Spirit upon your conscience, he who bids thee do this is no mere man, but the Son of God, and thou must say to him, "Good Lord, I beseech thee give me now the faith which thou dost ask of me. Give me the repentance thou dost command;" and he will hear thy prayer, and faith shall spring up within thee.

Did you never notice Christ's way of doing his work? His way is generally this—first, to give the command, then to help the heart to turn the command into a prayer, and then to answer that prayer by a promise. The Lord says, "Make you a new heart." That is clearly a command. But by-and-by you find the Psalmist David, in the fifty-first Psalm, saying, "Create in me a clean heart, O God." And then, if you turn to Ezekiel, you get the promise, "A new heart also will I give you." First, he commands you; next he sets you praying for the blessing; and then he gives it to you.

Take another; the command is, "Turn ye, turn ye, why will ye die, O house of Israel?" Then comes the prayer, "Turn thou me, and I shall be turned"; and then follows the blessed turning of which the apostle Paul speaks when he says that God has sent his Son to bless us by turning every one of us from his iniquity.

Take another case, and let it refer to purging. We find the Lord commanding us to "purge out the old leaven"; and straightway there comes the prayer, "Purge me with hyssop, and I shall be clean," and then on the heels of it comes the promise, "I will purely purge away thy dross." Or, take another kind of precept, of a sweeter sort, belonging to the Christian. You are continually told to sing: "Sing praises to God, sing praises: sing praises unto our King, sing praises." In another place we meet with the prayer, "Open thou my lips, and my mouth shall shew forth thy praise;" and in a third Scripture we have the divine promise, "This people have I formed for myself; they shall shew forth my praise." See, then,

the Master's way of going to work—he commands you to
believe, or repent; he then sets you a-praying that you may be
enabled to do it, and then he gives you grace to do it, so that the
blessing may really come to your soul; for everywhere Gospel
commands are uttered by Christ himself to men's hearts,
and they, receiving them, find the ability coming with the
command.

"But he is not here," says one, "he is not here." Verily I say
unto you in his name, he is here. His word is, "Lo, I am with
you always even to the end of the world": till this dispensation
shall be ended Christ will be where the Gospel is preached.
Where his message is honestly and truthfully delivered with the
Spirit of God, there Jesus Christ himself is virtually present,
speaking through the lips of his servants. Therefore, dear soul
with the withered hand, Jesus himself says to thee, "Stretch
forth thine hand." He is present to heal, and his method is to
command.

It is time for a few words upon another point, and that is
upon THE COMMAND ITSELF. The command itself was, "Stretch
forth thine hand." I notice about that command that it goes
to the very essence of the matter. It is not, "Rub your right
hand with your left"; it is not, "Show your hand to the priest,
and let him perform a ceremony upon it"; it is not, "Wash
your hand"; but it is, "Stretch it forth." That was the very
thing he could not do, and thus the command went to the very
root of the mischief. As soon as the hand was stretched out it
was healed; and the command went directly to the desired
mark.

Now, my Lord and Master does not say to any of you sinners,
"Go home and pray." I hope you will pray, but that is not the
great Gospel command. Paul stood at the dead of night, with
the trembling jailer, who hardly understood his own question,
when he cried, "Sirs, what must I do to be saved?" and Paul
according to the practice of some should have said, "We must
have a little prayer," or, "You must go home and read the
Bible, and I must further instruct you until you are in a better
state." He did nothing of the sort, but there and then Paul
said, "Believe in the Lord Jesus Christ, and thou shalt be
saved." There is no Gospel preached unless you come to this;
for salvation comes by faith, and by nothing short of it. That is

just the difficult point, you tell me. Yes, and at the difficult point this command strikes and says, "Stretch forth thine hand"; or in the case of the sinner, "Believe in the Lord Jesus Christ." For, remember, all that any of you ever do in the matter of eternal life, which has not faith in it, can be nothing after all but the effort of your carnal nature, and that is death. What can come of the movements of death but a still deeper death? Death can never produce life. Prayer without faith! What sort of prayer is it? It is the prayer of a man who does not believe God. Shall a man expect to receive anything of the Lord if he does not believe that God is, and that he is the rewarder of them that diligently seek him? "Oh, but I must repent before I believe," says one. What kind of repentance is that which does not trust God—does not believe in God? An unbelieving repentance—is it not a selfish expression of regret because of punishment incurred? Faith must be mixed with every prayer and every act of repentance, or they cannot be acceptable; and hence we must go right straight to this point, and demand faith, saying: "Believe and live;" "Stretch forth thine hand."

That stretching forth of the hand was entirely *an act of faith.* As a matter of sense and nature the man was powerless for it. He only did it because his faith brought the ability. "I do not understand as yet," says one, "how a man can do what he cannot do?" But you will understand a great many other wonderful things when the Lord teaches you; for the Christian life is a series of paradoxes; and for my own part I doubt an experience unless there is something paradoxical about it. At any rate I am sure that it is so—that I who can do nothing of myself can do everything through Christ which strengtheneth me. The man who is seeking Christ can do nothing, and yet, if he believeth on Christ, he can do everything, and his withered hand is stretched out.

But, in addition to its being an act of faith, it seems to me it was *an act of decision.* There sit the haughty, frowning Pharisees. Your imagination can easily picture those fine-looking gentlemen, with fringes to their garments, and phylacteries across their foreheads. There, too, are the scribes all wrapped up in their formal array—very grave and knowing men. Persons were almost afraid to look at them, they were so holy, and so contemptuous. See, there they sit, like judges of assize, to try the Saviour. Now, Christ does, as it were, single out this poor man with a withered hand to be his witness; and by his command he practically asks him which he will do—will he obey the Pharisees or himself? It is wrong to heal on the Sabbath day, say the Pharisees. What say you with the withered hand over yonder? If you agree with the Pharisees, of course you will decline to be healed on the Sabbath day, and you won't stretch out your hand; but if you agree with Jesus, you will be glad to be healed, Sabbath or no Sabbath. Ah, I see, you will stretch out your hand and break away from the tyrants who would keep you withered. The man did as good as vote for Christ when he stretched forth his hand. Many a soul has found peace when at last he has held up his hand and said, "Sink or swim, lost or saved; Christ for me, Christ for me! If I perish I will cling to his Cross-foot, and to him alone will I look; for I am on his side, whether he will have compassion upon me or not." When that act of decision is performed, then comes the healing. If you hold up your hand for Christ, he will make it a good hand though now it is all paralysed and drooping, like a dead thing. Unworthy as you are, he has the power, as you hold up your hand for him, to put life into it, and to give you the blessing your heart desires.

> *He that suffer'd in my stead,*
> *Shall my Physician be;*
> *I will not be comforted*
> *Till Jesus comforts me.*

When that is done, I do not doubt that, through faith in the physician, you will be quickened by divine power, and you will find healing at once.

So I will just lead you on, in the fourth place, to notice THIS MAN'S OBEDIENCE. We are told that he stretched forth his hand. Christ said, "Stretch forth thine hand": Mark says, "And he did so." That is to say, he stretched forth his hand. Now, observe that *this man did not do something else in preference to what Jesus commanded*, though many awakened sinners are foolish enough to try experiments. If, instead, the man had walked across the synagogue and brought himself up to Christ, the Master would have said, "I bade thee do no such thing. I bade thee stretch forth thy hand." Suppose he had then with his left hand begun to grasp the roll of the law as it stood in the synagogue, and had kissed it out of reverence, would that have been of any use? The Master would only have said, "I bade thee stretch forth thy hand." Alas, there are many, many souls that say, "We are bidden to trust in Jesus, but instead of that we will attend the means of grace regularly." Do that by all means, but not as a substitute for faith, or it will become a vain confidence. The command is, "Believe and live"; attend to that, whatever else you do. "Well, I shall take to reading good books; perhaps I shall get good that way." Read the good books by all means, but that is not the Gospel: the Gospel is, "Believe in the Lord Jesus Christ and thou shalt be saved." Suppose a physician has a patient under his care, and he says to him, "You are to take a bath in the morning; it will be of very great service to your disease." But the man takes a cup of tea in the morning instead of the bath, and he says, "That will do as well, I have no doubt." What does his physician say when he enquires—"Did you follow my rule?" "No, I did not." "Then you do not expect, of course, that there will be any good result, for you have disobeyed me."

So we, practically, say to Jesus Christ, when we are under searching of soul, "Lord, thou badest me trust thee, but I would sooner do something else. Lord, I want to have horrible convictions; I want to be shaken over hell's mouth; I want to be alarmed and distressed." Yes, you want anything but what Christ prescribes for you, which is that you should simply trust him. Whether you feel or do not feel, you should just come and cast yourself on him, that *he* may save you, and he alone. "But you do not mean to say that you speak against praying, and reading good books, and so on?" Not one single word do I speak against any of those things, any more than, if I were the physician I quoted, I should speak against the man's drinking a cup of tea. Let him drink his tea; but not if he drinks it instead of taking the bath which I prescribe for him. So let the man pray: the more the better. Let the man search the Scriptures; but, remember, that if these things are put in the place of simple faith in Christ, the soul will be ruined. Let me give you a text: did you ever hear it quoted properly? "Ye search the Scriptures, for in them ye think ye have eternal life;

but ye will not come unto me that ye might have life." That is where the life is—in Christ; not even in searching Scripture, good as the searching of Scripture is. If we put even golden idols into the place of Christ, such idols are as much to be broken as if they were idols of mud or idols of dung. It matters not how good an action is, if it is not what Christ commands, you will not be saved by it. "Stretch forth thine hand," says he; that was the way by which the healing was to come: the man did nothing else, and he received a gracious reward.

Notice, that *he did not raise any questions*. I think this man might very fairly have stood up in his place and said, "This is inconsistent, good Master. Thou sayest to me, 'Stretch forth thine hand.' Now, thou knowest that if I can stretch forth my hand there ails me nothing, and therefore there is no room for thy miracle. And if I cannot stretch forth my hand, how canst thou tell me so to do?" Have you not heard some of our friends, who like to make jests of holy things, and to scoff at our doctrines of grace, declare that we teach, "You can and you can't; you shall and you shan't"? Their description is right enough, though meant to ridicule us. We teach paradoxes and contradictions to the eye, if you only consider the letter; but if you get down into the innermost spirit, it is within these contradictions that the eternal truth is found. We know that the man is dead in trespasses and sins—steeped in a spiritual and moral torpor, out of which he cannot raise himself; yet do we by the Master's own command say, "Awake, thou that sleepest, and arise from the dead, and Christ shall give thee life;" or, in other words, we say to the withered hand, "Be thou stretched out," and it is done. The blessed result justifies that very teaching which in itself seems so worthy of sarcastic remark.

Notice further that what the man did was, that *he was told to stretch out his hand, and he did stretch out his hand*. If you had asked him, "Did *you* stretch out your hand?" perhaps he would have said, "Of course I did. Nobody else did." "Wait a minute, my good man. Did you of *yourself* stretch out your hand?" "Oh, no," he would say, "because I have tried many times before and I could not, but this time I did do it. Jesus told me to do it, and I was willing, and it was done." I do not expect that he could have explained the rationale of it, and perhaps we cannot either. It must, indeed, have been a very beautiful sight to see that poor, withered, limp, wilted hand, first hanging down, and then stretched out before all the people in the middle of the synagogue. Do you not see the blood begin to flow, the nerves gaining power, and the hand opening like a reviving flower? Oh, the delight of his sparkling eyes as at first he could only fix them upon the little finger and the thumb to see if they were really all alive! Then he turned, looked at that blessed One who had healed him, and seemed anxious to fall down at his feet and give him all the praise! Even so, we cannot explain conversion and regeneration and the new birth, and all that; but we do know this, that Jesus Christ says, "Believe," and we believe. By our own power? No. But as we will to believe (and he gives us that will) there comes a power to do according to his good pleasure.

I look around me, wondering where is the man or woman with the withered hand. To such I would say in my Master's name, "Stretch out that hand of thine." It is an auspicious moment. A great thing shall be done unto thee. Believe thou now. Thou hast said aforetime, "I never can believe." Now trust Jesus.

> *Venture on him, venture wholly;*
> *Let no other trust intrude,*
> *None but Jesus*
> *Can do helpless sinners good.*

Our Lord Jesus never casts away a sinner who trusts in him. There is this blessed thing about my Master—if you can get a crumb from under his table he will not take it from you, for he never casts out those that come. He never says, "Come here, you sir, you have no right to hope in my grace." Remember the woman in the press that dared not come to Christ before his face, but who came behind him, and touched the hem of his garment. She stole the cure from him, as it were, willy-nilly he, and what did he say? "Come here, my woman, come here, what have you been at? What right had you to touch my garment, and to steal a cure like this? A curse shall come upon thee." Did he speak thus in indignation? Not at all! He bade her come, and she told him all the truth, and he said, "Daughter, be of good cheer. Thy faith hath made thee whole." Get

at him, soul! Behind or before, push for a touch of him!
Make a dash at him. If there be a crowd of devils between you
and Christ, plough your way through them by resolute faith.
Though you be the most unworthy wretch that ever trusted
him, trust him now, that it may be told in heaven that there is a
bigger sinner saved to-day than ever was saved before. Such
a salvation will make Christ more glorious than he ever was;
and if yours is a worse case than he ever touched with his
healing hand to this day, well then, when he has touched and
healed you, as he will, there will be more praise to him in heaven
than he ever had before.

The last thing to consider is THE RESULT OF THIS STRETCHING
OUT OF THE MAN'S HAND IN OBEDIENCE TO THE COMMAND. He
was healed, and it was also *immediate*. The man had not to
stand there a long time, but his hand was straightway healed:
and yet the cure was *perfect*, for his hand was whole like unto
the other, just as useful as his left hand had been, with all the
extra dexterity which naturally belongs to the right. You
may depend upon it, that it was *permanently* healed; for,
though I have heard it said that saved souls fall from grace and
perish, I never believed it, for I have never read of any of the
cases which our Lord cured that they became bad again. I
never heard of a withered hand that was healed and was
paralyzed a second time. Nor will it ever be. My Master's
cures last for ever.

I remember seeing in the shop windows some years ago, that
there was to be had within a "momentary cure" for the
toothache. I noticed after a few months that the proprietor
of that valuable medicine, whatever it was, had discovered that
nobody wanted a *momentary* cure, and so the word "momentary" was changed for the word "*instantaneous*," which was a
great improvement. I am afraid that some people's salvation
is a momentary salvation. They get a sort of grace, and they
lose it again. They get peace, and by-and-by it is gone. What
is wanted is permanence, and there is always permanence in the
work of Christ. "The gifts and calling of God are without
repentance," and his healing is never revoked. O soul, dost
thou see, then, what is to be had at this moment of Jesus?
Healing for life; deliverance from the withering power of sin
through life and through eternity. This is to be had by cheerful

obedience to the matchless command: "Stretch forth thine hand," or, in other words, "Trust, trust, trust."

Only this week I was talking with one who said he could not trust Christ, and I said, "But, my dear friend, we cannot have that. Could you trust *me*?" Yes, he could trust me. "Why can you trust me and not trust the Lord Jesus? I will put it the other way. If you said to me I cannot trust you, what would that imply?" "Why," said he, "it would mean, of course, that you were a very bad fellow, if I could not trust you." "Ah," I said, "that is exactly what you insinuate when you say, I cannot trust Jesus; for he that believeth not hath made him a liar. Do you mean to say that God is a liar?" The person to whom I spoke drew back with horror from that consequence, and said, "No, sir, I am sure that God is true." Very well, then, you can certainly trust one who is true. There can be no difficulty in that; to trust and rest upon one whom you cannot doubt must follow as a matter of course upon your good opinion of him. Your belief that he is true is a sort of faith. Throw yourself upon him now. If the Son shall make you free, you shall be free indeed; and free you shall be at once if now you trust him.

XVII

"WHERE ARE THE NINE?"

"And one of them, when he saw that he was healed, turned back, and with a loud voice glorified God, and fell down on his face at his feet, giving him thanks: and he was a Samaritan. And Jesus answering said, Were there not ten cleansed? but where are the nine? There are not found that returned to give glory to God, save this stranger. And he said unto him, Arise, go thy way: thy faith hath made thee whole."—Luke 17: 15–19.

YOU have often heard the leprosy described: it was a very horrible disease, I should think the worst that flesh is heir to. We ought to be much more grateful than we are that this fell disease is scarcely known in our favoured country. You have also heard what an instructive symbol it is in human flesh of what sin is in the human soul, how it pollutes, how it destroys. I need not go into that sad subject. But here was a sight for the Saviour—ten men that were lepers! A mass of sorrow indeed! What sights our Lord still sees every day in this sin-defiled world! Not ten men that are sinners, nor even ten millions merely, are to be found all the world over, but on this earth there are a thousand millions of men diseased in soul. It is a miracle of condescension that the Son of God should set foot in such a lazarhouse as this.

Yet observe the triumphant grace of our Lord Jesus to the ten men that were lepers. It would make a man's fortune, it would crown a man with lifelong fame, to heal one leper: but our Lord healed ten lepers at once. So full a fountain of grace is he, so freely doth he dispense his favour, that the ten are bidden to go and show themselves to the priests because they are healed, and on the way to the priests they find it is so. None of us can imagine the joy they felt when they perceived that they were healed. Oh, it must have been a sort of new birth to them to find their flesh made fresh as that of a little child! It would not have been wonderful if the whole ten had hurried back, and fallen at Jesus' feet, and lifted up their voices in a tenfold psalm. The sad thing about it is that nine of them, though they were healed, went on their way to the priests in the coolest possible manner: we never hear of their return; they drop out of the story altogether. They have obtained a blessing, they go their way, and there is an end of them.

Only one of them, a Samaritan, returned to express his thanks. Misery has strange bedfellows; and so the nine lepers of the seed of Israel consorted with an outcast Samaritan: and he, strange to tell it, was the only one, who, seized by a sudden impulse of gratitude, made his way to his Benefactor, fell down at his feet, and began to glorify God.

If you search the world around, among all choice spices you shall scarcely meet with the frankincense of gratitude. It ought to be as common as the dew-drops that hang upon the hedges in the morning; but, alas, the world is dry of thankfulness to God! Gratitude to Christ was scarce enough in his own day. I had almost said it was ten to one that nobody would praise him; but I must correct myself a little: it was nine to one. One day in seven is for the Lord's worship; but not one man in ten is devoted to his praise. Our subject is *thankfulness to the Lord Jesus Christ*.

I begin with the point that I have already touched upon, namely, THE SINGULARITY OF THANKFULNESS.

Here note: *there are more who receive benefits than ever give praise for them*. Nine persons healed, one person glorifying God; nine persons healed *of leprosy*, mark you, and only one person kneeling down at Jesus' feet, and thanking him for it! If for this surpassing benefit, which might have made the dumb to sing, men only thank the Lord in the proportion of one to nine, what shall I say of what we call God's common mercies—only common because he is so liberal with them, for each of them is inestimably valuable? Life, health, eyesight, hearing, domestic love, the continuance of friends—I cannot attempt a catalogue of benefits that we receive every day; and yet is there one man in nine that praises God for these! A cold "Thank God!" is all that is given. Others of us do praise him for these benefits, but what poor praises! Dr. Watt's hymn is sadly true,

> *Hosannas languish on our tongues,*
> *And our devotion dies.*

We do not praise the Lord fitly, proportionately, intensely. We receive a continent of mercies, and only return an island of praise. He gives us blessings new every morning, and fresh every evening, great is his faithfulness; and yet we let the years roll round, and seldom observe a day of praise. Sad is it to see God all goodness, and man all ingratitude! The tribe who receive benefits may say, "My name is legion"; but those who praise God are so few that a child may write them.

But there is something more remarkable than this: *the number of those who pray is greater than the number of those who praise*. For these ten men that were lepers all prayed. Poor and feeble as their voices had become through disease, yet they lifted them up in prayer, and united in crying: " Jesus, Master, have mercy on us!" They all joined in the Litany, "Lord, have mercy upon us! Christ, have mercy upon us!" But when they came to the Te Deum, magnifying and praising God, only one of them took up the note. One would have thought that all who prayed would praise, but it is not so. Cases have been where a whole ship's crew in time of storm has prayed, and yet none of that crew have sung the praise of God when the storm has become a calm. Multitudes of our fellow-citizens pray when they are sick, and near to dying; but when they grow better, their praises grow sick unto death. The angel of mercy, listening at their door, has heard no canticle of love, no song of thankfulness. Alas, it is too sadly true that more pray than praise!

I put it in another shape to you who are God's people—*most of us pray more than we praise*. You pray little enough, I fear; but praise, where is that? At our family altars we always pray, but seldom praise. In our closets we constantly pray, but do we *frequently* praise? Prayer is not so heavenly an exercise as praise; prayer is for time, but praise is for eternity. Praise therefore deserves the first and highest place; does it not? Let us commence the employment which occupies the celestials. Prayer is for a beggar; but methinks he is a poor beggar who does not also give praise when he receives an alms. Praise ought to follow naturally upon the heels of prayer, even when it does not, by divine grace, go before it. If you are afflicted, if you lose money, if you fall into poverty, if your child is ill, if chastisement visits you in any form, you begin to pray, and I do not blame you for it; but should it be all praying and no praising? Should our life have so much salt, and so little sweet in it? Should we get for ourselves so often a draught from the rock of blessing, and so seldom pour out a drink-offering unto the Lord Most High? Come, let us chide ourselves as we acknowledge that we offer so much more prayer than praise!

On the same head, let me remark that *more obey ritual than ever praise Christ*. When Jesus said, "Go shew yourselves to the priests," off they went, all ten of them; not one stopped behind. Yet only one came back to behold a personal Saviour, and to praise his name. So to-day—you will go to Church, you will go to Chapel, you will read a book, you will perform an outward religious action: but oh, how little praising God, how little lying at his feet, and feeling that we could sing our souls away for gratitude to him who hath done such great things for us! External religious exercises are easy enough, and common enough; but the internal matter, the drawing out of the heart in thankful love, how scarce a thing it is! Nine obey ritual where only one praises the Lord.

Once more, to come yet closer home, *there are more that believe than there are that praise:* for these ten men did believe, but only one praised the Lord Jesus. Their faith was about the leprosy; and according to their faith, so it was unto them. This faith, though it only concerned their leprosy, was yet a very wonderful faith. It was remarkable that they should believe the Lord Jesus though he did not even say, "Be healed," nor speak a word to them to that effect, but simply said, "Go shew yourselves to the priests." With parched skins, and death burning its way into their hearts, they went bravely off in confidence that Jesus must mean to bless them. It was admirable faith; and yet none of the nine who thus believed ever came back to praise Christ for the mercy received. I am afraid that there is much of faith, better faith than theirs, which concerns spiritual things, which has yet to flower into practical gratitude. Perhaps it blooms late in the year, like the chrysanthemum; but certainly it has not flowered in spring-time, like the primrose and the daffodil. It is a faith which bears few blossoms of praise. I chide myself sometimes that I have wrestled with God in prayer, like Elias upon Carmel, but I have not magnified the name of the Lord, like Mary of Nazareth. We do not laud our Lord in proportion to the benefits received. God's treasury would overflow if the revenue of thanks were more honestly paid. There would be no need to plead for missions, and stir up God's people to self-denial, if there were praise at all proportionate even to our faith. We believe for heaven and eternity, and yet do not magnify the Lord as we should for earth and time. It is real faith, I trust—it is not for me to judge it, but it is faulty in result. Faith was only real in these lepers so far as their leprosy was concerned; they did not believe in our Lord's divinity, or believe for eternal life. So also among ourselves, there are men who get benefits from Christ, who even hope that they are saved, but they do not praise him. Their lives are spent in examining their own skins to see whether their leprosy is gone. Their religious life reveals itself in a constant searching of themselves to see if they are really healed. This is a poor way of spending one's energies. This man knew that he was healed, he had full assurance upon that point; and the next impulse of his spirit was to hie him back to where *he* stood who had been his glorious Physician, to fall at *his* feet, and praise *him* with a loud voice, glorifying God. Oh, that all my timorous, doubting hearers may do the same!

I have said enough, I think, upon the scantiness of thanksgiving. Let us go over those points again. More receive benefits than praise God for them; more pray than praise; more obey ritual than praise God with the heart; and more believe, and receive benefits through faith, than rightly praise the Giver of those benefits.

Briefly let us note THE CHARACTERISTICS OF TRUE THANKFULNESS. This man's simple act may show the character of praise. It does not take the same shape in everybody. Love to Christ, like living flowers, wears many forms; only artificial flowers are all alike. Living praise is marked by *individuality*. This man was one of ten when he was a leper; he was all alone when he returned to praise God. You can sin in company, you can go to hell in company; but when you obtain salvation, you will come to Jesus all alone; and when you are saved, though you will delight to praise God with others if they will join with you, yet if they will not do so, you will delight to sing a solo of gratitude. This man quits the company of the other nine, and comes to Jesus. If Christ has saved you, and your heart is right, you will say, "I *must* praise him; I *must* love him." You will not be kept back by the chilly state of nine out of ten of your old companions, nor by the worldliness of your family, nor by the coldness of the Church. Your personal love to Jesus will make you speak even if heaven, and earth, and sea are all wrapt in silence.

You have a heart burning with adoring love, and you feel as if it were the only heart under heaven that had love to Christ in it; and therefore you must feed the heavenly flame. You must indulge its desires, you must express its longings; the fire is in your bones, and must have vent. Since there is an individuality about true praise, come, brothers in Christ, let us praise God each one in his own way!

> Oh, may the sweet, the blissful theme,
>   Fill every heart and tongue,
> Till strangers love thy charming name,
>   And join the sacred song!

The next characteristic of this man's thankfulness was *promptness*. He was back to Christ almost immediately; for I cannot suppose the Saviour lingered at the village-gate for hours that day. He was too busy to be long on one spot: the Master went about doing good. The man was back soon; and when you are saved, the quicker you can express your gratitude the better. Second thoughts are best, but this is not the case when the heart is full of love to Christ. Carry out your first thoughts; do not stop for the second, unless indeed your heart is so on flame with heavenly devotion that second ones consume the first. Go at once, and praise the Saviour. What grand designs some of you have formed of future service for God! What small results have followed! Ah, it is better to lay one brick to-day than to propose to build a palace next year! Magnify your Lord in the present for present salvation. Why should his mercies lie in quarantine? Why should your praises be like aloes, which take a century to flower? Why should praise be kept waiting at the door even for a night? The manna came fresh in the morning; so let your praises rise betimes. He praises twice who praises at once; but he who does not praise at once praises never.

The next quality of this man's praise was *spirituality*. We perceive this in the fact that he paused on his way to the priests. It was his duty to go to the priests: he had received a command to do so; but there is a proportion in all things, and some duties are greater than others. He thought to himself: I was ordered to go to the priests; but I am healed, and this new circumstance affects the order of my duties: the first thing I ought to do is to go back, and bear witness to the people, glorifying God in the midst of them all, and falling down at Christ's feet. It is well to observe the holy law of proportion. Carnal minds take the ritualistic duty first; that which is external outweighs with them that which is spiritual. But love soon perceives that the substance is more precious than the shadow, and that to bow at the feet of the great High Priest must be a greater duty than to go before the lesser priests. So the healed leper went first to Jesus. In him the spiritual overrode the ceremonial. He felt that his main duty was in person to adore the divine Person who had delivered him from his fell disease. Let us go first to Jesus. Let us in spirit bow before HIM. Ah, yes! Come to our services, join in our regular worship: but if you love the Lord, you will want something besides this: you will pine to get to Jesus himself, and tell him how you love him. You will long to do something for him by yourself, by which you can show forth the gratitude of your heart to the Christ of God.

True thankfulness also manifests itself in *intensity*. Intensity is perceptible in this case: he turned back, and with a loud voice glorified God. He could have praised, could he not, in a quieter way? Yes, but when you are just cured of leprosy, and your once feeble voice is restored to you, you cannot whisper out your praises. You know it would be impossible to be coolly proper when you are newly saved! This man with a loud voice glorified God; and you, too, feel forced to cry—

> *Fain would I sound it out so loud*
> *That earth and heaven should hear*.

Some of our converts are very wild at times, they grow extravagant. Do not blame them. Why not indulge them? It will not hurt *you*. We are all of us so very proper and orderly that we can afford to have an extravagant one among us now and then.

Oh, that God would send more of that sort to wake the Church up, that we, also, might all begin to praise God with heart and voice, with soul and substance, with might and main! Hallelujah! My own heart feels the glow.

In true thankfulness, next, there is *humility*. This man fell down at Jesus' feet: he did not feel perfectly in his place until he was lying there. "I am nobody, Lord," he seemed to say, and therefore he fell on his face. But the place for his prostration was "at his feet." I would rather be nobody at Christ's feet than everybody anywhere else! There is no place so honourable as down at the feet of Jesus. Ah, to lie there always, and just love him wholly, and let self die out! Oh, to have Christ standing over you as the one figure overshadowing your life henceforth and for ever! True thankfulness lies low before the Lord.

Added to this there was *worship*. He fell down at Jesus' feet, glorifying God, and giving thanks unto him. Let us worship our Saviour. Let others think as they like about Jesus, but we will put our finger into the print of the nails, and say, "My Lord and my God!" If there be a God, he is God in Christ Jesus to us. We shall never cease to adore him who has proved his Godhead by delivering us from the leprosy of sin. All worship be to his supreme majesty!

One thing more about this man I want to notice as to his thankfulness, and that is, *his silence as to censuring others*. When the Saviour said, "Where are the nine?" I notice that *this man did not reply*. The Master said, "Where are the nine? There are not found that returned to give glory to God, save this stranger." But the adoring stranger did not stand up, and say, "O Lord, they are all gone off to the priests: I am astonished at them that they did not return to praise thee!" We have enough to do to mind our own business, when we feel the grace of God in our own hearts! If I can only get through my service of praise, I shall have no mind to accuse any of you who are ungrateful. The Master says: "Where are the nine?" but the poor healed man at his feet has no word to say against those cruel nine; he is too much occupied with his personal adoration.

Let us consider now THE BLESSEDNESS OF THANKFULNESS. This man was more blessed by far than the nine. They were healed, but they were not blessed as he was. There is a great blessedness in thankfulness.

First, *because it is right*. Should not Christ be praised? This man did what he could: and there is always an ease of conscience, and a rest of spirit, when you feel that you are doing all you can in a right cause, even though you fall far short of your own desire. At this moment magnify the Lord.

> *Meet and right it is to sing,*
> *In every time and place,*
> *Glory to our heavenly King,*
> *The God of truth and grace.*
> *Join we then with sweet accord,*
> *All in one thanksgiving join!*
> *Holy, holy, holy Lord,*
> *Eternal praise be thine.*

Next, there is this blessing in thankfulness, that *it is a manifestation of personal love*. I love the doctrines of grace, I love the Church of God, I love the Sabbath, I love the ordinances; but I love Jesus most. My heart never rests until I can glorify God personally, and give thanks unto the Christ personally. The indulgence of personal love to Christ is one of the sweetest things out of heaven; and you cannot indulge that personal love so well as by personal thankfulness both of heart and mouth, and act and deed.

There is another blessedness about thankfulness: *it has clear views*. The thankful eye sees far and deep. The man healed of leprosy, before he went on glorifying God, gave thanks to Jesus. If he had thanked Jesus and stopped there, I should have said that his eyes were not well open; but when he saw God in Christ, and therefore glorified God for what Christ had done, he showed a deep insight into spiritual truth. He had begun to discover the mysteries of the divine and human Person of the blessed Lord. We learn much by prayer. Did not Luther say, "To have prayed well is to have studied well"? I venture to add a rider to what Luther has so ably said: To have praised well is to have studied better. Praise is a great instructor. Prayer and praise are the oars by which a man may row his boat into the deep waters of the knowledge of Christ.

The next blessedness about praise is that *it is acceptable to*

Christ. The Lord Jesus was evidently pleased; he was grieved to think the other nine should not come back, but he was charmed with this one man that he did return. The question, "Where are the nine?" bears within it a commendation of the one. Whatever pleases Christ should be carefully cultivated by us. If praise be pleasant to him, let us continually magnify his name. Prayer is the straw of the wheat, but praise is the ear. Jesus loves to see the blade grow up, but he loves better to pluck the golden ears when the harvest of praise is ripe.

Next, notice, that the blessedness of thankfulness is that *it receives the largest blessing*, for the Saviour said to this man what he had not said to the others, "Thy faith hath made thee whole." If you would live the higher life, be much in praising God. Some of you are in the lowest state as yet, as this man was, for he was a Samaritan: but by praising God he rose to be a songster rather than a stranger. How often have I noticed how the greatest sinner becomes the greatest praiser! Those that were farthest off from Christ, and hope, and purity, when they become saved, feel that they owe the most, and therefore they love the best. May it be the ambition of every one of us, even if we be not originally among the vilest of the vile, yet to feel that we owe Jesus most; and therefore we will praise him most: thus shall we receive the richest blessedness from his hands!

I have done when I have said three things. Let us learn from all this to *put praise in a high place*. Let us hold praise-meetings. Let us think it as great a sin to neglect praise as to restrain prayer.

Next, *let us pay our praise to Christ himself*. Whether we go to the priests or not, let us go to *him*. Let us praise him personally and vehemently. Personal praise to a personal Saviour must be our life's object.

Lastly, if we work for Jesus, and we see converts, and they do not turn out as we expected, do not let us be cast down about it. *If others do not praise our Lord, let us be sorrowful, but let us not be disappointed.* The Saviour had to say, "Where are the nine?" Ten lepers were healed, but only one praised him. We have many converts who do not join the Church; we have numbers of persons converted who do not come forward to baptism, or to the Lord's Supper. Numbers get a blessing, but do not feel love enough to own it. Those of us who are soul-winners are robbed of our wages by the cowardly spirits who hide their faith. I thank God of late we have had many avowing their conversion; but if the other nine would come, we should need nine Tabernacles. Alas for the many who have gone back after professing their faith! Where are the nine?

So you that hold cottage meetings, you that go round with tracts, you are doing more good than you will ever hear of. You do not know where the nine are, but even if you should only bless one out of ten, you will have cause to thank God.

"Oh," says one, "I have had so little success; I have had only one soul saved!" That is more than you deserve. If I were to fish for a week, and only catch one fish, I should be sorry; but if that happened to be a sturgeon, a royal fish, I should feel that the quality made up for lack of quantity. When you win a soul it is a great prize. One soul brought to Christ—can you estimate its value? If one be saved, you should be grateful to your Lord, and persevere. Though you wish for more conversions yet, you will not despond so long as even a few are saved; and, above all, you will not be angry if some of them do not thank you personally, nor join in Church fellowship with you. Ingratitude is common towards soul-winners. How often a minister has brought sinners to Christ, and fed the flock in his early days! but when the old man grows feeble they want to get rid of him, and try a new broom which will sweep cleaner. "Poor old gentleman, he is quite out of date!" they say, and so they get rid of him, as gipsies turn an old horse out on the common to feed or starve, they care not which. If anybody expects gratitude, I would remind them of the benediction, "Blessed are they that expect nothing, for they will not be disappointed." Even our Master did not get praise from the nine: therefore do not wonder if you bless others, and others do not bless you. Oh, that some poor soul would come to Christ now, some leper to be healed of sin-sickness! If he does find healing, let him come out, and with a loud voice magnify the Lord who has dealt so graciously with him.

XVIII

THE DEVIL'S LAST THROW

"And as he was yet a coming, the devil threw him down, and tare him."—Luke 9: 42.

OUR Lord Jesus Christ taught the people much by his words, but he taught them even more by his actions. He was always preaching, his whole life was a heavenly discourse on divine truth; and the miracles which he wrought were not only the proofs of his deity, but the illustrations of his teaching. His wonders of mercy were, in fact, acted sermons, truths embodied, pictorial illustrations appealing to the eye, and thus setting forth Gospel teaching quite ás clearly as vocal speech could have done. What he did of old to the bodies of men should be received as a prophecy of what he is to-day prepared to do to the souls of men. I am sure I shall not be straining the meaning of the text, or the intention of the miracle, if, instead of preaching about the youth possessed of the devil, and dwelling only upon that wonderful display of power, I endeavour to show that there are parallel cases at this time in the world of mind.

I suppose that we have never seen Satanic possession, although I am not quite sure about it; for some men exhibit symptoms which are very like it. Certainly, in our Saviour's day it was very common for devils to take possession of men and torment them greatly. It would seem that Satan was let loose while Christ was here below that the serpent might come into personal conflict with the appointed seed of the woman, that the two champions might stand foot to foot in solemn duel, and that the Lord Jesus might win a glorious victory over him. Since his defeat by our Lord, and by his apostles, it would seem that Satan's power over human bodies has been greatly limited; but we have still among us the same thing in another and worse shape, namely, the power of sin over men's minds.

That this is akin to the power of the devil over the body is clear from holy Scripture. "The God of this world hath blinded the eyes of them that believe not." "The spirit that now worketh in the children of disobedience," says the apostle Paul. Satan works in all ungodly men, as a smith at his forge; do you wonder that they sometimes curse and swear? I know passionate men in whom the fiercest of devils appear to rave and rage; and I could point out others whose love of lying betrays the presence of the father of lies. One blasphemes and uses such filthy language that we are sure his tongue is set on fire of hell, even if the prince of devils is not ruling it. Whether this is the devil, or whether it is altogether the man himself, I am not going to argue; but the drink-devil, whose name is legion, is certainly among us to this day, and we hear persons tell us that they are anxious to escape from its power, and yet they return to it, rushing to intoxication as the swine rushed into the sea when the demons had entered into them.

Need I mention another form of this evil in the shape of unchastity? How many a man there is—alas, it is true of women too!—struggling against a fierce passion, and yet that passion conquers them; the unclean desire comes upon them like a hurricane bearing all before it, and they yield to it as the sere leaf yields to the blast. Nay more, they rush into a sin which they themselves condemn, of which already they have tasted the bitter fruit: they could not be more eager for it if it were the purest of all enjoyments. As the moth dashes again into the candle which has burned its wings, so do men hurry into the vice which has filled them with misery. Men practise differing sins, but their sins all manifest the same evil power. Unless Christ has set us free we are all in some shape or other under the dominion of the prince of darkness, the master of the forces of evil.

This poor young man was brought into a most horrible condition through the influence of a Satanic spirit. He was a lunatic: reason had been dethroned. He was an epileptic, so that if left alone he would fall into the fire or into the water. You have yourself seen persons in fits of epilepsy, and you know how dreadful would be their danger if they were taken in a fit in the middle of a street, or by the side of a river. In this youth's case the epilepsy was only the means by which the

demon exercised his power, and this made his condition seven-
fold worse than if it had been simply a disease. This afflicted
one had become deaf and dumb besides, and very violent, so
that he was capable of doing a great deal of mischief. In all
the Holy Land there was only one who could do anything for
him! There was one name by which he could be cured, and only
one. It was the name of Jesus.

The Lord Jesus had disciples who had wrought miracles in
his name, but they were baffled by this extraordinary case.
They tried what they could do, but they were utterly defeated,
and gave up the task in despair; and now there remained only
one Person beneath the canopy of heaven that could touch this
child's case and drive out the devil. Only one person could now
answer the poor father's prayers: every other hope was dead.
That is just the state in which we are: there is but one name
under heaven whereby we must be saved. Many are the pre-
tended salvations, but only one is real.

> *There is a name high over all,*
> *In hell, and earth, and sky.*
> *Angels and men before it fall,*
> *And devils fear and fly.*

That one name is the name of Jesus, the Son of God, to whom
all power is given, and He can deliver any man from the
dominion of evil, whatever form it may have assumed, and
however long established the dominion may be. Nothing else
can rescue a man from the thraldom of his sin but the word of
Jesus. When the word of power is spoken from his divine
mouth all things obey; but none out of the ten thousand voices
of earth can deliver us from evil. We are shut up to heaven's
unique remedy: God grant that, being so shut up, we may
avail ourselves of it.

This poor lad, although nobody could cure him save Jesus,
had a father that loved him, and nobody could tell the sorrow
of that father's heart because of his poor son. The father had a
sharp struggle to get his son to the disciples, for epileptic
persons who are also insane are hard to manage. Alas, the Lord
Jesus Christ was away! The parent's heart was heavy when he
found that the great Healer to whom he looked was for a while
absent. But when Jesus came down from the mountain-top

the poor demoniac had this one great advantage—that he had friends to aid in bringing him to Christ. Perhaps it is a wife who cannot bear that her husband should remain out of Christ, or a husband who pines till his spouse is turned unto the Lord, and in either case it is a great help. How often a mother bears a secret anguish in her breast for her unconverted sons and daughters! I have known a sister in the family to be the only one who knew the Lord, and she has pleaded with the Lord day and night, entreating him to bless the whole of her household. Frequently a servant in the house becomes its best helper, or it may be a neighbour who has seen the ungodly conduct of his neighbours never ceases to pray for them. When some few get together to bring a specially hard case before Jesus, it is blessed work: for desperate cases grow hopeful under the influence of prayer.

My first point shall be that OUR HOPES ARE ALL AWAKENED. Here is a poor youth, but bad as he is, terribly possessed as he is, he is coming to Christ! Prayer has been offered for him by his father, and Jesus is near. All looks well! We will take the case of a sinner who is in a similar condition: prayer has been offered for him, and that prayer has, in some measure, been heard. We have in this congregation, I trust, some who are coming to Christ, and I am right glad of it. Coming to Christ is not the best possible condition, for the best condition is to have already come to him. For a hungry man to be coming to a dinner is not enough: he must actually reach the table and eat. For a sick man to be coming to an eminent physician is hopeful, but it is not enough; he must get to that physician, take his medicine, and be restored. That is the point. To be coming to Christ is not enough: you must actually come to him, and really receive him; for to such only does he give power to become the sons of God.

This poor child was coming, and so are some here: that is to say, they have begun to hear the Gospel with attention. They did not aforetime go anywhere on the Sabbath. You might see the man any time before one o'clock in his shirt-sleeves. Half this city of London is in that condition every Sunday morning, because they look upon the day as simply their own day, and not the Lord's day. They have very short memories, and do not "remember the sabbath-day to keep it holy:"

they forget all about its being the Lord's day, and do not reverence it. This is shameful conduct towards God. If a man on the road were to meet with a poor beggar, and give him six out of seven shillings which he had with him, the beggar would be a wicked wretch if he afterwards knocked the man down and stole the other shilling. Yet there are multitudes of people to whom God gives six days out of seven, and nothing will satisfy them but they must have the seventh all to themselves, and rob God of it. The man I refer to has begun to read the Word of God in an earnest way. He thought at one time that it was about the dullest book in the world. He even dared to turn it into a jest, and all because he never read it; for those who deny the inspiration of Scripture are almost always people who have never read it for themselves. It is a book which carries conviction within itself to candid minds when they carefully peruse it. Assuredly this man is coming to Christ, for he searches the Scriptures.

I feel sure he is coming to Christ, for he has begun to mend in many respects. He has dropped his frequent attendance at his usual place of worship, namely, the public-house. He keeps more at home, and is therefore sober. Plenty of people in London need no bell to fetch them into the temples of their gods. We see in some of our Churches and Chapels persons going in twenty minutes or half-an-hour after service begins; but look at the temples of Bacchus at one o'clock, and at six in the evening, and see how punctual are his votaries! Drink seems to be the water of life to them, poor creatures that they are! But now our friend of whom we are so hopeful is not seen waiting at the posts of the doors—the "Blue Posts," I mean. Thank God, he is looking to another fountain for comfort.

Note also that he has dropped his blasphemy and his unchastity. He is a purer man in mouth and body than he used to be. He is coming to Christ. But, as I said, coming is not enough. The thing is really to reach the Lord Jesus and to be healed by him. I pray you, do not rest short of this.

Still, this is all hopeful, very hopeful. The man is a hearer; he is also a reader of the Scriptures; he has begun to mend a bit; and now he is a thinker, too, and begins to be a little careful about his soul. While he is at his labour, you can see that there is something working in his brain, though once it was filled with vanity and wickedness. He has a weight, too, at his heart, a burden on his mind; he is evidently in earnest; so far as he knows the teaching of Scripture he is deeply affected by it. He has learned that he will not cease to exist when he dies; but that he will continue to be when yonder sun becomes black as a burnt-out coal. He knows that there will be a day of judgment, when throngs upon throngs, yea, all the dead, shall stand before the judgment-seat of Christ to give an account of the things which they have done in the body; he thinks this over, and he is alarmed. He chews the cud upon divine truth, and finds time for solitary meditation. That man is coming to Christ, for there is no better evidence of the face being set towards Christ and heaven than a thoughtful state of mind.

And I have heard that the other night he began to pray. If so, I know that he is coming to Christ, for prayer is a sure token. He has not yet cast himself fully at the feet of Jesus, but he cries, "Lord, save me," and I am as glad as the birds on a spring morning. The angels are watching; they are leaning from the battlements of heaven to see whether it will end rightly, and you and I are very hopeful, especially those of us who have been praying for this man; for since we see that there is some change in him, and he begins to think and pray, we look for his salvation, as men look for flowers when April showers are falling.

And now I will read the text again,—"As he was yet a coming, the devil threw him down, and tare him." By this OUR FEARS ARE AROUSED. What a sight it must have been! Here is the poor father bringing his lunatic son, and friends are helping him; they are getting him near the Saviour, and he is just coming to him who can cure him, when, on a sudden, he is taken in a fearful fit, worse than he had ever suffered before. He is cast down, thrown about, dashed to and fro; he wallows on the ground: he seems to be flung up and down as by an unseen hand, we fear that he will be torn to pieces. See! he falls down like a dead man, and there he lies. As the crowd gathers around him, people cry, "He is dead." Does it not seem a dreadful thing that when hope was at its brightest all should be dashed aside?

I have observed this thing hundreds of times. I have seen men, just when they were beginning to hear and beginning to

think, taken on a sudden with such violence of sin, and so fearfully carried away by it, that if I had not seen the same thing
before I should have despaired of them; but, having often seen
it, I know what it means, and I am not so dismayed as a raw
observer might be; though I must confess that it half breaks
my heart when it happens to some hopeful convert whom I
hoped to receive into the Church, and to rejoice over. We mourn
when we hear that the man who was somewhat impressed has
become worse than aforetime, and has gone back to the very
vice from which we had rescued him. The case runs on the
same lines as our text—"As he was a coming, the devil threw
him down, and tare him."

How does the devil do this? Well, we have seen it done in this
way: When the man had almost believed in Christ, but not
quite, Satan seemed to multiply his temptations around him,
and to bring his whole force to bear upon him. There is a
wicked man in the shop, and the devil says to him, "Your
mate is beginning to be serious: ridicule him. Tempt him all
you can. Treat him to strong drink. Get him away to the
theatre, the music-hall, or the brothel." It is wonderful how
the ungodly will lay all kinds of traps for one who is escaping
from his sins. They are fearfully set on keeping him from Christ.
This is a free country, is it not? A wonderfully free country
when a Christian man in the workshop has to run the gauntlet
for his very life to this day. The devil finds willing servants,
and they worry the poor awakened one; is there any wonder
that, as he has not yet found Christ and is not yet saved, he
should for the time be carried away by these assaults, and feel
as if he could not go further in the right road?

I have known in addition to all this that Satan has stirred
up the anxious one's bad passions. Passions that lay asleep
have suddenly been aroused. Moreover, the man has become
thoughtful, and from that very fact doubts which he never
knew before have come upon him. He begins to mend, and now
he finds a difficulty in getting his needle through where the rent
was made. He finds that tearing is easier work than mending,
and that running into sin is a much more easy thing than rising
out of the black ditch into which he has fallen. So now, the
disease which before had been concealed in more hidden and
vital parts, seems to be thrown out upon the surface, and the

sight is sickening. This, however, is not always a bad sign. Doctors rather prefer it to an inward festering. I have seen a man almost converted—well-nigh a believer in Christ, on a sudden become more obstinate in his opposition to the Gospel than ever he was before. A man that was quiet and harmless and inoffensive before has, under the influence of Satan, just when we hoped the best things of him, turned round in a rage against the people who sought to do him good, and he has spoken opprobriously of the Gospel which a little while before he seemed anxious to understand. Sometimes such persons act as if they were reckless and profane; just as boys, when they go through a graveyard, whistle to keep their courage up. Have you not discovered that a man is never so violent against a thing as when he is unwillingly convinced of the truth of it? He has to try and demonstrate to himself that he does not believe it by being very loud in his declarations: a secret something in his soul makes him believe, and he is mad because he cannot resist the inward conviction.

I will describe the usual way in which the devil throws men down and tears them. You need not listen to this unless you like, because it does not relate to all of you; but it is true of a sufficient number to render it needful for me to speak of it. It is a very curious thing that if there is a poor soul in London that is well-nigh insane through despair of heart he wants to talk to me. I am often sore burdened by the attempt to sympathize with the distracted. I do not know why they should be attracted to me, but they come to tell me of their evil state of mind— people who have never seen me before. This fact gives me a wide field of actual practice and careful observation. I frequently meet with persons who are tempted with blasphemous thoughts. They have not yet laid hold on Christ, but they are trying to do so; and at this stage of their experience most horrible thoughts pass through their minds. They cannot prevent it: they hate the thoughts, and yet they come, till they are ready to lose their reason.

I will tell you what happened to me. I was engaged in prayer alone in a quiet place one day when I had just found the Saviour, and while I was in prayer a most horrible stream of blasphemies came into my mind, till I clapped my hand to my mouth for fear that I should utter any one of them. I was so brought up that I do not remember ever hearing a man swear while I was a child; yet at that moment I seemed to know all the swearing and blasphemy that ever was in hell itself; and I wondered at myself. I could not understand whence this foul stream proceeded. I wrote to my venerable grandfather who was for sixty years a minister of the Gospel, and he said to me,—"Do not trouble about it. These are no thoughts of yours; they are injected into your mind by Satan. The thoughts of men follow one another like the links of a chain, one link draws on another; but when a man is in prayer the next natural thought to prayer is not blasphemy; it is not, therefore, a natural succession of our own thoughts. An evil spirit casts those thoughts into the mind." Thus should we treat these diabolical thoughts. Whip them by hearty penitence, and send them off to where they came from, far down in the deeps. Thoughts of this sort, seeing you loathe them, are none of yours. Perhaps when you know this, it may help to break the chain; for the devil may not think it worth his while to worry you in this way any more, when he cannot by this means lead you to despair: he seldom wastes his time in spreading nets when the birds can see them. Therefore, tell Satan to begone, for you can see him, and you are not going to let him deceive you.

When this does not answer, I have known Satan to throw the coming sinner down and tear him in another way. "There," says he, "did you not hear the preacher speaking about election? You are not one of the elect." "Perhaps I am not," says one. Perhaps you are, say I, and I think that whether you are one of the elect or not, you had better come, on the ground that Jesus says—"Him that cometh to me I will in no wise cast out." If you come, he will not cast you out, and then you will find that you are one of the elect. You need not trouble about predestination: you will see *that* clearly enough very soon. If any man had a ticket to go to a meeting, and he said, "I do not know whether I am ordained to get in or not," I should think it very probable that he was not ordained to enter if he sat at home in the chimney-corner and did not make the attempt to go; but if, having his ticket, he walked to the place and went in, I should feel sure that he was ordained to go in. You will know your election when you have obeyed your calling. Go you to Christ because you are commanded and invited, and leave the deeper question to be answered by the facts.

Satan will throw men down and tear them in another way. "Ah!" says he, "you are too big a sinner." I make short work of that. No man is too big a sinner. "All manner of sin and of blasphemy shall be forgiven unto men."

"Oh but," says Satan, "it is too late." Another lie of his. It is never too late so long as we are in this world, and come to Jesus for pardon. Generally in the case of young people he puts the clock back, and says "It is too soon"; and then when they get old he puts the clock on, and says, "It is too late." It is never too late as long as Jesus lives, and the sinner repents. If a sinner were as old as Methuselah, if he came to Christ and trusted him he would be saved.

"Oh but," the devil says, "it is no use your trying at all. The Gospel is not true." Ay, but it is true, for some of us have proved it. I could bring before you, if it were necessary, men and women who lived in sin and wallowed in it, and yet the Lord Christ has saved them by his precious blood. They would rejoice to tell you how they have been delivered from the reign of sin by faith in Jesus, though they could never have delivered themselves. Conversion is the standing miracle of the Church; and while we see what it works every day in the week, we are confident and sure. When men that were passionate, dishonest, unchaste, covetous, become holy, gracious, loving, pure, generous, then we know that the Gospel is true by the effect which it produces. A lie would never produce holiness and love. Out of the way, devil! It is all in vain for you to come here with your falsehoods; we know the truth about you, and about the Gospel, and you shall not deceive us.

And then the devil will come with this—"It is of no use. Give it up; give it up." Many and many a man who has been on the brink of eternal life, has been thrown down and torn with this, "It is of no use; give it up. You have prayed, and you have not been answered: never pray again. You have attended the house of God, and you have become more miserable than ever: never go again. Ever since you have been a thinking man and a sober man, you have had more trouble than ever you had. See," says the devil, "what comes of your religion." Thus he tries to induce the newly awakened to give it up. But oh, in God's name let me implore you do not turn from it, for you are on the brink of the grand discovery. Another turf turned, and there is the golden treasure. After all your striving—your long striving—never give up the search until you have found your Saviour; for your Saviour is to be found. Trust in him this day, and he is yours for ever.

As our hopes have been awakened and our fears have been aroused, let us look on the scene till OUR WONDER IS EXCITED. Did you notice when I was reading in the ninth chapter of Mark, how Jesus healed this poor child? He did *heal* him, he healed him of all that complication, healed him of the devil's domination, healed him of the epilepsy, healed him of being deaf and dumb, healed him of being a lunatic, healed him of pining away; and in one moment that young man was completely saved from all his ills. He could speak; he could hear; he was cured of his epilepsy, and was no more a lunatic, but a happy rational being. The whole thing was done at once. Wonder, and never leave off wondering!

"Can a man be changed all at once? It must take a long time," says one. I admit there are certain qualities which come only by education and patient watchfulness. There are certain parts of the Christian character that come of culture, and must be watered with tears and prayer. But let me assure you, not as a matter of theory, but as a matter which I have seen for thirty years, that a man's character may be totally changed in less time than it takes me to tell you of it. There is such power in the name of Christ that, if that name be preached and the Spirit of God applies it, men can be turned right round; for God can take away the heart of stone and give a heart of flesh. The child of darkness can be translated into the kingdom of light. The dead heart can be quickened into a spiritual existence, and that in a single moment, by faith in Jesus Christ. When that poor epileptic child was healed, it is said that the people were amazed. But how much greater will be our amazement if we see the Lord Jesus work such a miracle upon you! You have struggled to get better, you have prayed to get better, and all seems to be unavailing. Now, just trust Christ, the blessed Son of God who reigns in heaven, who died for sinners, and now lives for sinners. Only trust him, and this blessed deed is done, you become a new creature in Christ

Jesus, and commence a holy life which shall never end. This wonder can be performed *now*.

The most charming point about it was that the Lord Jesus said, "Thou dumb and deaf spirit, I charge thee, come out of him, and enter no more into him." Enter no more into him— there is the glory of it! Though the epileptic fit was ended, yet the young man would not have been cured if the devil had returned to take possession of him again. The Saviour's cures endure the test of years. "Enter no more into him" preserved the young man by a life-long word of power.

I never dare to preach to anybody a temporary salvation. "Believe in the Lord Jesus Christ and thou shalt be saved," for ever. When God saves a man he *is* saved: not for weeks and years, but eternally. Now, this is a salvation that is worth your having, and worth my preaching. I will tell you a story of Christmas Evans which I like to tell on this point. Christmas Evans was once describing the prodigal's coming back to his father's house, and he said that when the prodigal sat at the father's table his father put upon his plate all the daintiest bits of meat that he could find; but the son sat there and did not eat, and every now and then the tears began to flow. His father turned to him and said, "My dear son, why are you unhappy? You spoil the feasting. Do you not know that I love you? Have I not joyfully received you?" "Yes," he said, "dear father, you are very kind, but have you really forgiven me? Have you forgiven me altogether, so that you will never be angry with me for all I have done?" His father looked on him with ineffable love and said, "I have blotted out thy sins and thy iniquities, and will remember them no more for ever. Eat, my dear son." The father turned round and waited on the guests, but by-and-by his eyes were on his boy, they could not be long removed. There was the son weeping again, but not eating. "Come, dear child," said his father, "come, why are you still mourning? What is it that you want?" Bursting into a flood of tears a second time, the son said, "Father, am I always to stop here? Will you never turn me out of doors?" The father replied, "No, my child, thou shalt go no more out for ever, for a son abides for ever." Still the son did not enjoy the banquet; there was still something rankling within, and again he wept. Then his father said, "Now, tell me, tell me, my dear son, all that is in thy heart. What do you desire more?" The son answered, "Father, will you *make* me stop here? Father, I am afraid lest, if I were left to myself, I might play the prodigal again. Oh, constrain me to stay here for ever!" The father said, "I will put my fear in thy heart, and thou shalt not depart from me." "Ah! then," the son replied, "it is enough," and merrily he feasted with the rest. So I preach to you just this—that the great Father when he takes you to himself will never let you go away from him again.

Whatever your condition, if you trust your soul to Jesus, you shall be saved, and saved for ever.

> *Once in Christ, in Christ for ever:*
> *Nothing from his love can sever.*

"But what if we fall into great sin?" says one. You shall not abide in great sin. You shall be kept and preserved by that same power which has begun the good work, for it will surely carry it on even to the end.

I have been speaking about the devil throwing some down and tearing them when they are coming to Christ. Are there any of you who do not know anything about it? Well, I am glad that you do not. I have endeavoured to help those that are terribly tormented; but if you are not so tried, do not wish to be. When I saw two or three of the good fish-people from Newhaven here recently in their picturesque costumes, they reminded me of a story that I heard about an old fish-wife who used to live near Edinburgh. A young man visited her, and began speaking to her about her soul. She was going out, and she took up her great load of fish to carry on her back, much more than most men would like to carry. The young man said to her, "Well, you have got a great burden there, good woman. Did you ever feel a spiritual burden?" She put down her load and said, "You mean that burden which John Bunyan speaks about in the *Pilgrim's Progress*, do you not?" "Yes," he said. "Well," she said, "I felt that burden before you were born, and I got rid of it, too; but I did not go exactly the same way to work that John Bunyan's pilgrim did."

Our young friend thought that she could not be up to the mark to talk so, for he fancied that John Bunyan could not make a mistake. "Well," she said, "John Bunyan says that

Evangelist pointed the man with the burden on his back to the wicket-gate, and when he could not see the gate, Evangelist said, 'Do you see that light?' And he looked till he thought he saw something like it. 'You are to run that way—the way of that light and that wicket gate.' Why," she said, "that was not the right direction to give a poor burdened soul. Much good he got out of it; for he had not gone far before he fell into the Slough of Despond, up to his neck in the mire, and had like to have been swallowed up. Evangelist ought to have said, 'Do you see that cross? Do not run an inch, but stand where you are, and look to that; and as you look your burden will be gone. I looked to the cross at once and lost my load.'" "What!" said the young man, "did you never go through the Slough of Despond?" "Yes," she said, "I have been through it far too many times; but let me tell you, young friend, that it is a deal easier to go through the Slough of Despond with your burden off than it is with your burden on." There is much blessed truth in this story. Do not any of you be saying to yourselves, "How I wish I could get into the Slough of Despond!" If you say that, you will get in, and then you will say, "How I wish I could get out of the Slough of Despond!" I have met with persons who fear that they never were saved because they have not experienced much terror. I meet with others who say that they cannot be saved because they experience too much terror. There is no pleasing people. Oh that they would look to Jesus whether or no!

After I was preaching Jesus Christ from this platform once, there came a man into the vestry who said to me, "Blessed be God that I entered this Tabernacle. I come from Canada, sir. My father, before he found true religion had to be locked up in a lunatic asylum, and I always thought that I must undergo a similar terror before I could be saved." I said, "No, no, my dear friend, you are to believe in the Lord Jesus Christ, and if you do that, despond or not despond, you are a saved man."

This Gospel I preach to you. Believe in the Lord Jesus Christ. Trust him quietly, humbly, simply, immediately. Trust him to make you a holy man—to deliver you from the power of the devil and the power of sin, and he will do it: I will be bound for him that he will keep his word. Jesus is truth itself, and never breaks his word. He never boasts that he can do what he cannot do. He has gone into heaven, and he is therefore "able to save them to the uttermost that come unto God by him, seeing he ever liveth to make intercession for them." Only trust him. There is hope for you if you will trust the wounded, bleeding, dying, risen, living Saviour. He will battle for you, and you shall get the victory.

XIX

UNBINDING LAZARUS

"And when he thus had spoken, he cried with a loud voice,
Lazarus, come forth. And he that was dead came forth,
bound hand and foot with graveclothes: and his face was
bound about with a napkin. Jesus saith unto them, Loose
him, and let him go."—John 11: 43, 44.

IN many things our Lord Jesus stands alone as a worker. No
other can unite his voice with the fiat which says, "Lazarus,
come forth." Yet in certain points of gracious operation the
Master associates his servants with him, so that when Lazarus
has come forth he says *to them*, "Loose him, and let him go."
In the raising of the dead he is alone, and therein majestic and
divine: in the loosing of the bound he is associated with them,
and remains still majestic; but his more prominent feature is
condescension. How exceedingly kind it is of our Lord Jesus
to permit his disciples to do some little thing in connection
with his great deeds, so that they may be "workers together
with him." Our Lord as frequently as possible associated his
disciples with himself; of course, they could not aid him in pre-
senting an atoning sacrifice, yet it was to their honour that they
had said, "Let us go that we may die with him," and that in
their love they resolved to go with him to prison and to death.

Our Lord understood the fickleness of their character, yet
he knew that they were sincere in their desire to be associated
with him in all his life-story whatever it might be. Hence,
when he afterwards rode into Jerusalem in triumph, he alone
was saluted with Hosannas; but he sent two of his disciples to
bring the ass on which he rode, and they cast their garments
upon the colt and they set Jesus thereon, and as he went they
spread their clothes in the way. Thus they contributed to his
lowly pomp, and shared in the exultation of the royal day.
Further on, when he would keep the feast, he expressly dwells
upon it that he would keep it with them; for he said, "With

desire I have desired to eat this passover *with you* before I suffer." He sent Peter and John to prepare that passover, he directed them to the large upper room furnished, and there he bade them make ready. Anything that they could do they were allowed to do.

Their Lord was willing to have led them further still; but through weakness they stopped short. In the garden he bade them watch with him on that dreadful night, and he sought sympathy from them.

> *Backward and forward, thrice he ran,*
> *As if he sought some help from man.*

He cried in sorrowful disappointment, "Could ye not watch with me one hour?" Ah, no! They could go to the brink of the abyss with him, but they could not descend into its deeps. He must tread the winepress alone, and of the people there must be none with him; yet as far as they could go he disdained not their dear society. He allowed them according to their capacity to drink of his cup, and to be baptized with his baptism; and if their fellowship with him in his sufferings went no farther, it was not because he warned them back, but because they had not the strength to follow. According to his own judgment they were intimately associated with him, for he said to them, "Ye are they which have continued with me in my temptations."

Our Jesus Christ still delights to associate us with him as far as our feebleness and folly will permit. In his present work of bringing sinners to himself, he counts it a part of his reward that we should be labourers together with him. As a father smiles to see his little children imitating him, and endeavouring to assist him in his work, so is Jesus pleased to see our lowly efforts for his honour. He is glad to save sinners at all, but most of all glad to save them by the means of those already saved. Thus he blesses the prodigal sons and the servants of the household at the same moment. He gives to the lost salvation, and upon his own called and chosen ones he puts the honour of being used for the grandest purposes under heaven. It is more honourable to save a soul from death than to rule an empire. Such honour all the saints may have.

The chief subject of this discourse is our association with

Christ in gracious labour; but we must on the road consider other themes which lead up to it. First, then, this chapter records A MEMORABLE MIRACLE. Perhaps that writer is correct who speaks of the raising of Lazarus as the most remarkable of all our Lord's mighty works. There is no measuring miracles, for they are all displays of the infinite; but in some respects the raising of Lazarus stands at the head of the wonderful series of miracles with which our Lord astonished and instructed the people. Did he raise the naturally dead? So doth he still raise the spiritually dead. Did he bring back a body from corruption? So doth he still deliver men from loathsome sins. The life-giving miracle of grace is as truly astounding as the quickening miracle of power. As this was in some respects a more remarkable resurrection than the raising of Jairus's daughter, or of the young man at the gate of Nain, so there are certain conversions and regenerations which are to the observing mind more astonishing than others.

I notice the memorableness of this miracle in *the subject of it*, because the man had been dead four days. To give life to one of whom his own sister said, "Lord, by this time he stinketh," was a deed fragrant with divine power. Probably the sisters had perceived the traces of decay upon the body of their beloved brother before they buried him, for it is more than supposable that they delayed the funeral as long as possible under an undefined hope that perhaps their Lord would appear upon the scene. In that warm climate the ravages of decay are extremely rapid, and before many hours the loving sisters were compelled to admit, as Abraham had done before them, that they must bury their dead out of their sight.

Surely it were an easier task to make a new man altogether out of the earth than to take this poor corrupted corpse which has turned to worms' meat and make it live again. This was the stupendous miracle of divine power which our glorious Lord performed upon his friend Lazarus. Now, there are some men who are symbolized by this case: they are not only devoid of all spiritual life, but corruption has set in; their character has become abominable, their language is putrid, their spirit is loathsome. They are so far gone from original righteousness as to be an offence to all, and it does not seem possible that ever they should be restored to purity, honesty, or hope. When the

Lord in infinite compassion comes to deal with them and makes them to live, then the most sceptical are obliged to confess, "This is the finger of God!" What can it be else? Such a profane wretch become a believer! Such a blasphemer a man of prayer! Such a proud, conceited talker, receive the kingdom as a little child! Surely God himself must have wrought this marvel! Now is fulfilled the word of the Lord by Ezekiel,— "And ye shall know that I am the Lord, when I have opened your graves, O my people, and brought you up out of your graves" (Ezek. 37 : 13). We bless our God that he does thus quicken the dry bones, whose hope was lost. However far gone a man may be, he cannot be beyond the reach of the Lord's right arm of mighty mercy. The Lord can change the vilest of the vile into the most holy of the holy! Blessed be his name, we have seen him do this, and therefore we have cheering hope for the worst of men!

The next notable point about this miracle is *the manifest human weakness of its worker*. He who has to deal with this dead man was himself a man. I do not know of any passage of Scripture wherein the manhood of Christ is more frequently manifested than in this narrative. The Godhead is, of course, eminently conspicuous in the resurrection of Lazarus, but the Lord seemed as if he designedly at the same time set his manhood to the front. The Pharisees said, according to the forty-seventh verse, "What do we? for *this man* doeth many miracles." They are to be blamed for denying his Godhead, but not for dwelling upon his manhood, for every part of the singular scene before us made it conspicuous. When our Lord had seen Mary's tears, we read that he groaned in spirit and was troubled. Thus he showed the sorrows and the sympathies of a man. We cannot forget those memorable words, "Jesus wept." Who but a man should weep? Weeping is a human speciality. Jesus never seems to be more completely bone of our bone and flesh of our flesh than when he weeps.

Next, our Lord made an enquiry—"Where have ye laid him?" He veils his omniscience: as a man he seeks information —where is the body of his dear departed friend? Even as Mary in after days said about himself, "Tell me where thou hast laid him," so does the Lord Jesus ask for information as a man who knows not. As if to show his manhood even more fully, when they tell him where Lazarus is entombed he goes that way. He needed not to go: he might have spoken a word where he was, and the dead would have risen. Could he not as easily have wrought at a distance as near at hand? Being man, "Jesus therefore again groaning in himself cometh to the grave." When he has reached the spot he sees a cave whose mouth is closed by a huge stone, and now he seeks human assistance. He cries, "Take ye away the stone." Why, surely he who could raise the dead could have rolled away the stone with the self-same word! Yet, as if needing help from those about him, the man Christ Jesus reminds us again of Mary at his own sepulchre, saying, "Who shall roll us away the stone?"

That done, our Lord lifts up his eyes to heaven, and addresses the Father in mingled prayer and thanksgiving. How like a man is all this! He takes the suppliant's place. He speaks with God as a man speaketh with his friend, but still as a man. Did not this condescending revelation of the manhood make the miracle all the more remarkable? The time came when the flame of the Godhead flashed forth from the unconsumed bush of the manhood. The voice of him who wept was heard in the chambers of death-shade, and forth came the soul of Lazarus to live again in the body. "The weakness of God" proved itself to be stronger than death and mightier than the grave. It is a parable of our own case as workers. Sometimes we see the human side of the Gospel, and wonder whether it can do many mighty works. When we tell the story, we fear that it will appear to the people as a thrice-told tale. We wonder how it can be that truth so simple, so homely, so common should have any special power about it. Yet it is so. Out of the foolishness of preaching the wisdom of God shines forth. The glory of the eternal God is seen in that Gospel which we preach in much trembling and infirmity. Let us therefore glory in our infirmity, because the power of God doth all the more evidently rest upon us. Let us not despise our day of small things, nor be dismayed because we are manifestly so feeble. This work is not for our honour, but for the glory of God, and any circumstance which tends to make that glory more evident is to be rejoiced in.

Let us consider for a few moments *the instrumental cause of this resurrection.* Nothing was used by our Lord but his own word of power. Jesus cried with a loud voice, "Lazarus, come forth!" He simply repeated the dead man's name, and added two commanding words. This was a simple business enough. It is marvellous that such poor preaching should convert such great sinners. Many are turned unto the Lord by the simplest, plainest, most unadorned preaching of the Gospel. They hear little, but that little is from the lip of Jesus. Many converts find Christ by a single short sentence. The preacher owned no eloquence, he made no attempt at it; but the Holy Spirit spoke through him with a power which eloquence could not rival. Thus said the Lord "Ye dry bones live"; and they did live. I delight to preach my Master's Gospel in the plainest terms. The power to quicken the dead lieth not in the wisdom of words but in the Spirit of the living God. The voice is Christ's voice, and the word is the word of him who is the resurrection and the life, and therefore men live by it. Let the Spirit of God rest upon us, and we shall be endowed with power from on high: so that even the spiritually dead shall through us hear the voice of the Son of God, and they that hear shall live.

The result of the Lord's working must not be passed over, for it is a main element of wonder in this miracle. Lazarus did come forth and that immediately. The thunder of Christ's voice was attended by the lightning of his divine power, and forthwith life flashed into Lazarus and he came forth. Bound as he was, the power which had enabled him to live enabled him to shuffle forth from the ledge of rock whereon he lay, and there he stood with nothing of death about him but his grave-clothes. He quitted the close air of the sepulchre and returned to know once more the things which are done under the sun; *and that at once*. To me it is one of the great glories of the Gospel that it does not require weeks and months to quicken men and make new creatures of them; salvation can come to them at once. The man who stepped into this Tabernacle steeped in rebellion against his God, and apparently impervious to divine truth, may nevertheless go down those steps with his sins forgiven, and with a new spirit imparted to him, in the strength of which he shall begin to live unto God as he never lived before.

Do you speak of a nation being born at once, as if it were impossible? It is possible with God. The Divine Power can send a flash of life all round the world at any instant to quicken myriads of his chosen. We are dealing now with God, not with men. Man must have time to prepare his machinery, and get it into going order; but it is not so with the Lord. If you and I had to feed five thousand, we should need to grind the corn at the mill, and bake the bread in the oven, and then we should be a long time in bringing the loaves in baskets; but the Master takes the barley cakes and breaks, and as he breaks the food is multiplied. Anon he handles the fish, and lo, it seems as if a shoal had been in his hands instead of "a few small fishes." Behold! the vast multitude receives refreshment from the little stock which has been so abundantly increased. In all your work of love, trust in the unseen power which lay at the back of the manhood of Christ, and still lies at the back of the simple Gospel which we preach. The everlasting word may seem to be weak and feeble; it may groan and weep, and seem as if it could do no more; but it can raise the dead, and raise them at once.

The effect which this miracle produced upon those who looked on was very remarkable, for many believed in the Lord Jesus. Besides this, the miracle of raising Lazarus was so unquestioned and unquestionable a fact that it brought the Pharisees to a point—they would now make an end of Christ. They had huffed and puffed at his former miracles; but this one had struck such a blow that in their wrath they determined that he should die. No doubt this miracle was the immediate cause of the crucifixion of Jesus: it marked a point of decision when men must either believe in Christ or become his deadly foes. If the Lord be with us, we shall see multitudes believing through Jesus; and if the rage of the enemy becomes thereby the more intense, let us not fear it: there will come a last decisive struggle, and mayhap it shall be brought on by some amazing display of the divine power in the conversion of the chief of sinners.

Secondly, I beg you to observe A SINGULAR SPECTACLE. A notable miracle was unquestionably wrought; but it required a finishing touch.

The man was wholly raised, but not wholly freed. See, here is *a living man in the garments of death!* That napkin and other grave-clothes were altogether congruous with death, but they were much out of place when Lazarus began again to live. It is a wretched sight to see a living man wearing his shroud. Yet we have seen in this Tabernacle hundreds of times people quickened by divine grace with their grave-clothes still upon them. Such was their condition that unless you observe carefully you would think them still dead; and yet within them the lamp of heavenly life was burning. Some said, "He is dead, look at his garments;" but the more spiritual cried, "He is not dead, but these bands must be loosed." It is a singular spectacle: a living man hampered with the cerements of death!

Moreover, he was *a moving man bound hand and foot*. How he moved I do not know. Some of the old writers thought that he glided, as it were, through the air, and that this was part of the miracle. I think he may have been so bound that though he could not freely walk yet he could shuffle along like a man in a sack. I know that I have seen souls bound and yet moving; moving intensely in one direction, and yet not capable of stirring an inch in another. Have you not seen a man so truly alive that he wept, he mourned, he groaned over sin; but yet he could not believe in Christ, but seemed bound hand and foot as to faith? I have seen him give up his sin determinedly, and crush a bad habit under his foot, and yet he could not lay hold on a promise or receive a hope. Lazarus was free enough in one way, for he came out of the tomb, but the blinding napkin was about his head; and even so it is with many a quickened sinner, for when you try to show him some cheering truth he cannot see it.

Moreover, here was *a repulsive object, but yet attractive*. Mary and Martha must have been charmed to see their brother, even though wrapped in grave-clothes. A man fresh from the sepulchre robed in a winding-sheet is a sight one would go a long way not to see, but such was Lazarus. Mary and Martha felt their hearts dancing within them since their dear brother was alive. So have we come near to a poor sinner; it was enough to frighten anybody to hear his groans, and to see his weeping, but yet he was so dear to every true heart that we loved to be with him. I have sometimes spoken with broken-hearted sinners, and they have pretty nearly broken my heart; and yet, when they have gone out of the room, I have wished to see a thousand like them. Poor creatures, they fill us with sorrow, and yet flood us with joy.

Moreover, here was a man *strong, and yet helpless*. He was strong enough to come forth from his grave, and yet he could not take the napkin from his own head, for his hands were bound, and he could not go to his house, for his feet were swathed. Unless some kind hand unbound him he would remain a living mummy. He had strength sufficient to quit the grave, but he could not be quit of his grave-clothes. So have we seen men strong, for the Spirit of God has been in them, and has moved them mightily; they have been passionately in earnest even to agony in one direction, yet the new-born life has been so feeble in other ways that they seemed to be mere babes in swaddling clothes. They have not been able to enjoy the liberty of Christ, nor enter into communion with Christ, nor work for Christ. They have been bound hand and foot: work and progress have alike been beyond them. This seems a strange sequel to a miracle. The bands of death loosed, and strength bestowed, but not the power to undress himself. Such anomalies are common in the world of grace.

This brings us to consider A TIMELY ASSISTANCE which you and I are called upon to render. O for wisdom to learn our duty, and grace to do it at once.

Let us consider *what are these bands which often bind newly regenerated sinners*. Some of them are blindfolded by the napkin about their head; they are very *ignorant*, sadly devoid of spiritual perception, and withal the eye of faith is darkened. Yet the eye is there, and Christ has opened it; and it is the business of the servant of God to remove the napkin which bandages it, by teaching the truth, explaining it, and clearing up difficulties. This is a simple thing to do, but exceedingly necessary. Now that they have life we shall teach them to purpose. Besides that, they are bound hand and foot, so that they are compelled to *inaction;* we can show them how to work for Jesus. Sometimes these bands are those of *sorrow*, they are in an awful terror about the past; we have to unbind them by showing that the past is blotted out. They are wrapped about by many a yard of *doubt*, mistrust, anguish, and remorse. "Loose them, and let them go."

Another hindrance is the band of *fear*. "Oh," says the poor soul, "I am such a sinner that God must punish me for my sin." Tell him the grand doctrine of substitution. Unwrap this cerement by the assurance that Jesus took our sin, and that "by his stripes we are healed." It is wonderful what liberty comes by that precious truth when it is well understood. The penitent soul fears that Jesus will refuse its prayer; assure it that he will in nowise cast out any that come to him. Let fear be taken from the soul by the promises of Scripture, by our testimony to their truth, and by the Spirit bearing witness to the doctrine which we endeavour to impart.

Souls are very often bound with the grave-clothes of *prejudice*. They used to think so and so before conversion, and they are very apt to carry their dead thoughts into their new life. Go and tell them that things are not what they seem: that old things have passed away, and behold all things have become new. The days of their ignorance God winked at, but now they must change their minds about everything, and no more judge according to the sight of the eyes and the hearing of the ears. Some of them are bound with the grave-clothes of evil *habit*. It is a noble work to aid a drunkard to unwind the accursed bands which prevent his making the slightest progress towards better things. Let us tear off every band from ourselves that we may the more readily help *them* to be free. The bonds of evil habits may still remain upon men that have received the divine life until those habits are pointed out to them and the evil of them is shown and so they are helped by precept, prayer, and example to free themselves. Who among us would wish Lazarus to continue wearing his shroud? Who would wish to see a regenerate man falling into ill habits? When the Lord quickens men the main point of the business is secured, and then you and I can come in to loose every bond which would hamper and hinder the free action of the divine life.

But why are these bandages left? Why did not the miracle which raised Lazarus also loosen his grave-clothes? I answer because *our Lord Jesus is always economical of miracles*. False wonders are plentiful: true miracles are few and far between. In the Church of Rome such miracles as they claim are usually a lavish waste of power. When St. Swithin made it rain for forty days that his corpse might not be carried into the church it was much ado about very little; when St. Denis walked a thousand miles with his head in his hands one is apt to ask why he could not have journeyed quite as well if he had set it on his neck; and when another saint crossed the sea on a table-cloth it would appear to have been an improvement if he had borrowed a boat. Rome can afford to be free with her counterfeit coin. The Lord Jesus never works a miracle unless there is an object to be gained which could not be obtained in any other way. When the enemy said, "Command that these stones be made bread," our Lord refused, for it was not a fit occasion for a miracle. Lazarus cannot be raised out of the grave except by a miracle, but he can be unstripped without a miracle, and therefore human hands must do it. If there is anything in the kingdom of God which we can do ourselves it is folly to say, "May the Lord do it," for he will do nothing of the sort. If you can do it you shall do it; or if you refuse the neglect shall be visited upon you.

I suppose that those bands were left *that those who came to unwind him should be sure that he was the same man who died*. Some of them may have said, "This is Lazarus, for these are the grave-clothes which we wrapped about him." From coming so near to Lazarus they would be equally well assured that he was really alive! They marked his breathing, and the flush which reddened his cheek. For some such cause our Lord permits the quickened sinner to remain in a measure of bondage, that we may know that the man is the same person who was really dead in trespasses and sins. He was no sham sinner, for the traces of his sins are still upon him. You can see by what he says that his training was none of the best; the relics of the old nature show what manner of man he used to be. We know that he is alive, for we hear his sighs and cries, and we perceive that his experience is that of a living child of God. Those desires, that searching of heart, and that longing to be soundly right with God—we know what these mean. It is a great help to us in discerning spirits, and in being assured of the work of God upon any person, to come into living contact with those imperfections which it is to be our privilege to remove under the guidance of the Holy Ghost.

Moreover, I still think that the main object was *that these disciples might enter into rare fellowship with Christ*. They could each say, not proudly but still joyfully, "Our Lord raised Lazarus, and I was there and helped to unloose him from his grave-clothes." Perhaps Martha could say in after-life, "I took the napkin from my brother's dear face," and Mary could add, "I helped to unbind a hand." It is most sweet to hope that we have done anything to cheer, or to teach, or sanctify a soul. Will you not earn a share in this dear delight? Will you not seek the lost sheep? Will you not sweep the house for the lost money? Will you not at the very least help to feast the long-lost son? This, you see, *gives you such an interest in a saved person*. Those who are very observant tell us that those whom we serve may forget us, but those who do us a service are fast bound to us thereby. Many kindnesses you may do for people and they will be altogether ungrateful, but those who have bestowed the benefit do not forget. When the Lord Jesus sets us to help others it is partly that they may love us for what we have done, but still more that we may love them because we have rendered them a benefit. Is there any love like the love of a mother to her child? Yet did the little child ever render a pennyworth of service to the mother? Certainly not. It is the mother that does everything for the child. So then the Lord binds us to the new converts in love by permitting us to help them. Thus is the church made all of a piece and woven together from the top throughout by the workmanship of love. O you who are devoid of love, it is evident that you do not labour with pure desire to benefit others, for if you did you would be filled with affection for them.

Let us ask—*why should we remove these grave-clothes?* It is enough reply that the Lord has bidden us do so. He commands us to "Loose him, and let him go." He bids us comfort the feeble-minded and support the weak. If he commands it we need no other reason. I hope you will set to work at once, for the King's business requireth haste, and we are traitors if we delay.

We should do this because it is very possible that we helped to bind those grave-clothes upon our friend. Some of the people who were at Bethany that day had assisted in the burial of Lazarus, and surely those should loose Lazarus who helped to bind him. Many a Christian man before his conversion has helped to make sinners worse by his example, and possibly after his conversion he may by his indifference and want of zeal have aided in binding new converts in the bonds of doubt and sorrow. At any rate, you have said of many a person,

"He will never be saved!" Thus you have wrapped him in grave-clothes; the Lord never told you to do *that*—you did it of your own accord; and now that he bids you remove those grave-clothes, will you not be quick to do it?

I remember when somebody lent a hand to take the grave-clothes off from me, and therefore I desire to loose the grave-clothes of others. If we cannot repay what we owe to the precise individual who wrought us good, we can at least repay it by working for the general benefit of seekers. "There," said a benevolent man, as he gave help to a poor man, "take that money, and when you can pay it back give it to the next man whom you meet who is in the same plight as yourself, and tell him he is to pay it to another destitute person as soon as he can afford it; and so my money will go travelling on for many a day." That is how our Lord does. God grant that you and I may not be negligent in this heavenly service.

Lastly, A PRACTICAL HINT. If the Lord Jesus Christ employed the disciples in relieving Lazarus of his grave-clothes, do you not think he would employ us if we were ready for such work? Yonder is Paul: the Lord Jesus has struck him down; but the lowly Ananias must visit him and baptize him, that he may receive his sight. There is Cornelius: he has been seeking the Lord, and the Lord is gracious to him, but he must first hear Peter. There is a wealthy Ethiopian riding in his chariot, and he is reading the Book of the Prophet Isaiah, but he cannot understand it till Philip comes. Lydia has an opened heart, but only Paul can lead her to the Lord Jesus.

When the prodigal came home, the father did not say to one of his servants, "Go and meet him,"—No; we read "when he was yet a great way off, his father saw him, and had compassion, and ran, and fell on his neck and kissed him." He did all this himself. The father personally forgave him, and restored him; but we read further on "the father *said to his servants*, Bring forth the best robe, and put it on him; and put a ring on his hand, and shoes on his feet: and bring hither the fatted calf, and kill it; and let us eat, and be merry." The loving father might have done all this himself, might he not? Oh yes, but then he desired that all the servants in the house should be of one accord with him in the joyful reception of his son. The great Lord could do everything for a sinner himself, but he does not do so because he wishes all of us to be in fellowship with him.

Come, fellow-servants, bring forth the best robe. I am never happier than when I preach the righteousness of Christ, and try to put it upon the sinner. "What!" cried one, "you cannot put it on!" So the parable says—"Bring forth the best robe *and put it on him.*" I not only bring it out and show it; but by the Holy Spirit's help I try to put it on the sinner. I hold it up before him, just as you hold up a friend's great-coat to help him to put it on. You are to teach him, comfort him, cheer him, and, in fact, help him to be dressed like one of the family. Then the ring, can we not bring it forth? Surely the father should have put the ring upon his son's hand. No, he bids his servants do that. He cries to them, "Put a ring on his hand"; introduce him into fellowship, gladden him with the communion of saints. You and I must conduct the new convert into the joys of Christian society, and let him know what it is to be married unto Christ, and joined unto his people. We must put honour upon these reclaimed ones, and decorate those who once were degraded. Nor must we fail to put shoes on his feet! He has a long journey to go; he is to be a pilgrim, and we must help to shoe him with the preparation of the Gospel of peace. His feet are new in the Lord's way: we must show him how to run on the Master's errands. As for the fatted calf, it is ours to feed the restored ones; and as for the music and the dancing, it is ours to make the hearts of penitents glad by rejoicing over them.

There is plenty to be done: try and do some of it now. Commence a holy ministry for the converted who are not yet brought into liberty. There are children of God who have not yet a shoe to their feet; there are plenty of shoes in the house, but no servant has put them on. When I come to look, I see some brethren who have not the ring on their hand. Oh, that I might have the privilege of putting it on! I charge you, by the blood that bought you, and by the love that holds you, and by the supreme bounty which supplies your need, go forth and do what your Master graciously permits and commands you to do; loose Lazarus, bring forth the best robe and put it on him, put a ring on his hand, and shoes on his feet, and let us all eat and be merry with our Father.

XX

GOOD CHEER FROM CHRIST'S CALL

"And they came to Jericho: and as Jesus went out of Jericho with his disciples and a great number of people, blind Bartimæus, the son of Timæus, sat by the highway side begging. And when he heard that it was Jesus of Nazareth, he began to cry out, and say, Jesus, thou son of David, have mercy on me. And many charged him that he should hold his peace: but he cried the more a great deal, Thou son of David, have mercy on me. And Jesus stood still, and commanded him to be called. And they call the blind man, saying unto him, Be of good comfort, rise; he calleth thee. And he, casting away his garment, rose, and came to Jesus. And Jesus answered and said unto him, What wilt thou that I should do unto thee? The blind man said unto him, Lord, that I might receive my sight. And Jesus said unto him, Go thy way; thy faith hath made thee whole. And immediately he received his sight, and followed Jesus in the way."—Mark 10: 46–52.

THE blind man described in this narrative is a picture of what I earnestly desire that every hearer and reader of my sermons may become. In his first condition, Bartimæus was a type of what the sinner is by nature—blind, hopelessly blind, unless the healing Saviour shall interfere, and pour in upon him the light of day. It is not, however, to this point that we shall now turn our thoughts, but to his conduct while seeking sight. This man, by God's great mercy, so acted that he may be held up as an example to all who feel their spiritual blindness, and earnestly desire to see the light of grace.

Several of the blind men of Scripture are very interesting individuals. There was one of them, you remember,—the man born blind—who baffled the Pharisees by answering them with cool courage mixed with shrewdness and mother wit. Well might his parents say that he was of age, for he had all his wits about him. Blind as he had been, he could see a great deal; and when his eyes were opened, he proved beyond all dispute that his questioners deserved the name of "blind Pharisees" which the Lord Jesus gave them.

Bartimæus, the son of Timæus, is a notable character. There is a sharp-cut individuality and crispness of style about him which makes him a remarkable person. He is one who thinks and acts for himself, is not soon daunted nor easily swayed, makes sure of what he knows, and when he is questioned gives a clear reply. I suppose that, as he sat in the midnight darkness which was his perpetual lot, he thought much; and having heard that from the seed of David there had arisen a great Prophet who wrought miracles, and preached glad tidings to the poor, he studied the matter over, and concluded that his claims were true. A blind man might well see that fact, if at all familiar with Old Testament prophecy; and as he heard more and more of Jesus, and compared him with the prophetic description of the coming King, he felt convinced that Jesus was the promised Messiah. Then, he thought within himself, "If he were ever to come this way, I would announce myself as one of his followers. I would proclaim him King, whether others acknowledged his royalty or not. I would act as a herald to the great Prince, and shout aloud that he is the Son of David."

Then he further resolved to seek the pity of the Messiah, and beg for his sight, for it was foretold that the Messiah would come to open blind eyes. This resolution he had so long dwelt upon that, when the time did come, and he heard that Jesus passed by, he immediately availed himself of the opportunity, and cried out with all his might, "Thou son of David, have mercy on me." Oh, that you who read these lines would think over the claims of Jesus, and come to the same conclusion as the blind beggar of Jericho!

Learn a simple lesson from this man, I pray you. He made use of what senses he had. He could *hear* if he could not see. The man had no eyes, but he had ears and a tongue, and he took care to use the faculties which remained to him, so that, when the Saviour passed by, he cried to him with all his might; he made his confession of faith, and offered, at the same time, a personal petition for mercy as he cried aloud, "Thou son of David, have mercy on me."

I wish to drive at one point only, which will stand out clearly when I have finished; but I must go a little roundabout to compass my design. May the Holy Spirit dictate every word!

My first remark is, that this man is a pattern for all seekers, because HE SOUGHT THE LORD UNDER GREAT DISCOURAGEMENTS.

He cried to the Lord Jesus so loudly, so unceremoniously, and at so unseasonable a time, as others thought, that they checked him, and bade him hold his peace; but this was like pouring spirits upon a fire, and it only made him the more intense in his pleading.

Notice his first discouragement: *no one prompted him to cry to Christ.* No friend lovingly whispered in his ears, "Jesus of Nazareth passeth by. Now is your opportunity; seek his face!" Possibly you, dear friend, may have been so neglected that you have sighed out, "No man careth for my soul." Then yours is a parallel case to that of Bartimæus. Very few can fairly thus complain if they live among lively Christians, for, in all probability, they have often been invited, entreated, and almost compelled to come to Christ. Some even complain of Christian importunity, and are weary of it, not liking to be spoken to about their souls. "Intrusion" it has been called by some cavillers; but indeed it is a blessed intrusion upon a sinner, slumbering in his sin over the brink of hell, to disturb his slumbers, and arouse him to flee for his life. Would you not think it very ridiculous, were a house on fire, if the fireman declined to fetch anybody out of the house because he had not been introduced to the family? I reckon that a breach of courtesy is often a most courteous thing when the desire is the benefit of an immortal soul. If I say a very personal thing, and it arouses anyone to seek and find salvation, I know that he will never blame me on that score.

Still, a person may reside where there is no one to invite him to seek Jesus, and if so, he may recall the example of this man, who, all unprompted, sought the Saviour's aid. He knew his need without telling, and, believing that Jesus could give him his eyesight, he did not need pressing to pray to him. He thought for himself, as all ought to do. Will not you do the same, especially on a matter so weighty as the salvation of your own soul? What if you have never been the subject of friendly importunities and entreaties, yet you ought not to require them. You are possessed of your reason; you know that you are already sinful, and will be lost for ever unless the Lord Jesus saves you; does not common sense suggest that you should cry to him at once? Be at least as sensible as this poor blind beggar, and let the voice of your earnest prayer go up to Jesus the Son of David.

The discouragement of Bartimæus was still greater, for when he did begin to cry, *those around discouraged him*. Read the 48th verse, "*Many* charged him that he should hold his peace." Some for one reason, and some for another, charged him that he should hold his peace. They did not merely advise him, but they "*charged* him." They spoke like people in authority. "Be quiet, will you? Be still! What are you at?" Judging him to be guilty of a grave impropriety in disturbing the eloquence of the great Preacher, they would have hushed him to silence. Those who do not smart under a sense of sin often think awakened sinners are out of order and fanatical when they are only in earnest. The people near the blind beggar blamed him for his bad taste in shouting so loudly, "Thou son of David, have mercy on me."

But he was not to be stopped. On the contrary, we are told that "*he cried the more*," and not only the more, but "the more *a great deal*," so that it was time wasted to try to silence him. Here was an opportunity for having his eyes opened, and he would not miss it to please anybody. Folks around him might misjudge him, but that would not matter if Jesus opened his eyes. Sight was the one thing needful, and for that he could put up with rebuffs and reproaches. His manhood and determination were developed by opposition.

Friend, how is it with you? Can you defy the opinion of ungodly men, and dare to be singular that you may be saved? Can you brave opposition and discouragement, and resolve that, if mercy is to be had, you will have it? Opposers will call your determination obstinacy; but never mind, your firmness is the stuff of which martyrs are made. Bartimæus must have sight, and he will have sight, and there is no stopping him; he is blind to all hindrances, and pushes through. He had been begging so long that he knew how to beg importunately. He was as sturdy a beggar with Christ as he had been with men, and so he followed up his suit in the teeth of all who would stave him off.

There was, however, one more discouragement that must have weighed on him far more than the want of prompting and the presence of opposition, *Jesus himself did not answer him at first*. He had evidently, according to the run of the narrative, cried out to Jesus many times, for how else could it be said "he cried the more a great deal"? His cry had waxed stronger and stronger, but yet there was no reply. What was worse, the Master had been moving on. We are sure of that, because we are told in the 49th verse that Jesus, at length, "stood still," which implies that, before this time, he had been walking along, speaking as he went to the crowd around him. Jesus was passing away, passing away without granting his desire, without giving a sign of having heard him.

Are you, my friend, one who has cried for mercy long, and found it not? Have you been praying for a month, and is there no answer? Is it longer still? Have you spent weary days and nights in waiting and watching for mercy? There is a mistake at the bottom of the whole affair which I will not explain just now, but I will tell you how to act. Even if Jesus does not appear to hear you, be not discouraged, but cry to him "the more a great deal." Remember, he loves importunity, and sometimes he waits a while on purpose that our prayers may gather strength, and that we may be the more earnest. Cry to him, dear heart. Be not desponding. Do not give up in despair. Mercy's gate has oiled hinges, and it swings easily; push at it again. Do have the courage of this poor blind man, and say, "Though for a while he may not hear me, yet still will I confess him to be the son of David, and so avow that he is able to save me, and still will I cry to him, 'Thou son of David, have mercy on me.'" Let this be your firm determination, and you too shall yet be saved.

Observe, in the second place, that there came a change over the scene. "Jesus stood still, and commanded him to be called." Here we see him under a warmer and brighter light for a moment; and we remark that, AFTER A WHILE, HE RE-CEIVED ENCOURAGEMENT.

The encouragement was not given to him by our Lord, but by the same persons who had formerly rebuked him. Christ did not say to him, "Be of good comfort," because the man was not in need of such a word. He was by no means backward, or disconsolate, or staggered by the opposition he had met with. Jesus Christ said, "Be of good cheer" in the case of the poor paralytic man who was let down by cords from the roof, because he was sad at heart; but this man was already of good courage, and therefore the Saviour gave him no superfluous consolation. The onlookers were pleased with the hope of seeing a miracle, and so offered their encouragements, which were not of any great worth or weight, since they came from lips which a few minutes before had been singing quite another tune.

At this time, I wish to give to all anxious souls, who are trying to find their Saviour, some little word of cheer, and yet I warn them not to think too much of it, for they need something far better than anything that man can say. The comfort given to Bartimæus was drawn from the fact that Christ called him. "Be of good comfort, rise; *he calleth thee*." To every sinner who is anxious to find Jesus this is a note from the silver trumpet. You are invited to Jesus, and need not therefore be afraid to come. In one sense or another, it is true of all who hear the Gospel, "He calleth thee," and therefore to every one of our hearers we may say, "Be of good cheer."

First, it is true that Jesus calls each one of us by *the universal call of the Gospel*, for its message is unto all people. Ministers are bidden to go into all the world, and preach the Gospel to every creature. You are a creature, and, consequently, the Gospel has a call for you, "Believe on the Lord Jesus Christ, and thou shalt be saved." We are bidden to preach the Gospel of the kingdom throughout all nations, and to cry, "Whosoever will, let him take the water of life freely." "Whosoever." There is no limit to it, and it would be a violation of our commission if we should attempt to enclose what God has made as free as the air, and as universal as manhood. "The times of this ignorance God winked at; but now commandeth all men everywhere to repent." This is the universal call, "Repent ye, and believe the gospel." In this there is comfort of hope for all who desire to come to God.

But there is still more comfort in what, for distinction's sake, we will name *the character call*. Many promises in the Word of God are directed to persons of a certain character. For instance, "Come unto me, all ye that labour and are heavy laden, and I will give you rest." Do you labour? Are you heavy laden? Then Christ specially calls you, and promises rest *to you* if you come to him. Here is another, "Ho, everyone that thirsteth, come ye to the waters." Are you thirsting after something better than this world can give? Then the Lord bids you come to the waters of his grace. "And he that hath no money, let him come." Is that you? Are you destitute of merit, destitute of everything that could purchase the favour of God? Then you are the person whom he specially invites. When we meet with a person whose case is thus anticipated, we are bound to bid him be of good cheer, because the Lord is plainly calling him.

Next, there is *a ministerial call*, which is made useful to many. At times, the Lord enables his servants to give calls to people in a very remarkable way. They describe the case so accurately, even to the little touches, that the hearer says, "Somebody must have told the preacher about me." When personal and pointed words are thus put into our mouths by the Holy Spirit, we may give our hearer comfort, and say, "Arise, he calleth *thee*." What said the woman of Samaria? "Come, see a man, which told me all things that ever I did: is not this the Christ?" When your inmost secrets are revealed, when the Word of God enters you as the priest's keen knife opened the sacrificial victim, laying bare your inward and secret thoughts and intents, you may say, "Now have I felt the power of that Word which is quick and powerful. Oh, that I might also know its healing power!" When a call to repentance and faith comes on the back of a minute personal description, you may assuredly gather that the Lord has sent this message especially to you, and it is your right and privilege at once to feel the comfort of the fact that Jesus calls *you*. "To you is the word of this salvation sent."

Yet there is another call, which overtops these three, for the universal call and the character call and the ministerial call are none of them effectual to salvation unless they are attended with the Holy Ghost's own personal and *effectual call*.

When you feel within yourself a secret drawing to Christ which you do not understand, but yet cannot resist, when you experience a tenderness of spirit, a softness of heart towards the Lord, when your soul kindles with a hope to which it was previously a stranger, and your heart begins to sigh and almost to sing at the same time for love of God, when the Spirit of God brings Jesus near you, and brings you near to Jesus, then we may apply to you this message, "Be of good comfort, rise; he calleth thee."

Thus have I tried to set this man before you as receiving comfort; but we shall see thirdly that HE OVERLEAPED BOTH DISCOURAGEMENT AND ENCOURAGEMENT, AND CAME TO JESUS HIMSELF.

Bartimæus did not care one whit more for the comfort than he did for the rebuffs of those around him. This is a point to be well observed. You who are seeking Jesus must not rest in *our* encouragements, but press on to Jesus. We would cheer you, but we hope you will not be satisfied with our cheering. Do what this blind man did. Let us read the text again: " Jesus stood still, and commanded him to be called. And they call the blind man, saying unto him, Be of good comfort, rise; he calleth thee. But (it should be "but" and not "and") he, casting away his garment, rose, and came to Jesus." He did not give them a "thank you" for their comfort. `He did not stop half a minute to accept or to reject it. He did not need it: he wanted Christ, and nothing else.

Whenever any man, with the best intentions in the world, tries to comfort you before you believe in Jesus, I hope you will pass him by, and press on to the Lord himself; for all comfort short of Christ himself is perilous comfort. You must come at once to Christ. You must hasten personally to Jesus, and have your eyes opened by him. You must not be comforted till he comforts you by working a miracle of grace. Even the consolation to be drawn from the fact of a man's being called requires much caution in its use, lest we do mischief with it. The true eye-salve is with Jesus himself; and unless the soul comes actually into personal contact with Christ, no other comforts ought to satisfy it, for they cannot save.

We read first that *he arose*. He had been sitting down before, wrapped up in his great cloak, in which he had often sat begging; and now that he heard that he was called, he, according to some versions, "leaped to his feet." The expression may be, perhaps, too strong; but at least he rose up eagerly, and was no laggard. His opportunity had come, and he was ready for it, nay, hungering for the boon. Now, I pray you, let neither discouragements nor comforts keep you sitting still, but rise with eagerness. Oh, be stirred up to seek the Lord!

Let all that is within you be aroused to come unto the Saviour.

The blind man was on his feet in far less time than it takes to tell; and as he rose, *he flung off his old cloak*, which might have hindered him. He did not care what he left or lost so long as he found his sight. His mantle had, no doubt, been very precious to him many a time when he was a poor beggar; but now that he wanted to get to Jesus, he flung it away as if it were nothing worth, so that he might get through the throng more quickly, and reach the One in whom his hopes centred. So, then, if anything impedes you in coming to your Saviour, fling it off. God help you to be rid of self and sin, and everything that is in the way. If any ill company you have been accustomed to keep, if any bad habit into which you have fallen, if anything dear as life, hinders you from simple faith in Jesus, regard it as an evil to be renounced. Off with it, and make a rush to him who calls you. Now, even now, draw near, and cast yourself at the Redeemer's feet.

Our Lord was well aware that this man knew his name and character, and so, without giving him further instruction, he addressed him in these words, "What wilt thou that I should do unto thee?" Our Lord's addresses to persons were usually based upon their condition. He knew that this man very clearly understood what he wanted, and so he put the question that he might openly give the answer. "What wilt thou that I should do unto thee?" "Lord," said he, "that I might look up," or, as our version has it, "that I might receive my sight." Go to Jesus, whether comforted or discouraged, and tell him what ails you. Describe your case in plain words. Do not say, "I cannot pray. I cannot find language." Any language will do if it be sincere. Give to him such words as come first to hand when your desires are fully awake. Tell him you are a wretch undone without his sovereign grace. Tell him you are a sinner worthy of death. Tell him you have a hard heart. Tell him you are a drunkard, or a swearer, if such be the case. Tell him all your heart. Then tell him that you need forgiveness and a new heart. Speak out your soul, and hide nothing. Out with it! It may be well to go into an enquiry-room to be helped by an earnest evangelist, but it is infinitely better to make your own chamber your enquiry-room, and there enquire of the Lord

himself on your own account. May the divine Spirit lead you
to do this *now*, if you have never accepted Jesus before.

Bartimæus received more than he had asked for. *He was made
whole, and so saved*. Whatever, therefore, had caused his blindness was entirely taken away; he had his sight, and he could
look up, a saved man. Do you believe that Jesus Christ is as
able to save souls as he was to heal bodies? Do you believe
that, in his glory, he is as able to save now as he was when he
was a humble Man here below? Why, if there be any difference,
he must have much more power than he had then. Do you
believe that he is the same loving Saviour now as he was when
here on earth? O soul, I pray you to argue this out with yourself,
and say, "I will go to Jesus straight away. I never find that
he cast out any; why should he cast out me? No bodily disease
baffled him, and he is Master of the soul as well as the body;
why should my soul-disease baffle him? I will e'en go and lie at
his feet, and trust him, and see whether he will save me or not.
Discouraged or encouraged, I will have done with men, and I
will go to the Saviour." That is the lesson which I would have
every unsaved soul learn. I would have him go beyond the
outward means of grace to the secret fountain of grace, even
to the great sacrifice for sin. Go to the Saviour himself, whether
others cheer you or frown upon you. Dejected, rejected,
neglected, yet come to Jesus, and learn that you are elected
to be perfected in him.

I want this man Bartimæus to be an example to all of us,
if we get a blessing from our Lord, and are saved. *Having
found Christ, he stuck to him*. Jesus said to him, "Go thy way."
Did he go his way? Yes; but what way did he choose? Read the
last sentence: "He followed Jesus in the way." The way of
Jesus was *his* way. He in effect said, "Lord, I do go my way
when I follow thee. I can now see for myself, and can therefore
choose my way, and I make this my first and last choice, that
I will follow thee in every pathway which thou dost mark out."
Oh, that everyone who professes to have received Christ would
actually follow him! But, alas, many are like those nine lepers
who received healing for their bodies, but only one of them
returned to praise him. Great numbers, after revival services,
are like the nine lepers; they declare that they are saved, but
they do not live to glorify God. How is this? "Were there not

ten cleansed?" In great disappointment we enquire, "Where
are the nine?" Alas, we ask with bleeding hearts, "Where
are the nine?" They are not steadfast in our doctrine and
fellowship, or in breaking of bread; they are neither active in
service nor exemplary in character. But this man was of a
nobler breed; immediately he received his sight, he "followed
Jesus in the way."

He used his sight for the best of purposes; he saw his Lord,
and kept to his company. He determined that he who gave him
his eyes should have his eyes. He could never see a more
delightful sight than the Son of David who had removed his
blindness, and so he stopped with him that he might feast his
eyes upon him. If God has given your soul peace and joy and
liberty, use your new-found liberty in delighting yourself in
his dear Son.

Bartimæus became Christ's avowed disciple. He had already
proclaimed him as the royal Son of David, and now he deter-
mines to be one of David's band. He enlists under the Son of
David, and marches with him to the conflict at Jerusalem. He
stayed with our great David in the hold, to share his persecu-
tions, and to go with him to death itself. We are told that he
went with Jesus in the way, and that way was up to Jerusalem,
where his Leader was soon to be spit upon, and to be mocked,
and to be crucified. Bartimæus followed a despised and
crucified Christ; friend, will you do the same? Will you fare
as he fared, and endure reproach for his sake? Brave men are
wanted for these evil times; we have too many of those thin-
skinned professors who faint if society gives them the cold
shoulder. Power to walk with a crucified Lord into the very
jaws of the lion is a glorious gift of the Holy Ghost; may it rest
on you to a full degree! May the Spirit of God help you!

This Bartimæus, the son of Timæus, is a fine man. When he is
once really aroused, you can see that he possesses a firm,
decided, noble manhood. Many nowadays bend to every
breeze, like the osier by the stream, but this man held his own.
It is our impression that he remained a steadfast and well-
known disciple of Jesus, for Mark, who is the most graphic
of all the Gospel writers, always means much by every stroke
of his pen, and he mentions him as Bartimæus, whose name
signifies "son of Timæus," and then he further explains that

his name really has that meaning. There might possibly have been a Bartimæus who was not the son of Timæus; Mark, however, writes as if Timæus was very well known, and his son was known too. The father was probably a poor believer known to all the church, and the son made his mark in the Christian community. I should not wonder if he was what we call "a character" in the church; known to everybody for his marked individuality and force of mind.

If you have been long in seeking salvation, and have become discouraged, may the Lord give you resolution to come to Jesus Christ this very day. Bring that firm, steadfast mind of yours, and bow it to Jesus, and he will accept you, and end your darkness. Under his teaching you may yet become a marked man in the church, of whom in after years believers will say, "You know that man, that grievous sinner while he was unsaved, that eager seeker when he was craving mercy, that earnest worker after he became a believer: he will not be put back by anybody. He is a true man, and gives his whole heart to our Lord. Gently would I whisper to each one of you, *Will not you be one of them?*